Doctors for Democracy

In 1990 a revolution in Nepal ushered in multiparty democracy and brought to an end the great power of the Hindu Monarchy. The activities of 1990 were sparked off by a group of medical professionals. Dedicated to the principle of "Health for All," they demanded the eradication of poverty, inequality, repression, and elite corruption. By insisting that scientific knowledge must prevail over traditional institutions, and that universal principles of truth, merit, human rights, and scientific efficacy were essential to democracy, they eventually challenged the moral basis on which Nepali society was organized. But the success of the revolutionaries placed health professionals in a dilemma, with repercussions far beyond Nepal. Can medicine be politicized and still claim to be an objective science? When does the scientific method infringe on the moral foundations of a nation? On the other hand, can health professionals in a poor, undemocratic country afford to steer clear of politics? Vincanne Adams, a leading medical anthropologist, writes penetratingly about the Nepali situation, and raises questions that are fundamental for anyone concerned with public health, scientific truth, and democracy in the developing world.

Cambridge Studies in Medical Anthropology 6

Medical anthropology is the fastest growing specialist area within anthropology, both in North America and in Europe. Beginning as an applied field serving public health specialists, medical anthropology now provides a significant forum for many of the most urgent debates in anthropology and the humanities. It includes the study of medical institutions and health care in a variety of rich and poor societies, the investigation of the cultural construction of illness, and the analysis of ideas about the body, birth, maturity, ageing, and death.

This series includes theoretically innovative monographs, state-of-the-art collections of essays on current issues, and short books introducing main themes in the subdiscipline.

Doctors for Democracy

Health Professionals in the Nepal Revolution

Vincanne Adams

Princeton University

CAMBRIDGE
UNIVERSITY PRESS

PUBLISHED BY THE PRESS SYNDICATE OF THE UNIVERSITY OF CAMBRIDGE
The Pitt Building, Trumpington Street, Cambridge CB2 1RP, United Kingdom

CAMBRIDGE UNIVERSITY PRESS
The Edinburgh Building, Cambridge CB2 2RU, United Kingdom
40 West 20th Street, New York, NY 10011–4211, USA
10 Stamford Road, Oakleigh, Melbourne 3166, Australia

First published 1998

Printed in the United Kingdom at the University Press, Cambridge

Typeset in 10/12pt Plantin [SE]

A catalogue record for this book is available from the British Library

Library of Congress cataloguing in publication data applied for
Adams, Vincanne, 1959–
    Doctors for democracy: health professionals in the Nepal revolution
    / Vincanne Adams.
        p.   cm. – (Cambridge studies in medical anthropology : 6)
    Includes bibliographical references (p.   ).
    ISBN 0 521 58486 8. – ISBN 0 521 58548 1 (pbk.)
    1. Medicine – Political aspects – Nepal.   2. Physicians – Nepal –
    Political activity.   3. Nepal – Politics and government – 1990–
    I. Title.   II. Series.
    RA413.5.N35A3   1998
    306.4′61′095496–dc21   97–18016   CIP

ISBN 0 521 58486 8 hardback
ISBN 0 521 58548 1 paperback

For Lydia Ke'olani

"The doctors have not politicized health . . . they have made clear the truth."

message written in the Bir Hospital medical register by a Nepali citizen to doctors on strike during the People's Movement, 1990

Contents

Illustrations

Acknowledgements

I am privileged to have met and been influenced by such wonderful people as I came to know while writing this book. First, I thank Dr. Mathura Shrestha, Dr. Bharat Pradhan, Nurse Meena Poudel and especially Dr. Mahesh Maskey for their visions, their patience and time and for sharing with me their commitment to their causes. A number of other health professionals stand out as particularly inspiring: Nurse Guna Laxmi, Dr. S. M. Dixit, Dr. Shankar Rai. There are numerous others whose names I do not mention but who were generous in their time and support of this project. Among Nepali colleagues, Krishna Bhattachan stands out as a major source of inspiration for this work. For suggestion that I study this movement, I am enormously grateful. For his family's extended generosity in welcoming me and my family as they would relatives in their homes and lives I am deeply indebted. My hope is that although some of these scholars may disagree with my analysis, they will find their concerns and their stories accurately told here and embrace my analysis as part of what I hope will be an ongoing debate about democracy and science in their country and in modernity more generally.

Several colleagues took the time to read the entire manuscript and provide me with extremely useful feedback. These include Emily Martin, Mahesh Maskey, Robert Desjarlais, David Gellner, Sharon Kaufman, and Angela Creager. I also benefited from feedback provided by Mary Des Chene, Stacy Pigg, and Pratyoush Onta who read small portions of the text or with whom I discussed some of the concerns raised here. Thanks to B. B. Shrestha, Jeffrey Montez de Oca and members of FS113. I alone take responsibility for the final product. Other fellow scholars in the field also deserve thanks, not only for talking over ideas but also for taking the time to ensure that I did not miss other aspects of Nepalese life which I might easily have forgotten about. These are Steve Mikesell and Jamuna Shrestha, Kathryn March and David Holmberg, Peter Moran, Richard Brown and Marget Sands, Helen Sherpa, and Krishna Pradhan. For their hospitality and friendship I also need to thank Chanda and Nanda Rai and family, Da Yangin Sherpani and family, Doma and

Mingma Sherpa. The staff at the United States Educational Foundation in Kathmandu were essential in making this project work and I also extend great thanks to them. I also extend thanks to the United States CIES, the Fulbright Foundation, for awarding me a Senior Research Scholar Award with which this research was conducted. I extend warm thanks to my colleagues in the Department of Anthropology as well as a group of fellow scholars from History, Molecular Biology, Psychology, Ecology and Evolutionary Biology, and Philosophy at Princeton University (Reality Check) for including me in what has proven to be an extraordinarily collegial, congenial, and intellectually stimulating academic environment within which to think about the relationships between science, truth, and what we take to be democratic social values. Thanks to Lynn Morgan for inspiration. Appreciation also to Barbara Metzger and Jo North for editorial suggestions. Finally, I offer my deepest thanks to my husband, John Norby, for his commitment to our partnership, our family, and my work, including his not so subtle realization of one promise of modernity by finding a way to telecommute to California from Princeton and Kathmandu.

1   Introduction

In 1989 Dr. Mathura Shrestha helped me and a group of US medical students to prepare a presentation for the Department of Community Medicine of Tribhuvan University Teaching Hospital on health conditions in a rural part of eastern Nepal. He taught us then about the ways in which medical practice in Nepal was different from that in the United States. "Community medicine is the priority here," he said, pointing out that sometimes even politics was a necessary part of health care. Social injustice could be a cause of ill health, and social injustice was particularly visible among Nepal's rural poor. Our job, accordingly, had been to find out what villagers considered their most important political, social, and health needs, and his had been to try to attend to them. Four years later, and three years since the democratic revolution in which he had played an important role, Dr. Mathura had been asked to serve as minister of health for the interim government that had come to power as a result of it. I guessed that his brief role as minister had been at least partially determined by his willingness to listen to the villagers' political demands.

Dr. Mathura's medicine, I learned, derived authority from its political stance, but it did so by asserting that medical truths were scientific and so they transcended the corruption and bias of politics. Political corruption was, after all, what had brought down their old government. I was anxious to see him again, hoping that he would want to take the time to tell me about the revolution and help me make sense of what seemed to me a sort of ironic combination of a politicized medicine which relied on *apolitical* notions of truth. As I entered the Department of Community Medicine office, I noticed a slogan on the wall, scrawled there as graffiti during the revolution: *Itihas le bhancha janata nai Nepal ko suruwat ho!* "History says the founder of Nepal is the public!" Criticisms of the king were also painted here, an offense punishable by imprisonment only four years earlier. No one here had yet wanted to paint over them.

Dr. Mathura greeted me and apologized for being late. He had been occupied with the administration of flood relief in connection with the failure of a dam in the southern part of the country. The dam had broken and the flood plains below it were submerged under millions of gallons of water. It was estimated that some 10,000 people had already died, and health professionals were concerned about the spread of cholera and starvation among the survivors. Dr. Mathura complained that the government was wasting foreign donations by dealing ineffectively with the disaster. In response, he mobilized teams of physicians and nurses to the area, offering help where politicans were unqualified or incapable of doing so. It was clear that he was, three years after the revolution, still engaged in the political battle for the survival of his democracy. For him, this was a battle on behalf of *truth* for the ordinary people of his country.

I knew that Dr. Mathura was not alone in his criticism of the government. On the day of my arrival a few weeks before, there had been a *chakka jam* ("wheel lock" – an interdiction against motorized traffic in the city) called by the leftist parties against the majority Congress party. That evening there had been tear gas, shooting, and young men in the streets inciting or running from more violence. People were angry, wondering if this new government was what they had fought for with their lives three years ago. For Dr. Mathura, the disaster relief effort epitomized the new government's failure; it was acting just like the old government, displaying self-interested favoritism rather than helping the common man – capitalizing on human tragedy to gain political prestige rather than alleviating human suffering by the efficient organization and dissemination of modern technology and know-how. Confronting this situation required medical help from experts – physicians – not politicians. So, while politicians were making use of the disaster for political gain, he was organizing volunteers, medical supplies, and monetary donations to fly relief teams down to the flood areas. He insisted that his interventions were not politically motivated, but he wasted no time in informing me of the failure of the current political regime to attend even to the most basic needs of the average citizen, let alone their extraordinary needs during this time of disaster. They were busy trying to win public support through public spectacles and announcements about the statistical grandiosity of the medical event – spectacles that would create loyal voters, while he was trying to save lives. Whereas he was working to establish medical needs as top priorities, the government was politicizing truths about the disaster, using a medical crisis for political ends.

"I am neither Communist [party] nor Congress," he said, despite the fact that most everyone who knew him publicly considered him a leftist. He considered himself a medical scientist – a physician whose concerns transcended political parties. The irony of his position, however, was that no matter how much he accused the new government of politicizing medicine, he himself had been a major contributor to this tactic.[1] During the revolution, he forced medical practice to attend to both politics and objective truth. He showed that you should always put politics to work for the truth. In fact, he showed that being a good doctor required this. In the process, he showed that putting medicine to work for politics was also required, for political solutions to medical problems demanded political action. But now he was arguing that if medical truth was used for politics it should be called corruption. Was there a difference, I wondered?

During the revolution, Dr. Mathura helped bring to life the politically activist medicine which he had introduced to me in 1989 when he showed me that social injustice can be a cause of ill-health. This, for him, was a modern and scientific approach to medicine. Becoming political had become for him a necessity for practicing medicine in a modernizing and developing nation like Nepal. He learned this, he explained, from his "Western" predecessors and teachers. He reminded me of a passage I had sent to him in an essay: Rudolf Virchow, writing about the 1848 typhus epidemic in Upper Silesia, Prussia, said that ". . . medicine is a social science, and politics nothing but medicine on a grand scale" (Taylor and Rieger 1984: 202).[2] His concern, like that of Virchow, was that more than any biological factors it was social, economic, and political inequality which led to the massive number of deaths and that only social, economic, and political reforms would help to end them. Then, he noted, as if an echo to Virchow's polemic, the World Health Organization and UNICEF convened their conference on Primary Health Care 130 years later in Alma Ata, Russia, and established that if universal health is to be achieved, medicine must attend to social, economic, and political needs. Health, they wrote, is a state of complete physical, mental, and social well-being, and not merely the absence of disease or infirmity; moreover, they claimed that health so defined was a fundamental human right, therefore the practice of medicine demanded activism and political will (Osmanczyk 1990: 31).[3] Dr. Mathura reminded me that Nepal had sent two representatives to that meeting, two people who helped formulate the international position. This was the perspective he still held, and the one which compelled him to fight, as a physician, for democracy in his country three years earlier. How then did he get from this position that welcomed the use of medical tools to fight political battles to one in which he felt that political uses of medicine constituted a corruption not only of politics but also of truth? When should a politicized medicine serving political goals be considered a corruption of medicine and when should it be considered the achievement of it? To answer this, I offer an introduction to this ethnography that explores the role played by biomedical health professionals in the democracy movement of Nepal in 1990 and thereafter.

As the political events between February 18 and May 16, 1990 escalated to the point of revolution, Nepali health professionals adopted what to them were the overtly politically and socially activist stances of Virchow and the Alma Ata Declaration, becoming revolutionaries for the sake of democracy. Backed by a history of political activism focused on establishing a multiparty elected government, doctors, nurses, and paramedicals (auxiliary health workers) became catalysts for a movement aimed to bring down what they saw as a repressive panchayat system,[4] to end underdevelopment and the corruption that nurtured it, and to establish the basis for a healthy democratic nation with full rights to political freedom. In the process, the movement would also bring an end to the absolute rule of the monarch. The oppositional activities of Nepali medical professionals made a decisive difference in the People's Movement. The voices of Nepali physicians were heard partly because of their political actions, including dissemination of information, strikes, and assertions of professional authority at strategic times and places. They alerted the news media about what they surmised was the government's use of bullets outlawed by the Geneva Convention; they protected leaders of the opposition from arrest by placing them under hospital bed rest; they made triage decisions which placed the lives of injured civilians above the needs and demands of soldiers and policemen by claiming medical expertise and by appropriating a *moral* and *scientific* high ground based on universal human rights. In doing so, health professionals were able to transform the revolutionary debate from a partisan one to one about universal truth. Their actions helped to inspire foreign democratic governments to threaten the withdrawal of aid unless the people's demands for political freedom were met. The highly visible protests of this cohort of scientific professionals dashed the king's hopes for a modern monarchical Nepal, for surely he recognized that a modern nation could not exist without support from rising professional scientific classes like theirs. A hunger strike by the physicians and other health personnel during the final days of the revolution helped compel the king to agree to a multiparty parliamentary democratic constitutional monarchy.

Many of the health professionals involved, particularly from the Department of Community Medicine at Tribhuvan University Teaching Hospital, had long espoused the argument of Alma Ata that the best medicine for Nepal was preventive, appropriate-technology, rural-based health care for the masses. Observing that social inequality and poverty were the root causes of ill health among the masses, some doctors reasoned that the most direct medical interventions they could promote were those of political and social reform. Politics, in their view, could be used to reveal and attend to objective truths and therefore could enhance medical practice without compromising scientific objectivity. This objectivity was born from the perceived efficacy of technical interventions provided by a scientific approach to social problems.

Dr. Mathura seemed right in pointing out how different this medicine was from that found in my own country. Although a commitment to politically attentive medicine is arguably often the "mainstream" view in schools of public health in centers of medical power, in many western industrialized, developed countries like the United States, a politicized medicine that actively offers politics as a cure is typically treated as marginal at best and problematic at worst. When attentive to politics, mainstream biomedical practitioners are often questioned about compromising their objectivity, as if political neutrality were a requirement of objectivity. Politically sensitive physicians are often subjected to criticisms of bias – of placing truth in the service of partisanism, whether the debate is on, for example medical insurance or the risks versus benefits of abortion. In this view, even though one could politicize medicine to serve objectivity, objectivity comes to stand for a perspective which is apolitical, which is above and beyond political bias. Objectivity and political neutrality are made to perform a fragile dance with one another. Political involvement is seen as capable of serving objective truth, but it can also be seen as corrupting it. True objectivity is often thought to carry with it certain assumptions of political neutrality. So had Dr. Mathura's criticisms of his government come to reflect our own conundrums around objective truth and politics? Had he cultivated his own similar sense of the need to transform politics into a technical – a politically neutral – category for social action?

I recalled that in the metropole, where powerful health development agencies have called for political commitment on the part of community members and recipient developing-country governments, there is a tendency to transform overtly political solutions into technical ones; political reforms that aim to redistribute power, wealth, and privilege to improve health are transformed into technical fixes that expressly evade political questions. This process of depoliticization reveals what Michel Foucault (1979) referred to as an effect of governmentality (also Ferguson 1994). Governmentality refers to the distinctly modern phenomenon arising with government institutions devoted to providing technical interventions that are assumed to be politically neutral because they are based on objective and scientific truth. This assumption of neutrality places science in a category of truth that is thought to transcend politics.

However, this view belies a much more subtle truth – that scientific neutrality is the practice of contested politics, wherein debates over truth stand in for debates over power (Ferguson 1994). Medical policy and development intervention can be instruments of governmentality, particularly when they treat something like social inequality as a technical problem with a technical solution, rather than a political problem with a political solution. When the Alma Ata Declaration embraced politics by generating calls for "political will" to support the Health for All goal, the attempt was to establish unbiased commitments to scientifically efficient medical strategies. The idea was that a form of medical politics existed which was essentially *non*-political – a form of politics not embroiled in contestations of power between different interest groups. This had to be the ideal, for clearly it became obvious to many that articulating the call for political will through local political institutions could derail primary health care programs entirely (Morgan 1993).

This book offers another case study of this unfolding ethnographic scenario at what some might refer to as the "periphery" of biomedical institutions of power. Nepali medical professionals adopted mainstream metropole health development priorities and in doing so held onto ideals of political impartiality while using them to deploy actual political solutions that were strong enough to overthrow a monarchy. Nepali professionals took up the call for a politicized medicine and remained committed to it, arguing that all medical practice and knowledge must be seen as political in part. At the same time, the events of the revolution also generated arguments against politicizing medicine, and these arguments are worth paying attention to because they attend to the problem – not just in Nepal – of the extraordinary fragility of this dance between objective truth and political neutrality, showing how one might be contingent upon the other. The Nepali case shows how very fine the line is between politically convenient truth and scientifically objective truth when political acts are called medical acts and medical truths are placed in the service of political regimes.

The health professionals in Nepal became revolutionary not just by invoking scientific objectivism but by invoking it as the foundation for a democracy. Democracy was taken as an objective set of institutions and practices – like science – replicable anywhere in the world if conditions were right and based upon fixed notions of universal truth. Moreover science, for them, was inherently democratic, and therefore becoming political to promote democracy was simply a matter of making scientific truth more visible. Medical professionals associated the objective qualities of their medical practice with the type of government and polity they hoped for. They took the position that a democracy – a political system that would foster equality, opportunity, the benefits of science, welfare, and wealth for all – was the best prescription for health. They also believed the reverse: that promoting scientific medicine would bring about a more democratic polity. This view that linked medicine to politics did not initially consider politics a corrupting influence on science, because it maintained that both, when practiced correctly, were democratic. Thus, what became particularly interesting about the stand of the medical professionals was their insistence on the visibility of the sources and beneficiaries of medical truths. And this, I show, may be where the troubles, like those encountered by Dr. Mathura in the wake of the flood, began.

While a politicized medicine enabled these professionals to help provoke and sustain a revolution for democracy, their desire to constantly politicize medical truths also became a source of some tension for some professionals in the years afterward. The reasons for unequal distributions of privilege were always clear to people in Nepal before the revolution; it was largely this inequality which lay behind the People's Movement. Many claimed that these inequalities were caused by corruption, and health professionals noted that corruption was found in all sorts of ways (false statistics, promotions through nepotism, politically motivated health policy, etc.) – in practices which disregarded truth for the sake of political and social favoritism. The latter were not scientific, therefore not democratic, bases for action. Nepali revolutionaries argued that a politicized medicine could reveal and therefore root out corruption. But the revolution to make political parties legal by ushering in a true democracy also made political parties a new basis upon which to gain access to privilege and, consequently, to offer new, but still inevitably unequal distributions of resources. Consequently, political parties came to be seen as the basis for new forms of corruption. Health professionals got caught in similar entanglements. By politicizing their medicine, medical professionals in the years after the revolution found themselves occasionally being accused of political bias for doing what they believed was simply scientifically prudent medicine. By 1993 the distinction between using politics as a medical weapon and using medical truth as a political tool had indeed become blurry. Mis-steps in the fragile dance were easily made.

Medical professionals called for a recognition of scientific universals during the revolution, but their very involvement in politics, and the politicization of medicine which ensued, had by 1993 made them vulnerable to the same sorts of charges of corruption once leveled at the king. Partisan constructions of truth were set in opposition to inviolable truths of medical science, which were believed to be above politics, but that stance had become increasingly difficult to sustain as party politics penetrated ever deeper into the public health, clinical, and even pedagogical practices of biomedicine.

As much as this story is about heroism in Nepal's democracy movement, then, it is also about the relationship between science, politics, and truth – in particular, about whether medicine can be politicized without undermining its claims to objectivity. The fact that this story takes place in Nepal raises equally important issues of cultural context. The commonly held Nepali professional's conviction that democratic politics and a scientific medicine (biomedicine) are inevitably linked takes interesting turns in the context of a cultural environment that still places high priority on the moral bases for social action. The linkage between democracy and medical science was for many Nepali professionals based on two ideas: the first was that truth could be universal because objective, and the second was that objective truths were constituted in a realm that was distinct from that of religion. Indeed, sacred moral knowledge and behavior were distinct from the moral knowledge and behaviors produced by the scientific mind. But the two were not entirely incompatible or separable in Nepal. As Nepal has become democratic, many believe that she can and must retain her identity as a nation marked by respect for and devotion to the morally sacred. This is expressed among Nepalis in religious behaviors that take place on a daily, weekly, monthly and annual basis (one need only reckon with the calendar of official holidays and daily work schedules to see the importance placed on religious ritual in everyday Nepali life), but also in behaviors which prioritize family responsibility, respect due persons in certain kinship and extra-kinship, including caste, relations to oneself creating a moral community (see Parish 1994). But morality is also expressed in appropriations of scientific rubrics that appeal to universal truth. For example, the doctors' collective interest in fighting for human rights as a weapon for democracy partially worked because they were as compelled by morally-based, scientifically objective concerns.

At its core, the Nepali commitment to a morally rich, religiously tolerant modernity led some to claim that they would have a distinctive Nepali democracy, wherein objective systems of government coexisted alongside sacred gods and the moral obligations towards them and others held by Nepali citizens. A democracy did not require the elimination of the sacred because its truths were generated and sustained in a realm beyond that of culture, in a realm of scientific objectivity. At the same time, it was felt among some that science's abundant truths could accord and fulfill the moral demands of a moral society, because truth, scientifically ascertained, did not lie about such things as equality and moral worth; its truths did not contradict those that upheld the moral sphere. In fact, however, the blurring of the domains was inevitable. I suggest here that it was partially this desire to retain a hold on the sacred quality of moral life among Nepalis that came to interfere with the "objective" functioning of a politicized medicine in the aftermath of the revolution. A politics of science became intertwined with a politics constructed around notions of sacred moral power and duty. New wine in old bottles of power. This basis for morality was in place for several hundred years in Nepal and continued to be sustained after the revolution regardless of its repackaging into institutions of objective science and democratic political parties. It was also sustained because it was deeply tied to Nepali desires for a distinctive national identity.

The unpredictable but intractable blurring of scientific and sacred politics points my analysis to one more final topic: the confrontation between Nepali convictions about the inherently democratic tendencies of science and postcolonial critiques of science which see it, and biomedicine, as ethnoscience and an instrument of Western hegemony. Nepali revolutionary medicine challenged my understanding of the debates about science in a global arena. Nepali medical professionals were promoting science at a time when intellectuals throughout the postcolonial world were criticizing it as an instrument of Western hegemony. Such criticisms focus on the cultural specificity of science truths and the neocolonialism of science's claim to universalist objectivity. Indeed some authors identify a fundamental incompatibility between sacred notions of truth and scientific, objectifying ones on grounds that both are culturally based. In the end, I note that the Nepali medical professionals provoked me to acknowledge the issue not of power but of privilege in relation to science versus sacred truths. The ability to propose social and political foundations of scientific truths has much to do with how much is at stake in adopting such a position. Nepali medical professionals opted for an objectivist science that was capable of providing insights about whose interests were served by one medical truth over another because their struggle for democracy depended on this sort of objectivity. Moreover, their ability to see this objectivity as compatible with their nationalist aspirations for retaining all that was good of their religiously rich and sacred nation cannot be dismissed by Western or postcolonial critics. Nepalis' very notions of democracy depended on it. Rather than paving the way for Western neocolonialism, good science they felt gave them the means to avoid such neocolonialism by giving them freedom. This freedom would infringe neither on their science nor their sense of moral duty to their nation, its gods, or their fellow citizens.

What this case shows is that the signs that circulate in medical cultures are often the same as those that circulate in political cultures as "science" and "democracy." This ethnography is a study of these valued signs that circulated in the 1990 revolutionary era of Nepal. It reveals the ways in which the logic of science itself became increasingly visible as being politically and culturally saturated, despite its claims to be above and beyond both culture and politics. At the same time, science was used by Nepalis to stabilize the democracy they hoped to establish and sustain. Signs like "democracy" and "science" are in the end revealed as cultural products – as free-floating signifiers deployed in the service of those who can make the best use of them, whether for the benefit of others or not. At the same time, democracy and science are enabling practices, and questions about their factualness can reveal much about the relative privilege of those who raise them.

Concluding, I suggest that we try to understand the political stance of Nepali medical professionals in the context of their struggle to construct a distinctive Nepali democracy – one that has what are perceived to be all the benefits of efficiency and fairness seen in many other democracies in the world, but still capable of nurturing those social and cultural institutions which make Nepalis feel "at home." Like the Nepali science advocated by Dr. Mathura, this sort of "neutral" institution called democracy (imagined to function something like a neutral science) may in fact be a distinctive democracy fraught, no less than any other, with conflicts and oppositionalism over, in their case, the meaning of *being* Nepali. Just as using science for politics is seen by some as a corruption of science, so too might we wonder whether promoting "Nepali" ways of life has the effect of appearing as a corruption of democracy. It forges a democracy infused with sensibilities of morality derived from those modeled after the relationships Nepalis historically had with their king, and their gods. Dr. Mathura's uneasiness with his new government's use of medicine to gain political power is perhaps a result of this blurring of sacred and secular, political and apolitical in the new democracy.

Before turning to a description of the chapters which follow, then, I offer the following notes concerning the context of my research. Although the view of events here is medico-centric – in fact at times doctor-centric – I try to discuss them in terms of the social contexts that made it possible for doctors and other medical professionals to make claims of truth and power. I have been doing research in Nepal since 1982, but most of my data for this book were collected over six months of intensive fieldwork in 1993, less intensive information gathering beginning in 1990, and another short visit in 1995. In 1993 I interviewed people mostly in the Kathmandu Valley and in a few of its surrounding villages, but in this book I draw from my experiences of living an additional two years over four different visits in various parts of Nepal, including in the village of Bandipur and city of Pokhara in central Nepal and villages in the Khumbu and Arun Valley regions of mountainous eastern Nepal. The interviews in 1993 were conducted in English and/or Nepali. I have tried to recount events as they were told to me by people who, three years before, had participated in the revolution – persons of different occupations within and outside the medical profession, including nurses, paramedicals (health assistants, assistant nurse midwives, rural health workers, and others), and medical students who were also involved in central ways in the movement.

I remind readers that the revolution was one in which nearly all urbanites and a vast representation of rural Nepalis from all walks of life participated. The fact that urban activities were the most important in the People's Movement should not obscure the fact that some twenty-two out of the country's seventy-five districts were fully involved in the movement with active protests, arrests, and injuries. Those who visit Nepal today will find, scattered among the many rural Nepalis who say that their prospects for social improvement today are no better than during the monarchical panchayat regime, others who will talk of their and their friends' and acquaintances' heroic participation in the People's Movement and of a new political freedom that has brought them closer to what they desire in development and modernity.

As far as possible, I have relied on other accounts of the movement, in particular Shaha (1992), Raeper and Hoftun (1992), K. C. (1993), FOPHUR (1990), and Brown (1996), to fill in gaps and locate in the larger activities events that doctors, other health professionals, and non-health professionals described. Inevitably, however, there are gaps in the coverage of events. Readers who are interested in more detailed accounts of the movement or accounts from a non-medical perspective should consult these other works.

Additionally, scholars of Nepal, inside and outside the country, will not find in my account much attention to the role and place of local healing traditions, shamanic and scholarly, in the health development of the country. One reason for this absence is that because these traditions were included in the category of what many biomedical professionals hoped to erase from the Nepali landscape as impediments to development my ethnographic work among them was seldom directed to healing traditions. Rather it was directed to the larger social patterns of corruption and backwardness that Nepalis identified in everyday social encounters. At the same time, I am very aware of the overwhelming presence of and belief in a wide variety of healing traditions among most Nepalis and know that these are not simply interpreted as "obstacles" to modernity but actively play a role in shaping the sort of modernity Nepalis bring to life. Indeed, if I were able to write a second book on the movement, it would be directed to the question of how so-called corruption is discursively linked to patterns of traditional healing which are identified as backward by developers. To the extent that some readers feel I have given this topic short shrift here I refer them to others who are already writing on the topic of traditional healers under conditions of modernity, specifically the work of Linda Stone (1986, 1989), Stacy Pigg (1990–1996), and Jean Langford (1995), among others.

Finally, many of those who live and work in Nepal will find some of the material here very familiar and cursory because I have tried to make the book accessible to the general reader. My hope is nevertheless that scholars of Nepal will find this story and the questions it raises a contribution to the ongoing debate over the nature and relationship of modernity, democracy, and science. I also hope that medical anthropologists in general will find that this book provides them with a useful case study of a problematic that has been of concern to the discipline nearly from its inception, addressing as it does the link between politics and medical knowledge and practice.

Chapters

I begin in chapter 2 with an overview of medical science as a domain of power in Nepal in light of the discussion of politics and medicine in "developing" countries more generally. Here I examine the argument that power in the modern era is unique, especially its deployment of notions of individualism and objectivity in medical settings. I also discuss the ways in which these concepts were employed by Nepali medical practitioners.

Chapter 3 offers a brief history of Nepali politics, focusing on the motivations and movement towards democracy that began over fifty years ago and the emergence of a central critique of corruption – a "corruption" that modern "scientific" solutions were expected to eradicate. I suggest that the patrimonial monarchy founded upon patronage, caste, and family or family-like relations came to be seen as a corrupt system that oppressed Nepalis and prevented them from fully achieving development. Demands for democracy revolved around a vision of a society that was free of corruption. This entailed a vision of Nepal as not "Western" but rather as scientific and universal – functioning like other democracies seen in the "West" but still culturally Nepali. The shift emerges as one that articulates notions of sacred duty to king and countrymen as problematic, while it espouses notions of scientific behavior based on objective and universalist criteria as morally correct. The shift in perception from monarchical politics to democratic politics entailed an internalization of critiques of "typical Nepali ways of doing things" and, because of that critique, produced a struggle in the revolutionary aftermath for typical Nepalis to find ways of being democratic without being "corrupt" – and even ways of being Nepali without being "corrupt."

Chapter 4 recounts the events of the period between February 18 and May 16, 1990, that brought down the monarchy, focusing on the activities of doctors, nurses, and paramedicals (auxiliary health workers of all kinds) and the significant moments when it was clear that their authority as scientific professionals was more potent than that of the king's armed forces. Chapter 5 offers an analysis of the motivations of the doctors involved in the political movement, and addresses the critique that politicizing medicine can corrupt its objectivity. Chapter 6 explores the complicated issue of politicizing medicine in historical and cross-cultural contexts.

In chapter 7 I examine the subtle way in which claims to scientific practice by doctors in Nepal are transposed onto the political landscape. I describe the problems that the health professionals in Nepal were having three years into their democracy negotiating the politicization of health without compromising the claims to scientific objectivity on which their practices rested. In the new multiparty democratic climate, political parties had taken the place of the palace as the origin of various forms of favoritism and corruption. The idea that political agendas corrupted scientific practice in medicine suggests that the old nexi of power in Nepal (tied to family, caste, reciprocity, and patronage) were still operating alongside new ones formulated in modern institutions.

The final chapter examines the implications of the issues developed in chapter 7 in terms of the critical claims made by postcolonial and other writers that science and biomedicine are instruments of Western hegemony. Nepali intellectuals say they desire a distinctive Nepali democracy, but such desires inevitably reproduce behaviors which were often called corrupt in the period just before the revolution. I suggest that analysis of the social and political *construction* of scientific and medical truths is celebrated by postcolonial authors critical of science who share with Nepali intellectuals the search for a basis upon which to build a nation with distinctive cultural character – a nation that rejects Western colonial notions of truth and attempts to retain a moral basis upon which to evaluate behaviors towards other family members, fellow citizens, and even towards the gods. But the critics' suggestion that science always signifies Western domination must itself be critically scrutinized in terms of

Nepali medical actions which hope to create a democracy imbued with moral sensibilities about duty, political engagement, and the uses of objective truth. Ultimately, the analysis in the final chapter leads to some observations about the debate in terms of the relationship between truth and privilege.

2 Medicine, science, and democracy in the developing world

This bid for power is not directed against any nation, class or race. It assails no particular way of government but the ways of creation, which have scarcely fluctuated within the memory of man. Clouds and wind, plant and beast, the boundless heavens themselves are to be subjugated. The stake is higher than dictators' seats and presidential chairs. The stake is the throne of God. To occupy God's place, to repeat his deeds, to recreate and organize a man-made cosmos according to man-made laws of reason, foresight and efficiency. . .   Robert Jungk 1954

The first achievement of the scientific spirit was to create reason in the image of the world; modern science has moved on to the project of constructing a world in the image of reason.   Gaston Bachelard 1934

In many ways, the participation of Nepali physicians in their revolution marked the rise of a professional class exercising a distinctively modern form of power in Nepal. Foucault (1988, 1981, 1973) argued that the role of professionals in modern European society was remarkable for their production and dissemination of truths around which modern people understood, organized, and lived their lives. The sort of power predominant in modern society was very different, he said, from that characteristic of the pre-modern European context, wherein the monarch's ability to rule was based on the capacity to engender loyalty through family ties, patronage, and alliances. Another mechanism of his royalty was of course not simply charisma but the ability to use the military as a repressive force. People afraid of the outcomes of being disloyal were compelled to do what the king required, and people obligated to him through patronage were constrained by his codes of conduct.

Foucault contrasted this power with what he called "micropower" found in the modern setting. Micropower was not repressive but productive. Its principal mechanisms emerged from self-disciplines of normalization, in which the normal was a product of institutions of the state (academies, laboratories, prisons, and the like). Professionals in specialized knowledge fields played an important role here. Being in a position to collect information about the populations they served, they used this information to produce truths, about what came to be seen as the "natural world" and also the "social world." From these truths, interventions could be designed. These truths became norms disseminated through micro-practices such as visits to the doctor to be weighed and measured so as to see where one fell in the normative line-up, reconstituting the family as the unit of surveillance for demographic and economic information and practice (Donzelot 1977). Thus in productive power Foucault sees two related processes: one involves the production of truths through a rational objectivism derived from scientific research methodologies (especially the social and physical sciences focused on populations), and another produces behaviors in a compliant public which is ever-attentive, in its individualistic priorities, to these scientifically produced "norms." Moderns are no longer subjects but rather citizens of the state, charged with responsibility for their own health care via an internalized responsibility for behaving "normally." Foucault identified the creation of a new subjectivity – one attentive to the notion of the self as an object that can be worked upon and forever improved. The body becomes the primary site for the expression of the subject, but it is objectified – made into an object upon which discourses of normalcy are articulated. Micropower is contingent upon subjects' considering themselves capable of being improved through disciplined adherence to truths put forward as scientific *facts*.

Obviously, physicians play an important role in modern societies. The basis of their power is their expertise, and therefore their ability to use force to compel normative behaviors is severely limited. The less force used, the more compliant moderns will be. People are self-responsible in the modern setting: the more they feel that they are in control of their bodies and their destinies, the more they will behave normally. They are organized by professional apparatuses; the modern state is more than technology, it is an "order of things" – an order designed by professional knowledge. Consequently, modernity has typically signified a shift in the nature of authoritative truth, shifting from truth established on the basis of sacred or spiritual knowledge to truth derived from scientific professional knowledge. The rise in belief in scientific truth is usually accompanied by a belief that sacred forms of truth are only relevant in certain social spheres designated as special, religious, or ritual moments of everyday life. Everyday life becomes less and less governed by moral obligations derived from sacred sources of authority and more and more governed by rational behaviors derived from scientific truth: the moral is subsumed by the rational (Weber 1958; Andreski 1983).

Scientific truths in the modern setting are thus a key to discipline and order. Social *control* is no longer the issue, particularly the sort of control effected through regimes of fear over the outcome of violating spiritual or sacred authority; control has given way to elaborate systems that strive for culturally uniform practices of self-*discipline*. We iterate, reiterate, and reinforce truth's power when we utter or behave in accordance with it. Of critical importance in the definition of modern truths is that they are typically formulated through *scientific* practices, established as objective and therefore taken as impartial and universally valid; in the nineteenth and twentieth centuries this has meant taking scientific "facts" as a basis for organizing one's life. The presumption is that modern truths cannot be challenged as subjective or partisan versions of reality because they have been "naturalized," they appear natural and self-evident.

Modern individuals

For the Nepali case, Foucault's insights are usefully complemented by the work of C. B. Macpherson, who noted the rise of a cultural spirit of "possessive individualism" in seventeenth-century European society – a spirit that remains one of the most striking characteristics of many industrialized Western nations today. Macpherson returned to the writings of Hobbes, the Levellers, Harrington, and Locke to show that theories about civil society and its potential undoing consistently invoked the notion of "natural law" to instantiate their philosophical arguments. He pointed out that possessive individualism was at the root of Locke's theory of civil society, particularly its need for a sovereign. Locke's claims about the "natural state" of man referred not to all men of all times but rather to men reared and socialized in a market society, where competitive individualism reigned. In his time the idea of possessive individualism justified the view (contrary to that of Hobbes) that men did not need a sovereign because they could, endowed with equal potential, govern themselves. His broad theory of equality between individuals presupposed, for example, the natural right of men to obtain and accumulate wealth unevenly; that some owned nothing but their labor was an artifact of their own failure, not society's.[1]

This idea of possessive individualism helps explain in a general way how individuals become the interlocutors for social and scientific discourses of normalcy and productivity in the context of emerging democratic sentiment. Many of these assumptions were shared by Nepal's revolutionaries, who saw individualism as a basis for social equality. Modernization in Nepal has placed increasing emphasis on the individual. Certainly individualism existed prior to the arrival of international development modernization forces (McHugh 1989), but it has since then emerged as an implicit ideal around which to organize democracy. In modern Nepal, it was believed that an emphasis should be placed on individual performance over the skillful ability to rise to positions of privilege through affiliations with others. Responsibility for social actions were thought best relegated to the individual (for example, in finding a person to blame for social disasters) as opposed to generalizing such responsibility to a large network of individuals through whom such actions emerged. This individualism is stressed even as others call for a restoration of historical ideals of collectivism (Parajuli 1992) as part of a revivalism for indigenous Nepali ways of life. I return to this in the next chapter.

Health development agencies have contributed to the emphasis on the individual as the unit of responsibility, rights, and duties in a modern society. This is particularly found in their very constructions of disease which place an emphasis on the "what" over the "who" in etiology and pathology. Rather than conceptualizing disease in terms of an intricate set of relationships between persons (and between persons and supernatural beings), biomedicine conceptualizes diseases in terms of objective agents which are not vested with the qualities of relational beings – the causes of diseases are things to which one has no moral obligation and to which one has no sense of sacred duty. This objectification of pathogenesis in the medical model transforms itself into elaborate rhetoric that places the individual at the center of the diagnostic and therapeutic system. The individual becomes responsible for his or her health, not the group and the focus on the group becomes nearly incidental to the process. This orientation is spelled out explicitly as a contingency of primary health care in the Alma Ata report which, for example, places enormous rhetorical emphasis on community needs and participation but then defines "community" as a collection of self-responsible individuals (WHO and UNICEF 1978: 21, cited in Morgan 1993: 68, emphasis added):

> [The community] helps to plan primary health care activities and subsequently it cooperates fully when these activities are carried out. *Such cooperation includes the acceptance by individuals of a high degree of responsibility for their own health care – for example, by adopting a healthy life style, by applying principles of good nutrition and hygiene, or by making use of immunization services.*

Nepali doctors fighting for democracy were fully indoctrinated in the Alma Ata philosophy. It formed a constitutive basis for medicine in Nepal, taking individual responsibility as a key to modern development. When operationalized for health delivery, however, it contrasted sharply with demands among recipients for decision-making in terms of collectivities. In Nepal, demands emerged from family, caste, ethnic group, and patronage networks (Justice 1987). The need to maintain social bonds with others through institutions which cultivated collectivist or dyadic social action, however, coexisted with the conviction that these institutions were obstacles to development and modernity. These collectivist tendencies emerged from a society that held enormous faith in the belief that behaviors towards others were invested with a moral sensibility – modeled upon the sort of relationship one would, by the logic of the sacred, have with the gods and the kindred through whom one's identity was ascertained.

By the time of the revolution, however, critics of collective-oriented social institutions had begun to distinguish between behaviors towards sacred gods from behaviors towards other humans like oneself (and even eventually from behaviors towards the king) who by the logic of science were equally susceptible to nature's pathogens. Behaviors that emphasized the bonds between persons, and showed collectivist preferences, became labeled nepotism, favoritism, source-force, and other words for "corruption"(see chapter 3). Critics knew that acting as individuals would disenfranchise and isolate them as "troublemakers" at worst, socially inept at best, until the time when popular sentiment deemed social affiliative behavior corrupt. The problem of being "left out" because one refused to work through social networks, because one operated as too much of an individualist, eventually did become seen as an obstacle to modernization in Nepal. Conceptualizing individualism as a problem came to be labeled as itself a problem, as a form of corruption, despite the assault this would have on traditional institutions of family, caste, ethnicity, and the religious institutions that mediated these relations. Some aspects of traditional Nepali culture, because they nurtured collective social interests, were thus seen as anti-modern. The love-hate relationship this cultivated around notions of the sacred and notions of moral duty became deeply intertwined with the ability for Nepalis to successfully fulfill their democratic dreams. How could one retain a sense of sacred traditions and morality while promoting a scientific system that labeled such behaviors as deviant, superstitious, and unhealthy? The answer can be partly seen in how doctors and other medical professionals articulated ideas about normalcy and pathogenesis for the average Nepali in terms of biomedical science.

Modern deviance

Biomedicine is known for its ability to reveal itself as modern by shifting the medical gaze from a focus on deviancy to a focus on normalcy. For example, efficacy in biomedicine is established around models of "the pathological" but the site of the pathological is increasingly in modernity revealed as an incursion into the realm of the normal. Whereas interventions were at one time focused simply on the visibly deviant, modern medicine increasingly extended its concerns into the realm of the normal as it pursued the study of more subtle differences within that realm. As the norm is more carefully scrutinized in relation to its own pathologies, more subtle and formally "hidden" differences are increasingly recognized as deviant and pathological. In biomedicine, examples include the shift away from the study of diseases as uniformly pathological for a population to the study of diseases specific to different age groups; eventually, specific pathologies of infants, adolescents, geriatrics become discovered, making what was once considered normal social life a new site for potential disease (Armstrong 1983). In psychiatry a similar shift occurred in the study of pathologies of marriage and female sexuality (Lunbeck 1994). Similarly, one might consider medicalization and the biologization of psychology, including the tendency to offer ever more refined scrutiny of the genome and a narrowing of definitions of normalcy, as examples of the way the normal becomes the site for identifying pathology. As the normal becomes more studied, so do we proliferate the ways in which and places we can find deviance.

Two insights might be garnered from this argument. The first is that rhetorics of difference are a foundation of the modern project and its truths. Creating interventions to deal with *difference* is thus one of the hallmarks of modernity. This is as true within the medical domain as outside of it in international development policy and action. It is as true for Nepali practitioners of biomedicine who deploy such techniques on behalf of the public they serve, as it is for the way in which Nepalis themselves are characterized as deviant by a metropole health development discourse. The second is that modern truths are ephemeral, even while remaining objective and universal in character. As new pathological explanations arise, they erase old ones in medical science, as in science generally; they do not coexist alongside old truths which might stand in a position of contestation with them (Kuhn 1962).

Modern truth

In the larger historical and international field, the fact that European modernity demanded *singular* truth, as opposed to the possibility of multiple coexisting truths regarding any one phenomenon, became important. The truth about the deviance of the Other emerged as part of a colonial project which could not sit comfortably with the possibility of non-Western notions of truth existing simultaneously with Western ones. Multiple coexisting truths about, say, the nature of reality or the body, were not possible. Scientific modernity held that only one truth could be in existence at a time, and if the Western world had truth right, the others' truths must be wrong. Truth in this modern sense is taken as singular and objective and universal despite the fact that it can be contested over time and even effaced by new truths. Scientific truths could be right, but only at the expense of other notions of truth found throughout the non-Western world; these became labelled as subjective, symbolic, and cultural. In Nepal, local knowledge was placed in contest with the scientific, but this move was itself socially contingent on global relations of development. What did this singularist truth conceal?

The role of medical and singular truth in modernity is elucidated in the work of Allan Young (1982, 1981) and Ronnie Frankenberg (1980, 1981), who, like Ludwig Fleck (1935) and Oswei Temkin (1949) before them, note that medical scientific truth about the pathological as against the normal is always socially and contextually contingent. Young and Frankenberg suggest, first, that social conditions determine who gets what diseases and when. When it comes to health, statistical facts are never "free-standing" numbers generated *sui generis*, but rather are tied in intimate ways with social relations. Second, they point out that diseases themselves and the statistics generated around them come to stand for named conditions and "facts" as a cultural result of the production of knowledge among medical professionals. Scientific production of medical truths about diseases, pathologies, and treatments is part of an elaborate system of production which is driven by the same apparatuses of modernity as are its other sciences and social institutions (including capitalism). Medical truths are themselves the product of social conditions and relations of production. Doctors' relationships to their patients, the medical infrastructure, the financing of research, and the class, ethnic, racial, and cultural relations which configure experiences of the body and health are the contingencies through which medical scientific truths are articulated. Medical truths are also, however, a product of the cultural systems that produce them in the sense that the available cultural constructions of reality find their way into the constructions of the natural world which science takes as given and then claims to "discover."

Arguably, the growth and expansion of biomedicine in non-Euro-American societies is a result of the expansion of apparatuses of European modernity and here too cultural differences came to be seen as deviance. Just as European modernity is a product of its colonial instruments of differentiating and pathologizing, medical models make use of notions of "difference" to ascertain development interventions. Maps of linear progress from the backward to the modern were invoked under colonialism to legitimate interventions by the "civilized" on behalf of the "uncivilized." In similar ways, the discourse of normality and abnormality finds its way into representations and understandings of non-Western societies in the form of distinctions between First and Third worlds (as political difference), industrialized and non-industrialized countries (as economic difference), developed and undeveloped or developing nations (as infrastructural difference), and even former colonizer and postcolonial worlds (a difference of subjectivity). In development discourse, representations of medical need in target societies reproduce the same indices of normalcy and deviance one finds in the "West" (Escobar 1995; Ferguson 1994; Pigg 1993). If infant mortality rates are lower in the United States than in Nepal, then the latter is represented as "different" and calling for interventions. Medical, like other, development interventions depend on the ongoing representation of the target communities as "different" and therefore needing intervention. Here too, differences come to be constructed in terms of health statistics and the pathologizing of traditional culture. Rampant disease prevalence or high infant mortality justify interventions, but so does the rampant belief in superstitious causes of disorders. Both are deviancies that can be eradicated. It is the social relations between wealthy and poor nations, between metropolitan US or World Bank social scientists and Nepali villagers, that offer representations of truth about medical need. But these truths are taken to be objective and universal facts, not the result of particular and socially, historically, and culturally specific relationships. Couched in the rhetoric of science rather than social relations, truths about medical needs become part of the apparatus of modernity exported from the Western-dominated metropole, while the contingencies of its origins disappear from view.

If modern *medical* truths are irretrievably socially and culturally constructed, contextually contingent truths, one might suggest this is not altogether surprising. After all, medicine is a science of the social, *designed* as a humanist intervention. Therefore one would expect to find in this science, more than in any other perhaps, a built-in reflexivity about the social production and impact of its truths – a reflexivity about the social agendas its truths serve, whether in the lab or in the clinic. Still, the idea of making medical truths socially useful is rarely equated with the idea that medical truths are socially constructed and therefore products of "culture" rather than "nature." On the contrary, even when put to social or even political purposes, medical knowledge is usually taken to be objective and potentially universally true. For example, even if a disease differentially affects different populations, the idea that it will manifest itself the same bodily way in these two populations, all else being equal, is rarely questioned. It is further assumed that making use of the "facts" of differential rates of infection to make claims about political or social inequality between populations will not undermine the "truth" about the disease entity or its "potential" to affect morbidity or mortality. In fact, however, calling attention to the political contexts which give rise to medical scientific truths by politicizing them for social and political purposes may run the risk of making them seem arbitrary – only conveniently true for a specific group of people at a specific time and place. Politicizing medicine can render the politics of its truth claims more visible. The clinically humanistic face of medicine makes medicine more vulnerable, as a science, to such interpretations than, say, other research sciences. Medicine, by its very nature, depends on a perception of its truths as objective, value-neutral, and politically neutral "facts", while more than other sciences it runs the risk of being seen as a socially driven producer of arbitrary truths always attentive to the social exigencies of the human encounter because at some level it must attend to politics and to social contingencies in order to make a real difference in human suffering. Nepali doctors confronted this issue, boldly.

Modern concealments

Health development can be seen as an instrument of modernity that depends upon mechanisms that hide its own political contingency. Among the ethnographers who have documented the uneasy relationships between development and politicization processes is James Ferguson (1994), who describes how international development programs in Lesotho succeed in introducing bureaucratic state political infrastructures in target communities by offering technical, so-called apolitical, interventions. Masked by the discourse of technical intervention were social problems arising from state–village relations, environmental degradation, class inequalities, Lesotho–South African relations, and Lesotho–foreign aid relations. Vicente Navarro (1984) also noted that health interventions presented as technical solutions often depoliticize local social problems. Ferguson shows, however, that despite the depersonalizing and instrumental discourse of technical intervention, rural development programs are always received and effected by local populations in terms of political relations. In a poignant example, he shows how a health clinic established as technical and apolitical was transformed into an instrument of the local political elite: "One informant was able to recall specific cases in which ambulance care was withheld from emergency patients due to their political affiliations with opposing parties" (1994: 212). A technical discourse that authorizes non-political interventions to modernize a population is here locally resignified as highly charged political discourse. The Nepal case is similar, with the additional fact that politics in Nepal is constituted in contextually unique ways. Closely intertwined with notions of corruption and nationalism, politics finds its way back into practices of modernity in the form of demands for various acts of social and political preference by medical practitioners. Nepali medical professionals who are activists typically aim to introduce technical interventions but they do so for political goals, and although this is not for them a corruption of the modern potential of their technical science but a mandate of it, it becomes so for some who observe the process.

Lynn Morgan's (1993) study of the establishment of primary health care programs in Costa Rica during the 1970s and 1980s is even more compelling as a comparative case, hence one I return to again and again. She shows how the rhetoric and implementation of programs for community participation in health, as advocated by international health development agencies, were undermined by the politics of this strategy, by the deliberate politicization of primary health care programs in general, and by the persistence of local hierarchies articulated through practices of paternalism. Community participation was invoked as a "technical" process measurable by numbers of participants and devoid of political meanings. She writes (1993:164), however, that citizens

> knew they could depend on the state to act paternalistically, just as they knew that only perfunctory compliance with participation programs was required.... Politicians ... associated health with democracy, [said] they wanted to strengthen health and democracy by fighting disease and communism (or the disease of communism). At the same time, many politicians insisted that health was above politics, and that they personally were interested only in the public welfare. Residents of La Chira found it difficult to accept the argument that participation in health was a weapon against communism, or indeed that communism posed a significant threat to democracy as they experienced it. The opinions of La Chira residents illustrated many of the contradictions inherent in the concept of participation as it was wielded by politicians in the capital and by international health planners.

The community participation called for by the Alma Ata Declaration and by the government of Costa Rica was not the same as that attended to by rural citizens, and to the extent that real participation in oppositional social struggles threatened government regimes these health programs were seen as a threat by those who held power. "Participation" for international health bureaucrats typically meant educating people to assume responsibility for their own health care, while for national health bureaucrats it usually meant obtaining compliance among villagers in implementing top-down programs that served the needs of government officials. Given the overwhelming perception among Costa Ricans that "participation" was the crux of "democracy," there was always the potential for villagers to see health participation as a way of expressing discontent over agricultural, industrial, or governmental exploitation. So the "community participation" that was a political rallying cry for politicians of the 1970s became the means of silencing potentially oppositional villagers living under new government regimes in the 1980s. "Health is not above politics," Morgan writes, "as international experts are beginning to acknowledge. Health is a profoundly political issue, but it is often in the interests of those who control health policy to perpetuate the illusion that health is immune from political considerations" (1989: 241).

The actions of the medical professionals in Nepal also reveal the problem of medical knowledge elucidated by these writers and other political economists of health (Hans Baer, Howard Waitzkin, Vicente Navarro, Lesley Doyal): that so-called objective truths are always constituted in a politically contested field of social relations. In a situation of social inequality, health development is likely to reproduce rather than eradicate the political arrangements that produce social inequality. This is partly because power is operationalized through the truth claims which are characterized as politically neutral (Escobar 1988, 1995) and objectively factual. If power here is distinctly modern, perhaps it is the more so in medicine because of its humanism and its ability to claim objectivity in the name of humanism. Thus modern medicine always walks a fine line between promoting social and political agendas via objective truth and concealing the presence of social inequalities that emerge from political arrangements that produce its truths.

In Nepal, the visibility of this fine line was highlighted by a growing desire on the part of Nepalis to infuse their medicine with politics, but only in order to make truth heard. It was hastened by desire on the part of Nepalis to infuse their actions with a sense of morality. These desires tied scientific truth to social affiliations which enabled Nepalis to express their sense of moral obligation to family, ethnic group, religion, etc. Since social affiliations were articulated in terms of social inequality but still authorized by Nepali notions of what made Nepal a sacred social landscape, politically neutral truth claims of biomedicine were never actually seen as free from political interest groups.

Thus far, I have contextualized modern medical power by noting that it is possessed of distinct qualities: an ability to offer objective truth claims, and an ability to conceal the political relations of production that produce such truths. I note here that the idea of objectivity is not unique to the modern Western episteme (on the contrary many non-Western epistemologies have it), but rather that this particular episteme is the one which arrived in Nepal as a part of its attempt to "modernize." Thus, secondly, I have noted that Nepalis' embrace of biomedicine as an instrument of modernity is not devoid of historical and cultural contingencies. That it arrived with development aid from the Western metropole (after a less intensive exposure to the British colonial project) and that it is internalized unevenly and in some conflict with traditional culture are important to this analysis. We might recognize that health development is, for many, a scientific apparatus of modernity and therefore an agent of Westernization. Modern subjects internalize notions of "normalcy" by thinking of themselves as objects upon which to erect modernity and as citizens who, in control of their destinies, must discipline themselves according to modern norms. They are both objectified and empowered by scientists and technical experts. Because modernity operates upon subjects who think of themselves as citizens, its functioning is often thought to depend on the elimination of non-modern subjectivity, for everything non-modern comes to be seen as deviant. But this elimination does not always occur. All sciences are susceptible to being shaped by the cultural and political contexts in which they are practiced. Modern medical sciences are invoked by Nepalis and others to achieve modernity while helping to insulate their nation-state from what they would call Western hegemony. Nepali medical professionals hope to establish an objectivist social system based on standards of efficiency, equality, and democratic representation while protecting their distinctive Nepali society and culture. But preserving their cultural distinctiveness often requires these agents of modernity to behave as "non-modern" subjects, being confronted with the awkward proposition that in order to be Nepali they must also see themselves as in at least some instances non-modern and deviant (Pigg 1992). Again, this proposition has become a central complication of Nepali modernity precisely because of the belief that one could separate sacred from scientific domains of truth.

Modern objectivity

On the one hand Nepali medical professionals' revolutionary activities must be seen as characteristically modern activities, relying on modern power and modern beliefs about relationships between health, develop-ment, and objective truth. In fact, one pillar of Nepali democracy was to be the authority of professionals claiming the political high ground through a rhetoric of science. The other, however, was to be the authority that derived from a moral universalist discourse called human rights, also built upon modern notions of objective truth but in this case articulated through a rhetoric of morality. In a democracy, these Nepalis hoped a meritocracy would replace the monarchy's nepotism and favoritism, a multiparty political system would mitigate the social inequalities of caste, ethnic, and class stratification nurtured by the palace, development according to scientific methods would mitigate poverty and perceived "backwardness," and the recognition of human rights as universal would eliminate political oppression and ensure the recognition of basic political freedoms.

On the other hand, modernity would emerge in Nepal within an existing culture and so it would retain a distinctive character. Many Nepalis believed that if objective and standardized rules were established upon scientific principles and everyone followed those rules, then they could not help but achieve modernity, wealth, health, and satisfaction. This was what was perceived as having happened in the "healthy" and "wealthy" Western nations because they had created social instruments allowing objectivist knowledge to take precedence over cultural and political knowledge and priorities. However, just as Western nations had their own nationalisms and cultures, so Nepalis imagined Nepal would retain its national and cultural distinctiveness by promoting a scientific society. Science was not a culture, they reasoned; it was merely a tool with which cultures could be enabled to flourish – a view effacing histories of colonialism.

It might be argued that, in espousing these views, Nepali physicians were demonstrating the neocolonialism to which Ashis Nandy (1983: xvi) calls attention in his description of modernity:

> Ultimately, modern oppression, as opposed to the traditional oppression, is not an encounter between the self and the enemy, the rulers and the ruled, or the gods and the demons. It is a battle between de-humanized self and objectified enemy, the technologized bureaucrat and his reified victim, pseudo-rulers and their fearsome other selves projected on to their "subjects".

Science was invoked as the panacea for "corruption and inefficiency" in Nepal, but for Nandy this science is built upon practices which dehumanize the subject by forging an internalized hatred for the self and everything that one does as tradition, calling it backward. Backwardness became a form of corruption for many urban and rural Nepalis. Inefficiency occurred because things were done non-scientifically – the wrong choices were made, the wrong people always got into decision-making roles because the system was driven by social and collective interests, by patronage concerns and reciprocity, favors for favors. The modern subject, however, would be able to avoid these practices by recognizing them as corrupt. Modern subjects had to learn to hate this part of themselves. Thus, subjects under modernity, for Nandy, became victims of a sort, reified by science as obstructions to truth. The unrecognized enemy of modernity is for Nandy the system of objectification itself.

So, while many Nepalis glorified tradition as a means by which to create a distinctive political culture and nation, many of these same Nepalis came to hold the idea that traditions (and particularly collectivist orientations) were an enemy within their midst by holding out for a science which could destroy them. The enemy became objectified as "other" even though it was an enemy within themselves. This objectification of the self is a feature of modernity most clearly articulated by science, for science is an object-making rationality, Nandy notes; it even makes an object of one's own subjectivity. Once available, any number of spheres of social life can be subjected to science's logic. This was particularly clear when Nepali medical professionals defined a moral basis for their democracy in a rhetoric of human rights. The idea of universal human rights demands a conception of the person as a universal object. This is a move that requires, by the logic of scientific reductionism, embracing the ideas that individuals are the unit of importance and that all individuals are at some level, acultural and bodily and in this sense universally uniform. The body as an object can be seen as universally the same, and therefore deserving the same rights. The body could be individually "universal," but at the level of "the social" it would become culturally specific. Human rights discourse requires, on some level at least, the presumption of individualism as the basic unit of humanness (even when "cultural survival" is its goal). The maneuver that brought together individualized bodies as objects under a rubric of universal human rights made it possible to distinguish between culture and science; culture was what led to violations against humans, but human rights were like science because they were in the realm of the factual. The idea that every human had the right not to be tortured, for example, was a given, a matter of unassailable fact, not a culture-specific and therefore "arbitrary" truth.

I take this view of a *world of objectivity* as problematic and historically contingent here, partly because its adoption caused difficulties for medical professionals who politicized their medical "facts." To be clear on the meaning of this notion of the cultural specificity of objective facts or an object-making rationality, I offer this passage from Shapin and Schaffer's historical analysis of the rise of this particular European Enlightenment issue in the context of Robert Boyle's promotion of the experimental method, a turning point in the rise of science as we know it today (and as Nepali medical professionals use it) (1985: 24, 23):

> Boyle and the experimentalists offered the matter of fact as the foundation of proper knowledge. In the system of physical knowledge the fact was the item about which one could have the highest degree of probabilistic assurance: "moral certainty." A crucial boundary was constructed around the domain of the factual, separating matters of fact from those items that might be otherwise and about which absolute, permanent, and even "moral" certainty should not be expected. . . . There is nothing so given as a matter of fact. In common speech, as in the philosophy of science, the solidity and permanence of matters of fact reside in the absence of human agency in their coming to be. Human agents make theories and interpretations, and human agents therefore may unmake them, but matters of fact are regarded as the very "mirror of nature."[2]

Human rights rhetoric in Nepal would, because articulated around the individual and because it conflated a moral issue with an objective and scientific one, also put universal rights into the category of the factual. It did this partially by making the rights of the individual count for more than demands upon the person made by family, caste, reciprocity, religious, ethnic, and monarchical privilege, in short, demands which "collectivize the person," and which are, as I show later, tied to notions of sacred moral duty as opposed to secular moral duty. In this way, the rhetoric of human rights would bring along with it the power of the "factual" and the associated moral certainty that came with secular notions of truth.

In Nepal, this rhetoric of objectivity elided the idea of culture as everyday practice. It treated family, monarchy, patronage, caste, reciprocity, and the moral sensibilities infused through them as impediments to "democratic freedom," and it reformulated culture as something found in an empty (although today highly contested) category of "nation" defined not in terms of everyday political and social practices and the social organization they spring from but in terms of nineteenth-century European notions of "high culture" in costume, art, music, and the sacred "traditional" institutions tied to gods and religion.

Human rights could be seen as political and politically constructed, but they usually appear apolitical when they are able to invoke truth the way that science does – as objective and universally valid. The rhetoric of universalism attached to human rights concerns among Nepalis was one in which not only notions of the individual but also notions of democracy and a democratic nation were given a central role. The very idea of a democracy was for Nepalis a combined effect of objectivist science and secular morality, again not sacred morality. Democracy became the imagined state wherein objective truths and a universal morality were expanded into society writ large – a utopian civil society whose principal cultural norms were those of science and objectivity, factually based principles of social organization which transcended culture and political bias but included and accommodated the culture (that remaining after corruption was eradicated) upon which the nation would be identified. Democracy was, in this sense, that social state wherein enough people believed in the idea of scientific truth to keep it going, and then behaved according to the self-discipline it demanded. Such a state, however, asked Nepalis to reject everything that stood for what was "bad" in their old society while remaining Nepali in all the ways that could accommodate scientific behavior and nationalist culture. This is one setting, then, for the modern events calling upon medical professionals to use truth for democracy in Nepal. First, though, I offer a closer look at Nepali history and power under conditions of the rise of modernity.

3   History and power in Nepal: secularizing morality

One of the first things Nepalis do whenever they have to negotiate with a government or state office is to ask themselves and their families "Whom do we know who works there?" The question signposts the fundamental belief that having a contact, preferably a relative or close friend in public office with power to render favours, is a legitimate avenue or right and proper way of getting things done.   Alex Kondos 1987

I remember to have actually heard a colleague of mine in the late king Mahendra's cabinet telling his Majesty in a fond manner how much he enjoyed remaining in the King's presence. This colleague of mine may have sounded naive but he was the most cunning of us all.
Rishikesh Shaha, cited in Kondos 1987

Nepal came into something close to its current form as the realm (*desa*) of the kings of Gorkha only in 1768 (Burghart 1984). In that year, one of the twenty-four rajas of the Gandaki area called Gorkha, Prithvi Narayan Shah, conquered the states, the trade depots, and beyond that the kingdoms and tribal territories as far north as the current border with Tibet, as far west as Kangra, south into the fertile plains of Uttar Pradesh, and as far east as Sikkim (Stiller 1973; Burghart 1984; Bista 1991; Shaha 1992). At the time of unification, the kingdom of Gorkha subjugated and incorporated an ethnically, religiously, and culturally diverse population, including scattered Hindu principalities and semi-autonomous tribal groups (Caplan 1971; Pfaff-Czarnecka 1997). The conquered included the Buddhist Tibeto-Burman-speaking peoples in the north and east, the Hindu Indo-Aryan-speakers of the southern and western regions, and multitudes of shamanistic-animistic and mixed Hindu and Buddhist peoples speaking unwritten languages mostly derived from one of these two dominant language groups throughout the mid- and high-montaine regions of the country.

Among the most important areas brought under the command of Prithvi Narayan Shah was the culturally and materially rich Kathmandu Valley. The inhabitants of the valley were the highly literate Newars, both

Buddhist and Hindu, and small groups of Buddhist immigrants from the high Himalayas and immigrant Hindus from the *terai* (jungle) to the south and from the plains of northern India. Prithvi Narayan Shah made Kathmandu his seat of power, deposing the divided Malla family that had previously ruled there (Gellner 1993). The people of Nepal at this time were farmers, herders, traders, craftsmen, soldiers, servants, menial laborers, migrant laborers, landlords, royalty, scholars, and priests, all brought together under an expansionist ruler.

The malarial jungle on Nepal's southern border with India and a fiercely strong army, among other things, kept colonial Britain out of the Gorkha kingdom for many years. In 1814, however, the British launched a successful incursion into the region and forced the king to sign the Treaty of Sagauli, which gave the East India Company and later the British government the privilege of maintaining a commercial officer in Kathmandu as an "advisor" to the king. Britain also acquired authority to involve itself in Nepal's foreign affairs and control over territories outside the area now called Nepal but once part of the Gorkha kingdom (English 1982; Joshi and Rose 1966; Shaha 1992). Although laborers in Nepal (including the weavers of southern Nepal and construction workers, mountain guides, and mercenary soldiers of the middle and high hills) were involved in economic relationships with global capitalism via the British, sometimes through Nepali and Indian middlemen in Nepal itself and sometimes as migrant labor in India, and although the Raj had a place in the realm of Gorkha, Nepal was technically never colonized (English 1982). Gorkha's isolation from the West was maintained partly by xenophobia and partly by its clever administrative skill. The rulers of Nepal established their nation as a Hindu kingdom and administered it with the tools of *dharma*, maintaining a cosmo-moral order, and a good deal of accommodation of local customary law, creating strong loyalties among its diverse populations (Hofer 1979; Burghart 1984; Whelpton 1992; Pfaff-Czarnecka 1997).[1]

The legacy of Prithvi Narayan Shah was still alive in 1990 Nepal in the form of absolute rule by his royal Hindu descendants, caste elitism, a patrimonial and hierarchical power structure, and a multiethnic but highly unified nation, but his family's hold on power had not been uninterrupted. Eventually, the overexpansionist tendencies of the Gorkha kings and the unwieldy diversity of subject populations, coupled with the vulnerabilities of successor transitions in the context of internal conflict among palace-tied ruling elites weakened the king's hold on power (Höfer 1979; Whelpton 1983). After only seventy years or so of successful rule, the throne was usurped by the aspiring Rana family, also Hindu. An ugly massacre orchestrated partially by Prime Minister Jang Bahadur Rana in

1846 enabled him to wrest control over the palace from the Shah successor, then only a youth.

Jang Bahadur Rana negotiated improved trade relations with the British empire and traveled to England and France as a guest of the British royal family. Whereas the British considered him a quasi-subject, albeit one who exemplified the exotic grandeur of the East, Jang saw himself as a revered guest and a statesman who harbored a good deal of suspicion about British expansionist intentions (Whelpton 1983). Jang nevertheless became infatuated with what he saw in England, and after his visit he imported British-style colonial architecture, which was quickly adopted by many elite Kathmandu families (Gellner 1993). More significant, he created the Muluki Ain, a Hindu legal code modeled on the British one.

The Muluki Ain became an important instrument of statecraft and nationalism during the Rana period. It was configured as an instrument of Hindu nationalism and state solidarity against the British rather than simply an imitation of their code (Höfer 1979; Leve n.d.). As Andràs Höfer has pointed out, the Muluki Ain created a Nepalese *national* caste hierarchy; all the kingdom's subjects were classified by *jat* ("kind"), which came to stand for "caste," whether this initially referred to caste, family, clan, or ethnic group. All subjects were made part of the caste hierarchy and given the rights and privileges and prohibitions appropriate to them as designated by Hindu custom. Even Buddhist subjects were incorporated into the Hindu kingdom as low caste (*matwali*, "alcohol drinking," therefore impure) – not twice-born but not untouchable castes. Under this legal code, everything from violations of land tenure to violations of commensality was delineated and accorded appropriate punishment.

The Muluki Ain was an effective instrument of national unification insofar as it was able to make Hinduism a uniform feature of nationalist sentiment (Burghart 1984; but cf. Gellner, Pfaff-Czarnecka, and Whelpton 1997). To do this, it had to cultivate a sense of unity within diversity. Joanna Pfaff-Czarnecka notes that "rather than seeking to establish a national unity through a vision of a culturally homogeneous population, the rulers sought to define a national identity which allowed for cultural variation but which had Hinduism as its major pillar" (1997). But the Muluki Ain, because it unified by internal differentiation, also created the basis for anti-caste and anti-Hindu elite sentiment (Bhattachan 1996; Gellner 1997b). By 1990, Hindu hegemony was actively sustained by Hindus holding political power and by a majority of the Nepali population, who viewed themselves as a "purer" Hindu nation than the Indians (Whelpton 1992). But, as Whelpton (1996) also notes, Hinduism was not only a midwife to Nepali nationalism, it was a source of its undoing; domination by caste elites and exclusion from access to privilege and power among Hindus became one of the reasons for the democratic revolution.

An even more significant instrument of statecraft was the sort of power that became prominent during Nepal's formative century-and-a-half as a Hindu kingdom. It was during the Rana period that many of the instruments of power associated with the Hindu monarchy were ossified in the Nepali way of life. The Ranas held power for 104 years, and most Nepalis believe that their rule had debilitating economic and social effects on the country.[2] Taxation systems which encouraged indiscriminate abuse by absentee landlords and great divisions between caste and other economic elites and the poor and caste subordinates emerged during the Rana era (Regmi 1978). The Ranas invested little in infrastructure or in social welfare. But what they lacked in material infrastructure, they made up for in the solidification of social superstructural linkages that were based on family bonds, reciprocal alliances between status equals, patronage relations between unequals, and a social nexus that tied all power to the palace.

Three years after India gained its independence from Britain in 1947, the forces conspiring against the reign of the Ranas in Nepal undertook a coup that would restore power to the Shah kings (Joshi and Rose 1966; Brown 1996). The movement originated with political activists residing in northern India, the founders of the Nepali Congress party and disgruntled low-status Ranas.[3] In 1950 they were joined by the Shah king Tribhuvan and his family, who had fled recently (Stiller 1993). By 1951, what some call the first democracy and others call the first steps toward democracy were taken as King Tribhuvan was restored to the throne. The Ranas were banished from holding the office of prime minister,[4] but because of their control over the army and their 104 years of intermarriage with the Shah family they remained an important part of the court. The king was back in power but the mode of power he, and consequently all Nepalis, used remained the same. Rejoicing over the restoration of the king buffered Nepalis' sense of urgency over criticizing the mode of power that was kept in place by him.

The four decades that followed the restoration of the Shah kings' power nevertheless saw a great deal of political experimentation. An early attempt at multiparty democracy was made by King Tribhuvan's son, King Mahendra (Joshi and Rose 1966). Only a few months after the elected government came into existence, however, it was disbanded, and as a result the king and his foreign advisers designed the panchayat system as an alternative that would bring Nepal halfway to democracy (Burghart 1993, 1994). This government consisted of the king and four tiers of elected councils or panchayats. Villagers elected local representatives, and these representatives in turn stood for higher offices (from village to district to zone to national level). By 1980 there was widespread sentiment in favor of a multiparty system, but a referendum for it failed to achieve enough votes, not without raising suspicions (Shaha 1993). Although members of the national panchayat were elected from the district levels with avowed, even if illegal, support for particular political parties, the government was still perceived by most Nepalis as dominated by a large and important body of ministers appointed by the king (28 of 140) and by the obligations of patronage and loyalty among elected members who knew that their own power depended on loyalty to the king. Government was largely perceived as belonging more to the king than to the people. The isomorphism between palace and political system during panchayat "democracy" thus led to a situation in which, according to Burghart, "the legal coherence of the 'personal,' the 'state' and the 'common' made sense in a lordly political culture, in which the public domain was personally represented by the sovereign, whose will was executed by his state agents for the common good of an indivisible body politic. His Majesty's Government legally and ritually represented the body politic" (1993: 7).

Rishikesh Shaha (1993) explains the Hindu king's instrument of statecraft this way: "Shrouded in the splendour of supreme majesty – the body of the King and the state [were] one and the same thing." One of the important reasons for the success of the Nepali monarchy, and perhaps one reason it lasted as long as it did, is the fact that the king ruled by means of instruments that wove together all Nepalis into a larger socio*moral* universe. This universe was invested with sacred power, meaning that all the way down to the lowliest villager Nepalis' sense of sacred duty to the king was intrinsically tied to their sense of duty to their country and their countrymen. This sacred duty was an outgrowth of a more profound sense among nearly all Nepalis that religious sentiment, spirituality, and respect for moral duty informed many acts of everyday life. It was also an outgrowth of the institutionalization of these sentiments in the everyday actions of patronage, reciprocity and family favoritism that, as we will see, became the micro and macrotechniques of power under Rana rule and panchayat democracy. Being involved in a patronage relationship, especially with someone in the palace, meant, for the average Nepali, being able to reveal one's sense of loyalty not only to one's countrymen but also to the king, since he was the grandest patron of them all. Being a loyal and dutiful citizen meant being involved in actions that conflated sacred duty (in a religious sense) with obligations to others, especially superiors and patrons. It was these institutions which came to be seen as undemocratic and "corrupt" over the years leading up to the revolution.

The shift from Rana politics to monarchical politics and then finally to panchayat democracy marked a dramatic transformation in the look of government, but again in significant ways the mode of power that emerged in the thirty to forty years before the revolution were still complexly articulated with a form of power that was solidified during the Rana era. The shift that was envisioned by some was from a government and polity that functioned on the basis of its sacred and moral power to one that functioned on the basis of its rational and objective instruments of knowledge (therefore a new kind of power).

Despite criticism as undemocratic, by 1990 the institutions of government *did* undergo dramatic changes during the panchayat era. Most significant was the development of rural institutions dealing with the judicial, fiscal, infrastructural, environmental, and cultural concerns of the monarchical state, and the increased opportunity for local Nepalis to meet their needs through these institutions. The basis for a modern "constitutive" political system in which the privileges and rights of citizens would take precedence over the needs of a body politic embodied in the king – in short, a democracy – was in fact made somewhat possible by the panchayat system (Burghart 1993; Adhikary 1995). This is partly because the arrival of the "development era" to Nepal, and its ideas of modernity, were simultaneous with the rise of panchayat institutions. In the next section I explore how, although the sort of power associated with the king came to be seen as a reason for revolution by 1990, it still remained in place through the panchayat era. The fact that this sort of power was associated with the palace and that the palace had been restored to its rightful owners in the early 1950s, removing the corrupt Rana userpers, is relevant. Nepalis' reverence for their monarch as a sacred symbol of the nation is deeply intertwined with the mode of power which was cultivated over several hundred years; it is a mode of power that gives the appearance of his being involved in personal relationships with each and every one of his subjects, much as would the father of a very, very large family (see also Bista 1991: ch. 4). It is through these institutions and modes of power that panchayat democracy came into existence.

Culture and Power

Rishikesh Shaha describes Nepal's pre-1990s government as a patrimonial monarchy wherein the king had complete power.[5] Being recognized as divine, as a descendant of Ram (an avatar of Lord Vishnu; the king is a partial incarnation of Vishnu, an amsavatara[6]) (Whelpton 1992: 9), he engendered a great deal of loyalty from his subjects, even from the non-Hindu Buddhist peoples of Nepal, many of whom paid homage to Hindu gods or considered them interchangeable with Buddhist figures. Belief in this kingly power was fairly uniform throughout all ranks of Nepali society (even among dissenters), with the result that the king came to stand symbolically for the state and for the people of the state. Shaha notes that particularly "the Royal Nepal Army regards the King as sole personification of the state, with the result that to the army it appears there is no such thing as loyalty to the state and the people as distinct from loyalty to the King as a person" (Shaha 1993: 25).

Given the allegiance of the military and the police, the power of the king was associated not only with sacred power but also with physical force and instruments of terror (guns, lathis, prison, torture, job sanctions or other exclusions). In this sense, the armed forces never really served the public, instead serving the king as its symbolic representation, and because they displayed little loyalty to the king's subjects, they engendered little loyalty from the average Nepali for holding this role. At the same time, rather than being respected as professionals serving the public, members of the army and police were admired as persons well-situated to receive favors and privileges from the palace. The perceived relationship between the king and his armed forces was typical of the relationships between the king and his other subjects.

Loyal subjects received rewards from their patrimonial elites – salaries, remuneration in kind, and access to resources and favors from the palace that were inaccessible to the less "connected."[7] This pattern was most apparent in the extensive landholdings and tax privileges given to loyal military officers during the Rana era (Whelpton 1992). Loyalty and obedience were repaid in material and social privileges. However, the reverse was also true: disloyalty to the king or threats to his power in any way were punishable both within the armed forces and outside of them (historically by death or exile) (Whelpton 1992: 211). This too was articulated in and through a sense of sacred duty to the father-cum-godlike figure of the king. Those who were loyal received rewards, and those who were not were denied them.

Networks of social obligation through which everything from business to affairs of state were conducted were modeled on the sort of relationships one ideally would find in a family. Beyond the family, such networks were modeled after that which could be found in the larger religious community of like-status and like-minded compatriots (*sangha*). In the best of circumstances, the titular head of this community-cum-family was the king himself. A connection with anyone in the palace, however, came to be thought of as almost as good as a connection with the king himself.

Patrimonialism was generated within social nexi in which relationships of patronage, reciprocity, and family connections were the basis for gaining privileges, protection, and all manner of rewards. This formed the mode of "politics" (*rajniti*) of the state, all the way down to its least-"connected" member. Power in this system was lodged in multiple systems of favoritism, each of which had its own logic but shared sensibilities of family-like ties, reciprocity, and access to privilege through social affiliations, preferably ascribed by birth but possible even if acquired through clever procedures of social endearment. The forms of favoritism included: giving priority to close relatives (*natabad*), to those already involved in reciprocal or family-like relationships (*krypabad*), and to "one's own people" (*aphno manche*), flattery or "currying favor" (*chakari*), and especially cultivating reciprocal obligations with status superiors. For most Nepalis, using these sorts of connections was part of what it meant to be Nepali, for these networks of social affiliation situated one in webs of relationships that ultimately tied one to the king – the symbol and body of the nation – or to the palace, the place from which most privileges came and which was thought to ideally form a microcosm for the ideal of the nation.

Alex Kondos wrote in 1987 about the system of favoritism, or partiality (following Caplan 1971), that calling upon a family connection with someone in a position to distribute resources or favors was, for Nepalis, the most secure way of obtaining them. This was because family was the idiom which organized many acts of everyday social life, and because family was one of the principal sites for expressing one's morality. Hindu caste, a system that promotes exclusion on the basis of kinship, reinforced the strength of the family as an organizing unit in Nepali society and it did so by being an institutionalized locus for realizing one's moral duty to the gods, one's family, one's nation, simultaneously. Thus, when people wanted to accomplish nearly any act which they could not do by themselves, they sought family help first, and when family connections were not available, the next best thing would be a friend who had been turned into someone who should behave like family through the formation of a dyadic bond of either patronage or balanced reciprocity.

The many ways that the moral idioms of family manifested themselves in the extradomestic domains of Nepali life were and are interesting and complex. Whereas reciprocity bonds are formed between status equals and exchanges often entail "like" goods (material or symbolic), patronage bonds are found between non-equals and rewards flowing in one direction are reciprocated with largely symbolic rewards (loyalty, political allegiance, flattery, etc.). All of these bonds and exchanges are legitimized for Nepalis by being infused with moral character; defaulting on a social obligation would be tantamount to insulting a family member. And, because the state was itself idealized as an extended family (albeit with different status ranked members therein), so too would defaulting on an obligation be a betrayal of the Nepali idealized sense of national pride. It would be "un-Nepali." It would be un-Nepali to leave one's social obligations of reciprocity unfulfilled, just as similarly it would be un-Nepali to abandon a family member to whom one was indebted or to whom one could extend help. So, given the extraordinarily hierarchized social organization of Nepal and the desire to idealize social transactions through idioms of the sacredness of the family, with all its moral obligations, it is not surprising that Nepalis cultivated a number of ways to create linkages which cross-cut these otherwise divisive hierarchies.

One of the premier strategies for establishing a patronage relationship with a status superior is *chakari* (flattery). Kondos (1987: 20) quotes an informant to suggest that there were probably two highly stylized sorts of *chakari* during the Rana period:

> To do the first kind of *chakari*, everyone would gather to a Rana compound, day after day, to salute, praise him and shout "*Sarkar!*" [government]. Sometimes he would pick out someone from the crowd and ask: who he is, where he is from, what he does and about his family and how they fared. If he was pleased with you and the way you phrased your answers, he would ask if he could help you, and your family, in any way. If your request was reasonable and well put, he would do. He did not beckon someone every time but we kept on doing *chakari* ever hoping that our turn would come. That's the first kind. When this kind of *chakari* was combined with *chakari* to an officer in the Rana's service, we have the second kind. After we presented ourselves many times at the compound we began to do *chakari* to one of his men also. We did that for some time. Many months would pass by. In good time, you would ask the officer if he could recommend you or your son to the Rana for a position in his section of the administration.

Kondos notes that *chakari* entails learning as much as possible about the person whom one wishes to shower with flattery, determining what he might consider useful information and discovering his daily routines so as to arrange to be conveniently in his presence. Ultimately, one aims to move from flattery to actual gift giving, which demands a return gift of some sort by the logic of the bond one has created and transformed into something that is meant to approximate one within the family.

Caplan pointed out that among villagers *chakari* was considered acceptable for establishing a basis for receipt of favors from someone outside one's local multiplex sphere of relationships – the multipurpose ties formed between persons who are in regular contact "as a part of a series of manifold obligations and counter-obligations" aroused by mutually beneficial exchanges (Caplan 1971: 272, following Gluckman 1955).

Within these multiplex spheres in Nepal, "the practice of *chakari* is considered a necessary and appropriate method of getting employment in the absence of such a personal link to the source of the appointment. It is recognised as demeaning to the supplicant, but no man loses esteem in the eyes of other local residents if he demonstrates weakness before and dependence on the administration. To do this is to merely accept reality" (Caplan 1971: 274; also in Bista 1991: 93).

Persons who had established connections to influential persons in Nepal were situated so as to be able to obtain rewards and privileges that would be otherwise unattainable. These persons were said to have *aphno manche* ("one's own people") connections. For example, if one needed any sort of privilege from a ministry, one would consider if one had *aphno manche* in that ministry on whom one could rely for processing one's request. If no family connections existed, one might consider *chakari* to create a basis for obtaining favors from a status superior. These family relations were usually the most promising sort of *aphno manche*, but beyond that persons who were in one's caste or ethnic group, and after them cultivated friends who could be brought into a morally obligated sense of duty, as would be true in the family, were sought. Thus, creating *aphno manche* relationships through marriage, politics, and a multitude of social events (worship events, parties, gambling, social clubs, sports, hobbies, etc.) was a primary strategy for economic, political, and social mobility.

By the 1980s being able to take advantage of personal connections through *natabad–kripabad* or *aphno manche* to gain advantage over competitors was called having *pahunch* or "source-force." Again, Kondos defines this: "'source' refers to the contact and 'force' refers to the contact's power being more potent or greater than that of your rival's contacts" (1987: 17). In general, Nepalis still refer to their economic and political status in life with reference to how much "source-force" they have or are able to take advantage of – a rhetoric that may even become commingled with beliefs about fate and *karma*, in the sense that in addition to being able to acquire advantageous connections in one's life through skillful social negotiation, it is also possible to be born with or without them. For many Nepalis, *karma* can become the ultimate explanation for why one has little "source-force," again tying social power to ideas about morality in a slightly different way.

In Nepal, being related by birth to someone in the palace and gaining an important social position on that basis was always considered not only legitimate but also highly desirable. It epitomized both intimate belief in the power of the sacred as it was invested in the institution of the family (especially among high castes) and it legitimized this sort of pattern in the extradomestic, extrapalace social spheres. Whelpton refers to the writings of the British Raj emissary, Kirkpatrick, who noted the importance of these sorts of familial links and the power associated with them among the historic *bharadari*, the ruling elite. These persons were given their positions on the basis of their familial connections with the ruling dynasty rather than on the basis of their demonstrated governing or administrative ability or their wealth or their numbers of supporters: "The leading members of this body, whether actually employed or not, appear to possess such a high authority in the state, as renders it nearly impossible for the executive government, in whatever hands that may be, to pursue any measures of an important nature in opposition to their advice" (Kirkpatrick, cited in Whelpton 1992: 20). (Kirkpatrick's critical tone should be noted.) Councils of *bharadari* persisted through the Rana period and beyond. Having *aphno manche* within this elite group guaranteed any Nepali access to privileges which would be otherwise unattainable. However difficult it was for non-high caste Nepalis to achieve such membership, it was not unheard of. In this and other ways, the power connecting palace to subject was expressed in relationships based on the related categories of caste, class, ethnicity, and religion, all of which tied persons together into morally-based networks.

For many Nepalis, *aphno manche* can refer to the system by which benefits accrue to one by birth or by social connection to persons in privileged caste or ethnic groups. One's caste is ascribed as one's family status, and it also refers in Nepal to the wider group of persons occupationally categorized within the Hindu status hierarchy (*varna*). All of one's relatives share one's caste,[8] but two persons of say, the sweeper caste from different villages may not be related. These two sweepers may, however, feel more closely related to one another than to, say, a Brahmin, especially where commensality is concerned. In other circumstances, a sweeper may feel more closely related to a Brahmin from his village, especially if he works for him, than to a sweeper from a distant village, especially where gaining political privileges is concerned. Because caste is also the Hindu label for ethnic identity in Nepal, non-Hindus of the same ethnicity generally feel a stronger sense of kinship with one another than with members of other castes. And, since ethnic identities are largely identified with religious and caste identity (as well as language and other culture), one's sense of moral and even sacred duty to members of one's "group" was easily aroused. At the same time, the creation of social bonds across status groups was what made this system of power so entrenched in Nepal. A Sherpa Buddhist villager from highland Nepal who felt he might benefit from a highly placed Hindu Brahmin from the Kathmandu valley, could establish a social bond with that Brahmin by offering him or someone in his family some benefit (beginning with *chakari*). Once the bond was cemented through exchanges of gifts and favors, the relationship would take on the qualities of those found within families, with their sense of reliability and trust, moral duty and even patriotic duty. Benefits of being born in a highly placed ethnic or caste group were more certain than those acquired by aspiring non-elites who had to work to establish the presence of elites in their *aphno manche* circles. But being able to establish bonds across such barriers remained an effective means of gaining privileges and resources within the system. *Aphno manche*, in this sense, is not isomorphic with caste or ethnicity; it defines a variety of pluralistic networks which determine one's access to resources and privilege.

Religious sensibility played an important role in *aphno manche* networks first by being, in an ecumenical sense, the foundation for legitimizing social obligations in reciprocity as sacred duties (through idioms of family) and second, in a sectarian sense, by enabling people to affirm social ties within their religious cohort as acts of religious duty. Religion in Nepal is not always marked by an either/or distinction between Buddhist and Hindu (or some other religion such as Christianity or Islam), although in *many* cases these are the relevant categories. As Stacy Pigg notes (personal communication) religion is more about what you "do" than it is something you "have" or "are." Religious affiliation can refer to one's ethnicity, which in Nepal can mean caste, linguistic group, endogamous group, or shared region of birth. For example, Thakalis will say they are Thakali by ethnic identity, and when asked for specific relationships to Hinduism or Buddhism they will give a variety of different answers depending upon where they live and what they consider the relevant identifiers at that time they are *doing* something that evokes religious identity (Fisher 1998). *Jat* (caste) and ethnic identity nearly always have customs which entail ritual practices (lifecycle rituals, honoring the dead, making offerings to the gods), but these can be as specific as to be limited to the family or as widely shared as to be practiced by an entire ethnic group. Moreover, for many Nepalis, showing deference for deities and holy figures who are formally outside one's ascribed "religion" is the norm. Religion can thus be a highly ambiguous category for Nepalis, cross-cutting languages, ethnic identities, and sometimes even kinship ties.

The more important consideration of religion among Nepalis is that although membership in one or another religious group was and remains sometimes variable, nearly all Nepalis in the pre-1990 era held deep-seated sentiments about the importance of the sacred and one's moral duty in everyday life. So, for example, nearly all Nepalis considered it important to pay respect to the gods and goddesses who were worshipped in the place they happened to be, whether they lived there or not, but particularly if they did. Nepalis uniformly expressed these religious sentiments by making offerings to deities (and spirits) and by interpreting their fortune and misfortune in terms of the actions of supernatural beings. Although different ethnic groups engaged in a wide variety of *different* practices for the worship of their own, or national-level, deities, almost all held the common belief that to be Nepali meant on some level to behave respectfully towards these beings. This shared religious belief was visible in varied ceremonies to honor lineage deities, or to placate local earth spirits, but it was uniformly expressed at the national level in the worship of the king, who was revered as a "living god", and to a lesser extent in the worship of the major Hindu deities. Because the palace was Hindu, the national character of Nepali religion took on Hindu performative characteristics, whether or not subjects were themselves Hindu. This is partly why the idiom of family is such an important basis for organizing social privileges; it follows the Hindu model of legitimizing family privilege by sacred designation. The fact that the king was Hindu and because Nepal was officially a Hindu monarchy also meant that persons who considered themselves high caste held greater access to privileges than those who did not. Acquiring high status Hindus in one's *aphno manche* group was usually advantageous. But even if one was not connected to powerful high-caste Hindus, again, one's social bonds within the extended family and across them with members of other caste and ethnic groups were themselves formulated around idioms of the sacredness of family. So, it was not uncommon for Nepalis from different caste and ethnic groups to form ritual brotherhood or sisterhood (*mit, mitini*) relationships as expressions of patronage or egalitarian bonds. Nor was it uncommon for Nepalis to invoke the help of the patrilineal gods to secure success in business as would a son invoke help from his father (Bista 1991).

Class position was and is also related to the social nexi of power that predominated in Nepal. If one is well connected to the socially "wealthy" (that is, those whose connections are strong and close to the palace), then one is likely to have greater access to monetary wealth – to a high class position. Class hierarchy and caste hierarchy are often, in this sense, commensurate, and often rationalized as an outcome of sacred privilege. For the most part, caste elites (Brahmins or Nepali Bahuns, Chettris, Thakuris, Ranas, Shahas, etc., and other high-caste families from rural Hindu or Hinduized groups) had more class privileges and resources than low-caste groups (including non-Hindus). Again, this power is typically embedded in palace affiliations, and the palace is itself an example of elite caste privilege and wealth. However, there are numerous high-caste families that are impoverished (particularly Brahmins in the terai) and increasing numbers of low-caste groups (notably some Tibetan, Sherpa and Thakalis) who have great wealth.

Class differences could be overcome by *aphno manche* affiliations and they, too, could be infused with a logic of sacred morality. Sometimes this took the form of a family's patronage of servant families, as in *jajmani* relations. Sometimes it took the form of extending favors to friends or persons who shared caste but not class status, often expressed in sentiments of moral obligations and sacred personal character.

A notion of class, in reference to economic status, has been used by politically active Nepalis for many years as a basis for generating revolutionary forces (Seddon 1987), and it was certainly articulated by the many covertly operating leftist parties in the country for nearly thirty years. But in Nepal "class" has other meanings which in some ways subvert this notion. One of the institutions created by panchayat democracy was the "class organization" of which five were established: ex-servicemen, workers, women, youth, and peasants. These organizations were designed to bring together people with common political interests (Burghart 1993), and political participation under panchayat democracy was at least in some regions articulated through these class organizations (local panchayats had elected representatives for women, youth, etc.). For the most part, however, they did not form the bases for political activities in favor of democracy that were seen in the immediately pre-revolutionary period. Nor did these classes ever take on the sort of unofficial cultural force of the sacred, as did other sorts of cross-caste affiliations. At the same time, a notion of economic class, articulated in terms of the haves and the have-nots (Pigg 1992), did form a basis of popular consciousness with regard to political dissent in the 1990 revolution. But even then, class was arguably never the most important criterion; it was the sense that so few had access to social positions of privilege, including status, that led people to consider a revolution. Access to privilege was not entirely articulated outside of ideas about sociomoral responsibilities to family and friends. By the time of the revolution, however, the terms of dissatisfaction had clearly become focused on economic differences which were not being effectively managed through idioms of moral and sacred family-like duty.

In all cases, access to wealth or status privileges not ascribed by birth came through social affiliations, reciprocal, and patronage ties that cross-cut or were formulated within the more formalized categories of caste, ethnicity, family, or religion. These social affiliations were and are at the core of wealth, even when it was also the product of "hard work" or "merit." "Hard work" in Nepal, in fact, often meant spending a lot of time creating and managing the source and force affiliations through which one obtained rewards in business. In essence, economic wealth was deeply intertwined with the sort of wealth one had in personal associations with other people (manifest as more than symbolic capital). Having friends who would provide one rewards was as valuable as having money and was a means of obtaining economic wealth. Money without social relations was useless. A Sherpa friend once told me that in Nepal "Friends are like cash-value documents. If you have so many friends in so many places, even if you are starving you will have no problems. Making a friend is making an investment; an investment means to make money. You give 10,000 say and you will expect to get back 15,000 at least. So, it's an investment if you spend some money for a friend, to be a friend. . ."

In the 1990s Nepal that I came to know, "source-force" also referred to the use of money to obtain rewards. But substituting cash for social connections in this way has a long history in Nepal. Caplan noted that villagers often used cash rather than kind (in services or goods) to create obligations in other villagers or persons within the local sphere, and this sort of substitution was considered morally correct, but the use of cash outside of such spheres was condemned. To use cash in order to obtain privileges from, say, a government representative was considered bribery (*ghus*) and totally different from the reciprocal relationships that linked together villagers (see Whelpton 1992: 189). This, Caplan explains, is because in one's local network social relationships were secure, predictable, and moral (Caplan 1971: 275), and therefore money was treated as a form of "in kind" substance. Outside of that sphere, where relationships are inherently tenuous and exploitative, money took on the quality of being "untamed" by social bonds, therefore potentially disruptive to them. By the same token, establishing friendships with social superiors in order to gain favors from them was considered not only essential but also morally appropriate. Thus, even when government communications were denouncing corruption (*bhrastachar*) and bribery (*ghus*), in the early 1970s, local Nepalis did not necessarily consider their uses of social connections to obtain rewards and resources problematic at all. This would change by 1990.

If Nepalis in the 1960s and 1970s clearly demarcated between corruption in the form of bribery (occurring outside one's local sphere of relations) and other social techniques of garnering privilege (on the basis of social reciprocity between friends or relatives), Nepalis of the 1990s, especially urban and even slightly educated rural Nepalis, often spoke about any and all sorts of favoritism or social influence in more ambivalent terms, notably linking the use of social connections to "corruption." They often spoke about *"source-force"* as a strategy that as often entailed payment of cash as it did use of social ties. In fact, however, although all use of social connections or cash payments to obtain privileges came to be seen by many as morally unacceptable, that it worked was undisputed. That one had to use them was also undisputed. And that one did not think of oneself as being corrupt in using them was also usually (though not always) undisputed. When necessary, it was always possible to interpret a cash outlay from a non-familiar as a "gift" leading to the furthering of a strong social bond that would engender the exchange of more favors, gifts, and social benefits, just as it was always possible to interpret the offering of a monetary sum between socially unfamiliar or familiar persons as "bribery." In the years leading up to the revolution, Nepali subjects interpreted monetary exchanges in a number of ways, certainly not always as corrupt. As often as the use of money was seen as an instrument that effaced the need for a strong social bond between bestower and recipient of rewards, from the perspective of the seeker of rewards or privileges, the use of money was often seen as a necessary first step in establishing a long-term relationship which might bring rewards even without cash outlays. The ability to read money as a gift worked at all levels of reciprocal transactions. In an exemplary case, Brown (1996: 31), notes that the average Nepali during the Mahendra administration frequently assumed that the distribution of monetary support to schools, hospitals, and other worthy causes was a personal donation from the king's own pocket as opposed to an appropriation of state funds. This was seen as an acceptable form of patronage and one that fit within the Nepali model for social affiliations and exchange. The money was a gift tied to an identifiable person who, in exchange for his expression of concern for his subjects, no less than one would expect from a living incarnation of a god, received loyalty.

Before the revolution, and, I will also argue, thereafter, power was exercised in and through social relationships and indexed by degrees of friendship, loyalty, and obligation, rather than abstract notions of efficacy, government resources, achievement, merit, bureaucratic or objective and neutral procedure. Similarly, the value of money varied in relation to the quality of the bond between persons exchanging it rather than vice versa, but by 1990 money came to be an instrument for strengthening bonds as often as it marked a violation of social responsibility in an act of bribery. By 1990, using money to cement social bonds was often seen as inherently corrupt, no matter who was exchanging or how close they were. As beliefs in standardized objective procedures and abstract notions of distributions of rewards and privilege became more common among Nepalis, so too were they more likely to see any attempt to obtain rewards and privileges through other methods as corrupt. Whereas it was once commonplace for money to be used as a tool for solidifying social relationships within limited social spheres, money eventually became thought of as potentially an instrument of corruption, especially within those limited social spheres. In a world wherein it was seen as morally and socially appropriate to use favoritism and partiality because such acts validated one's sense of moral duty to others, monetary exchanges could be seen as acts of friendship and reciprocal generosity. But in an idealized world wherein no favoritism or partiality affected the distribution of rewards and privileges, monetary exchanges were seen as corrupting.

Again, one of the important factors contributing to the maintenance of the system of patronage and reciprocity among Nepalis was perhaps that social networks between king and subject, patron and client, caste superior and inferior, and even networks cross-cutting caste and class divides, were networks which formed one of the bases upon which Nepalis considered themselves Nepali in a cultural sense. It was through one's social networks of affiliation with the king in particular that one expressed one's Nepali identity in a religious and moral sense. Because the king was revered as sacred, being connected to him through social networks guaranteed rewards in the same way that being connected to the gods by making offerings and promises to reciprocate brought rewards. This pattern of reciprocity was invested with sacred importance, tapping into Nepalis' sense of duty not only to the state and society but to the gods.[9] It was, moreover, a pattern that was replicated all the way down to the social affiliations one had with persons who were even distantly removed from the king.[10] To show respect towards the king was like showing respect to the gods, and by the same token treating a superior from whom one might obtain rewards with the same reverence shown a god or king would be not only a way of showing respect for others but also the most efficacious way of guaranteeing rewards from them. One's sense of duty towards and respect for the traditions upon which notions of the sacred, in a religious sense, were based carried over into one's relationships with one's family and beyond that with all others with whom one became connected in one's society, following the model provided by one's relationship to the king and his family. This sort of sociomoral character of one's relationships inscribed the metaphor of the family on the whole social system.

Nevertheless, by the 1990 revolution, Nepalis of all walks of life began calling this form of power corrupt. Using social affiliations to obtain rewards and resources was increasingly considered an abuse – and eventually a moral abuse – against one's fellow citizens. The transformation occurred partially at least as a product of the panchayat era of development which both made use of traditional modes of power to advocate development, but also criticized such modes of power. This left many Nepalis with a good deal of ambivalence about their traditional ways of conducting business and engaging in social life. On the one hand, such exercises of power came to be seen as an obstacle to development and the main reason for Nepali suffering. On the other hand, popular sentiment about one's personal relationships with the king and his palace still held such exercises of social affiliation as part of one's sacred duty as a Nepali citizen. Use of these relations to help friends and families was often thought to be morally appropriate, but this was coupled with an enormous antipathy towards this sort of relationship when it was used to promote what came to be called unfair favoritism as articulated by development programs and modernization advocates, or one's competitors.

Assessments of corruption – of calling any use of social affiliation for obtaining privileges corrupt – emerged with the rising professional and Westernized classes which internalized critiques from the West. The use of affiliations was increasingly seen as corrupt when compared with the sort of impartial system proposed by internal and external development agents. As Shaha notes, the sort of power common in Nepal contrasts with that believed to exist in a modern, Western context: "informal contacts [in Nepal] take precedence over formal procedures and power vests in the hands of persons or personalities [in Nepal] rather than in institutions" (1993: 31). But Nepalis in general took a fair amount of comfort in the belief that social networks tied one to the king, making one part of the greater Nepali family. It was upon the basis of such social connections that many Nepalis articulated their notions of respectable behavior – behavior that was in some sense religious. The relevant distinction with the West was seen as the sources of the strategies that generated the normative models for society: in the so-called developed West, normative ideals were believed to be handed down from scholarly scientific, impartial, and democratic institutions, whereas for all but the intelligentsia opposition in Nepal, the normative model was often the palace, taken as a paragon of family life with all its patrimonialism, demands for personal loyalty, as well as religious and moral obligation.

The use of social connections to obtain rewards through "unofficial" channels is commonplace in many Western democratic countries. In fact, one could argue that such an informal system of social partiality serves as the "shadow" institutional means by which most things from business to politics work in countries like the United States. At the same time, in the

United States at least, the use of such connections and the benefits that derive from them are nearly always thought of as being morally corrupt. People know that they exist and people make use of them regularly, but they also know that they may run the risk of being accused of favoritism, nepotism, influence peddling, etc. when they do. While there are clearly exceptions, in general, the more invisible people make such unofficial connections (for example, using alumni pull to obtain a job), the safer they feel. In Nepal, I would argue that this idea that there is an official way to do things and that using social affiliations should be seen as corrupt is rather new. I would argue that before the development era, this sort of social practice was "official" and publicly sanctioned. It was considered acceptable, within certain boundaries, to use influence and partiality towards family and friends because such practices functioned within social nexi involving family, caste, ethnicity, religion, and the moral sense of responsibility these engendered. The palace itself was a model of this patrimonial system, and from the palace all the way to the village it required social interdependencies and long-term obligations between persons. This system models society on the extended family. Few ordinary Nepalis knew much about the king or his family or had ever seen him face to face, but so long as one had face-to-face relations with someone who had connections with the palace or the royal family, or with someone who knew someone who had such connections, no matter how distant, then one could obtain rewards that devolved from the palace. As in most gift economies, the markers indicating wealth were, and are, associated with family, obligated friends, and reciprocal ties, and how close any of them are to the palace.

There is ample evidence that calling practices of favoritism and partiality corrupt is a Western development era impact. In fact, the term for "giving priority to family" is a Nepali-invented Sanskrit neologism for the Western concept of "nepotism": *natabad*. Giving priority to those deemed worthy on the basis of social status or social bonds came to be called *kripabad*, again a Sanskrit neologism corresponding to the Western concept of "favoritism." Even the word for corruption, *bhrastachar*, is a Sanskrit neologism (David N. Gellner, personal communication 1996).[11] The emergence of the blanket term "source-force" spoken by Nepalis in English to refer to the use of any social influence to obtain benefits is another sign of an internalized Western perception that such practices *should* be uniformly considered "corrupt." The persistent ambivalence about these concepts among many Nepalis might be another. The attitude of many Nepalis regarding the social-nexus-based practices of power is revealed in a telling case conveyed to me by a fellow Nepal scholar. When he asked one of his Newar friends if he knew what *kripabad* (favoritism) was, the friend "explained it as something like gratitude, and said, 'Yes, it is a good thing.' Then he went on to say, 'Actually, there's a good form and a bad form.' And he explained it as favouring friends, whereas *natabad* (familism, nepotism) is favouring relatives. Both he and his wife insist that ordinary people do understand these words, even the illiterate, because they have become extremely common with widespread political discussion" (David N. Gellner, personal communication, 1996). However great the ambivalence, one pole of the ambiguity took hold as the dominant discourse by the time of the revolution. The idea that corruption was bad, and that favoritism, familism, *aphno manche* and source-force could be called corrupt was widespread by 1990, and it was enough to constitute a powerful motive for revolution.

How did this happen? Although nurtured under Rana rule, this sort of power associated with the power of social affiliations was continued after restoration and to some extent cultivated under panchayat democracy. At the same time, the panchayat system set the stage for tremendous change. Because the panchayat era increasingly made use of a rhetoric of develop-ment to consolidate government power, Nepalis increasingly understood their social positions and underprivilege in terms of that rhetoric. By hanging on to a traditional mode of power derived from social affiliations and legitimized in the sort of relationship idealized in one's sacred ties to the king, the government's shortcomings in providing development were eventually seen by the intellectuals at first, and later by much of the public as a whole, as a result of this sort of power. In some ways, this might have been an expected outcome of a political system that was designed as an "indigenous alternative" to Western and Indian parliamentarianism (Whelpton 1997) – a system that would bring a monarchically organized nation into the twentieth century with all of its democratic strivings while hanging on to a mode of power distinctly non-modern in so far as it was constituted around sacred and moral sensibilities.

Development and Panchayat "corruption"

Since 1951, along with tourists and diplomats from the West, scores of bilateral and multilateral development aid providers have dramatically altered Nepal's cultural and social landscape. As Chaitanya Misra and Pitamber Sharma (1983: 1) tell it from a financial perspective:

> the story of foreign aid in Nepal is the story of a trickle turning into a torrent – an image that is more than literal in Nepal. The grant of Rs. 22,000 in the fiscal year 1951/52 from the United States Government under the Point Four Assistance Programme was to be the modest beginning of a multi-million rupee enterprise on which the

paraphernalia of Nepal's "development" would be contingent. The cumulative aid inflow into Nepal in the 30 year period between 1951/52 and 1979/80 has been a staggering Rs. 7734.4 million (roughly 13 million dollars per year).

By 1993 the cumulative amount that the United States alone had contributed to development aid in Nepal, a country no larger than the state of Florida, was over US $1 billion, with a USAID operating budget of $21 million a year in 1993.[12] And the United States was only *one* of the major donors. The total government estimate of foreign aid (grants and loans) to Nepal in 1990–91 was $286.5 million (at US$=Rs. 28), amounting to 40 percent of Nepal government expenditures.[13] Nearly all developed countries of the West, as well as India, the Soviet Union, China, and Japan, had diplomatic relations and foreign aid development programs in Nepal. Additionally, all of the major multilateral aid organizations had contributed enormously to Nepal, and international (non-profit) non-governmental organizations (INGOs) proliferated throughout the 1970s and 1980s. The shift in development policy towards privatization at the end of the United States' Reagan years, the effects of World Bank IMF structural adjustment programs which shifted emphasis to "user groups" and self-financing schemes for rural development and health-care institutions, and the increasing stress on a "people-centered, grass-roots" model for development in metropole agendas led to an enormous growth of in-country NGOs working under bilateral, multilateral, and international grants and loans. In 1994 it was reported that there were 6,000 local NGOs in Nepal, handling Rs. 2 billion ($400 million), or roughly one-twentieth of the amount of the operating budget of the government for 1994/95, all with the goal of "development."

Despite the enormous influx of foreign aid into Nepal, the outcomes have been less positive for Nepalis than most donors admit. Raeper and Hoftun (1992: 76) note that between 1951 and the late 1980s education levels rose from 2 percent to 40 percent, but fertility also increased so that the population grew from 8 million to 20 million in that same period and is now seen by some as being at crisis proportions. Per capita income in Nepal has not increased in proportion to rates of inflation, and therefore most of Nepal's people, rural subsistence agriculturalists, are arguably less well off than before the onset of development aid with a per capita income of only $160. Nepal's foreign trade deficit increased to Rs. 28,621.2 million ($564.1 million) by 1994, and this was set alongside enormous debts incurred through development aid (from India, Western nations, and multilateral lending institutions). With an annual gross domestic product of only about $2.7 billion, Nepal is still one of the poorest and least developed countries of the world. Infant mortality (under one year of age) has been reduced only slightly after forty years of aid and is still at 102 per 1,000 live births, and child mortality (under fives) is still at 197 per 1000.[14] Maternal mortality is 850 per 100,000 per year or one in thirteen (Maskey et al. 1994). Basic health indicators (especially morbidity from infectious diseases) are not greatly improved despite increases in the number of health professionals working in the public or private sectors on curative and preventive public health efforts. Medical programs designed and operated almost solely by foreign charities have shown the greatest success, but even these have had minimal impact on the overall health of the Nepali population. As the country itself becomes more indebted, the poverty of the majority classes is exacerbated, making such things as medicines, birth control, visits to clinics, and even more basic things such as education for children, basic nutrition, and clean water less rather than more attainable.

The visible failures of development notwithstanding, it had become for many Nepalis virtually synonymous with modernization, and in the years leading up to the revolution it came to stand, along with democracy, for everything that the Nepali people felt they needed in order to be happy, prosperous, and free (Bhattachan 1995). Most of the new technical professionals of Nepal are supportive of the efforts at development, even though many of them are vocal critics of the strategies thus far adopted by development planners. They argue that development projects are designed with the interests of donor institutions rather than those of local recipients in mind (IDS 1983; Dixit 1992; Gyawali 1991; see also review by Clarke 1990).[15] For example, the pursuit of uniform and quantifiable comparable outcomes is inconsistent with the desire to meet the specific needs of local people and to deal with local problems which are often culturally and physically unique. The critics point out that by the time the development aid is processed through the grinding mills of the government and development experts, all that is left for the people is the dust on the grinding stone. They note that few large development organizations remain accountable to the people once the projects have begun and that many development projects are adopted solely to provide contracts for donor-country companies (whether for construction work or for products used in construction or expensive foreign advisers). Planning at the national level is often severely hampered by the constraints of a dependent economy; long-term national planning must always be carried out in terms of priorities determined by donor schedules and interests (Wildavsky 1976; Justice 1987). Although the situation is changing, gross inequalities have typically existed between the pay rates of Nepalis and their foreign counterparts despite often equal qualifications – a criticism which reflects not simply a desire for personal gain but also a concern for an increase in Nepal's GDP.[16]

But the development industry in Nepal survives this critique because of the large class of urban professionals trained in development epistemologies which it created. These professionals define Nepal's crises and apply solutions to them consistent with Western development-industry interests (Pigg 1993). Most of the criticisms of development aid are therefore aimed not at stopping modernization but at rooting out the obstacles to it, and only rarely is discontinuation of all foreign aid seen as the most viable solution to the problems of underdevelopment (but see Himal 1989 and 1992 and other issues, and I note that this sentiment is proliferating). Most internal critics embrace foreign aid insofar as it can contribute to a better society. Their rejection of aid is targeted at rooting out failed programs in order to make room for better ones. Often these failures are blamed on corruption. Better technical and scientific expertise than has hitherto been seen – especially technical programs which provide an alternative to corruption – is still largely thought capable of solving Nepal's problems.

Since the 1950s Nepalis have received training in the technical areas considered vital to Nepal's development – including agricultural and forestry sciences, medicine, economics, engineering, and policy. The technical and scientific knowledge Nepalis have brought home has tended to be applied to development concerns, especially infrastructural projects (dams, roads, bridges) and health programs (clinical and public health for both rural and urban care) rather than the creation of laboratory academic or commercial enterprises, giving Nepali science an appearance different from sciences in industrialized settings. Nevertheless, Nepalis have in many ways embraced the same belief in the efficacy of science as found in these other countries. Development apparatuses deployed over the past thirty to forty years in Nepal have articulated a meaning of modern science and truth for rural and urban Nepalis. Particularly the belief that if they embrace development, they will be modern and they will be less reliant on what was often referred to as corruption – the use of social affiliations to obtain rewards and privileges.

Villagers experience development in the numerous indicators of it in their rural homes – village health personnel, immunization teams, foreign researchers, agricultural experts, deforestation experts, road construction crews, hydroelectric technicians – or, often, in the absence of these indicators as an unfulfilled foreign aid promise. They know that they are supposed to have certain things, and they know that they do not yet have them (Pigg 1992; Stone 1986). Urbanites too experience modernity as an increase in infrastructure and technically sophisticated possibilities, many of which they actually already make use of (from pharmaceuticals to satellite television), although they are also likely to experience the limitations on these resources imposed by social class which they are likely to read as unfulfilled development promises.

One of the important institutions through which the expectations of modernization have been aroused was the panchayat government. The employment of technical experts was both managed and manipulated through this system's governance. And the widespread growth in expectations for development came from the presence of these experts. Because the panchayat system of government became articulated from the early 1960s onward with the cause célèbre of government – development – it is not surprising that this system was also the target of blame for development's failures and omissions. The balance of power lay sometimes with foreign aid objectives and sometimes with local ones, which means that at least some of the time, development aid was being articulated in and through the institutions of social affiliation that came to be considered corrupt when and if programs failed.

This process of failure and the explanations of blame it engendered occurred at all levels. At the highest levels, the government was constantly pressured by multilateral and bilateral aid institutions to implement policies that would bring about development more quickly and more efficiently. This meant promoting technical solutions to technical problems, internalizing a critique that blamed development failures on corruption, yet conforming to foreign aid demands that local aid recipients and program officers not destabilize the current (seemingly stable) government system (the monarchy).[17] This came to be seen as a form of external profiteering, keeping foreign development agencies and their local national advisors in business without keeping them accountable to local recipients. Inside the country, foreign aid entering Nepal was processed through the Social Service National Coordination Committee (SSNCC), an institution putatively devoted to ensuring coordination among donor projects and some measure of conformity with at least national governmental objectives. Seemingly critical for successful development in Nepal, this council was directed by the queen, but it is said to have become a means of ensuring that privileges for development contracts went to those connected to the palace, that appropriate amounts of "commission" (*baksheesh*) were distributed to Nepali governmental agents, and that projects would be implemented in a manner that would ensure continued support of the current government.

All the way down to the village level, it was argued that panchayati officials made use of development aid resources as bargaining chips among constituents. Projects begun in any village or region always had the stamp of approval and "sponsorship" of the local government official, whether or not he was in fact instrumental in securing the resources, and this essentially meant he was receiving a "commission" (baksheesh).[18] Promises of more development resources became a useful political currency, especially during election years. As local politicians were able to ride into political offices on the bandwagon of development promises, so too were failed development projects the impetus behind villagers' perceptions that these politicians were corrupt. For nearly thirty years the panchayat regime promoted and benefited from its close alliances with development apparatuses, and thus government became an important site for the expression of both development aspirations and, necessarily, development frustrations. It was probably inevitable that by 1990 rural and urban Nepalis alike, distraught with their lack of development, chose to articulate their anger in the form of demands for a new political system. It was probably also inevitable that for a king whose panchayat regime held power on the platform of development and modernization, it would be impossible to oppose a revolution claiming to bring better techniques of modernity, better science, to the citizens of his land. The medical professionals probably made this dilemma highly visible to him.

Kondos (1987) argues convincingly that the systems of influence being critiqued and called corruption in the late 1980s in fact constitute a cultural rule by which Nepali society is organized: partiality. The idea of impartial decision-making and distribution of resources is perhaps, he notes, distinctly a Western ideal (seldom achieved in practice in the West). Though ideas about unfairness have long been articulated by Nepali intellectuals for forty years, the popular spread of the Western-derived critique of corruption – corruption based on the use of family connections or other forms of social partiality – was not apparent throughout Nepali society until the late 1980s, when development rhetoric had penetrated to the farthest reaches of the countryside and extended to all sectors of the urban milieu.

Stacy Pigg (1993) shows that contemporary villagers in Nepal have come to think of themselves as "backward" because of rhetoric employed by international and national purveyors of development. They have also internalized ideas about the obstacles to development in terms provided by that rhetoric – villagers' lack of education, their traditional lifestyle, their inability to use development resources, and the bankruptcy of their backward ways – and consequently they have also learned to use an index of corruption that also attacks traditional ways of doing things. They use this index to mark of their own modernity and to gauge how well their politicians treat them, displacing development accusations of corruption on to the targets development rhetoric itself tends to identify as sources of corruption. If they fail to achieve development, many villagers reason, it is not because the development program itself is poorly designed or built to fail, nor is it entirely because they are ignorant. Rather, it is because they are being abused by someone or some people who are corrupt. Development literature itself often displaces the blame for failed development on to the targets of the aid. When it does not, it tends to place blame on the next tier of local culture – the local national intermediaries who themselves rise to power from development resources. This tendency also added to villagers' willingness to blame their suffering from lack of development on local, corrupt panchayati politicians.

Pigg notes that villagers feel excluded from access to development in the same way that they have been made to feel excluded by caste hierarchies in the past. Accordingly, I suggest, following Kondos, this transition involved a critical shift in the way that Nepalis felt and feel about institutionalized use of "social connections." Whereas villagers in the past knew that using techniques of *chakari*, familism, favoritism, and *aphno manche* both reinforced and enabled one to evade the exclusions of caste hierarchies, in the panchayat era such strategies came to be articulated as unfair exclusion from development, enabling some people to reap its rewards while others were persistently denied them.

Thus, while panchayat institutions provided an apparatus for development, they also made the problem of uneven development more visible. Panchayat institutions are seen as having paved the way for revolution by failing to provide enough development and by systematically silencing oppositional voices (Adhikary 1995: 14):

> For nearly three decades, development discourse infused with nationalism was a device for Panchayat politicians to quiet alternative views. National media highlighted government promises and exaggerated development achievements, sustaining this process. However, as the Nepalese people increasingly noticed the discrepancies between the proclaimed gains of development and the realities they experienced, even the normally quiet people in the hills began to protest.

Political intellectuals in the decade before 1990 had been voicing opposition to patrimonialism, and many knew that this would result in calls for the removal of the person who symbolized "corrupt" strategies and for a Western-style government. As Kondos (1987: 28) put it:

> What is significant in the Nepali situation is that whilst the westernized intellectuals articulate their views on corruption in the context of their evaluations of planned development, often claiming that the negative outcomes of development programmes are largely due to administrative corruption, they are also using this opportunity to be highly critical of the mode of government as a whole, and in this way pressing for a new form of government along the lines their predecessors did in 1951.

It is no wonder that the desires for social change became articulated around notions of a democracy born of the institutions exported from foreign nations, for it was arguably a foreign, and largely Western, view of the social problems that provided Nepali political activists within and outside the panchayat system with a sense of what was wrong and needed to be fixed in Nepali society. Even those who were educated in socialist countries adopted the critique articulated by metropole- and Western-dominated aid agencies. In place of the patrimonialism, the Nepalis who called for a revolution wanted an *impartial* system. As early as 1951, according to Kondos (1987: 25), foreign educated Nepalis wanted "an administration that would operate in terms of a set of rules and regulations aiming at theoretical neutrality both in their formulation and application. . . . In other words, what was desired, was an administration based on the notion of rationality as theorised by Weber and which is generally seen to characterise administrations in contemporary Western societies." The same was true in 1990. The new political system, because it would not operationalize power through the same nexi of social relationships that were used in the old regime, would be democracy: *bahadul prajatantra*, multiparty democracy. It would be the solution to Nepal's problems; it would eliminate corruption and usher in true development.

Ironically, considering the influence of Western development rhetoric in particular in defining patrimonialism and the reciprocal exchanges found in familism, favoritism, and partiality as the enemy of democracy because they were the enemy to standardized objective rules and procedures (scientific, legal, etc.), calls for a democracy were also articulated around fears of Western hegemony. Some intellectuals envisioned a Nepali democracy as a unique one, making use of principles that held universal appeal because they were derived from universal truths and therefore capable of nurturing a local democracy that would be distinctively Nepali in character. Dr. M. Maskey played an important role in the movement as an organizer of the health professionals. He told me about this vision:

We think that the democracy we have fought for will be different from the democracy of the West. We have seen the way that it works in the Soviet Union and China, and we have seen the democracies of the West and we will take something from both of these and make a democracy that is our own. We will take the best from each system, but, you know, the West – and especially the United States – we have seen how many problems there are with your society and we don't want the crime and the problems you have. So many people haven't even any family. For a philosophical perspective, you should look at the book *What Is Living and What Is Dead in Indian Philosophy*, by Debi P. Chattopadhyaya, to see what philosophical tradition and renewal are desired to shape the features of Nepali characteristics in the new age. They may provide a glimpse . . . indirectly . . . of the philosophical basis of continuity and change . . . about the things that are unique to Nepal in our religion and in our society.

Adopting the logic of modern science articulated by development planners (Alvarez 1988), many Nepalis came to believe that all failures of development were attributable to factors external to science itself – that is, to culture – and therefore backward culture was the obstacle that had to be overcome to achieve modernization. But many of these same Nepalis held on to the idea that a distinctive Nepali culture could be retained after a revolution that brought modernity and that it would retain national character and, more importantly, remain invested with cultural sensibilities about sacred and moral duty in their hoped-for democracy. Thus patterns of corruption (although themselves embedded in culture) were targeted as the obstacles to development, while "culture" was bracketed as something which would give Nepal a unique national character. Multiparty democracy would serve as a constitutive institution enabling this combination of rational and objective social process with unique and morally rich Nepali culture.

Eradicating corruption as a motivation for Nepali democracy

For many urban professionals who were already elite by caste, class, and ethnic standards, the People's Movement of 1990 was a movement to gain freedom of expression, particularly freedom of political expression without fear of (often) violent repression. These professionals recognized that poverty and social inequality in the countryside were a reason for political change, but without freedom to speak out against the current regime, their interests were compromised. For most rural Nepalis, the need for democracy was inextricably intertwined with the desire for an end to poverty and for advancement towards the "development" that might contribute to the achievement of this goal. The thing that tied these urban and rural goals together for educated urban Nepalis was a desire for an end to what they saw as corruption, for in their view it was corruption more than anything else that impeded freedom, social equality, and development. As Dr. A. M., a physician and writer, put it:

> The king was the most responsible person, his being king comes with responsibility. It comes with our culture that the most powerful man is the most revered. And when the people have seen over thirty years how the palace is involved in all of this corruption. And the educated people were quite clear about the palace role.. . . A democracy was what we had in mind, but our motivations were different [from those of the masses]. We didn't have a problem with [lack of] food. We had problems with our expression, democratic freedom, creativity, that kind of cultural and educational renaissance and a nation-building challenge, and for industries that will allow entrepreneurship.

Educated and aspiring Nepalis from both the rural village or town and the capital wanted to see a complete overhaul of the system by which opportunities were made available. They wanted a system in which performance was more important than patronage, rewards were allocated according to merit, and achievement was measured by "objective" standards. Shaha exemplified this view in his comment that *darshan*, the blessing of a status superior (the ultimate one being from the king), "is antithetical to the spirit and methods of institutionalisation and modernisation" (1993: 11). In the old system, *darshan* guaranteed privilege much more efficiently than whatever versions of "objective merit" might be generated from institutionalization and modernization, but in the 1980s, dreams of democracy that had been imported partially as development agendas, made *darshan* into corruption – a morally problematic practice leading to partiality.

The logic resonating between the dominant political parties operating illegally by the late 1980s was clear: development was the panacea for Nepali social problems, development was only possible in a modern system that used scientific methods for organizing social life, and such modernization was possible only in a truly free democracy wherein objective standards were the basis for distribution of privileges. Sometimes the more sanguine argued the reverse – that democracy was the panacea and was possible only in a truly developed society. In either case, the paramount idea held by Nepali activists at the time of the revolution and shared by many Nepalis across the country was that only if "source-force," *aphno manche*, nepotism, and favoritism – corruption – were eradicated would development or democracy be possible.

The idea that there was a standard and ethical way to provide opportunities as opposed to a corrupt way that relied on "source-force" appeared in statements like the following one by D. U., a high-level administrator in the Nursing Faculty at Teaching Hospital:

I was pressured by the minister of health many times, but I was a very strong woman. I tell you very frankly, they asked me to enroll certain people in the nursing school even though they had failed their exams. They tried several times and failed, but I was pressured to accept them. These students were from his caste group and were like family members to him, but he used the argument that they were from an underrepresented caste and should therefore have different standards applied. I said, "Do you want a failed nurse to be a nurse to you? Would you like that kind of nurse to give you your injections?" I told him if he wanted to be this kind of minister of health, I would write on the application of that candidate that I have done this because I was ordered to accept her. "But before you do that for your own people, for aphno manche, you must do that for everybody who has failed in that batch. You must bring all the people back. I don't consider only your people to be eligible," I told him. I had my resignation already written in my bag. I knew that they would fire me, but you know, he was a high school teacher before, and he completely turned around. He said I was perfectly right, so from then on they did not bother me with that kind of demand.

Many others were not so lucky, and many professionals resigned over what they considered to be the use of undue social influence. In the years prior to the People's Movement, numerous Nepalis offered the same criticisms, identifying traditional strategies which emphasized favoritism towards family and social reciprocity as corrupt and as the major reason for Nepal's underdevelopment. Elements of this view, which I have argued arose as an internalization of Western critiques of Nepali traditional culture, are exemplified in a book by Dor Bahadur Bista, one of Nepal's premier anthropologists, *Fatalism and Development: Nepal's Struggle for Modernization* (1991). Here, he argues that the Brahminical worldview imposed on Nepal's populations by conquering Hindus from the plains of India in the eighteenth century has produced a widespread fatalism that is inimical to development because it nurtures various forms of corruption. He suggests that adopting "Brahminism" (in Nepal, "Bahunism") is only one of many possible ways of participating in a caste society, but it is a way that reinforces class stratification and impedes development by encouraging dependency. He points to a number of practices that lead to dependency instead of independent achievement. *Aphno manche*, he says, impedes cooperative action and results in factionalism and corruption. *Chakari* leads to a type of "sycophancy" extended to all those in positions of power. Despite his suggestion that the truly historic Nepal did not have these problems of favoritism or bahunism, he occasionally invokes the West as a model for Nepal's future. In the West, he says, "it is not who you know but what you know," whereas in Nepal "it is not what you know but who you know" that brings privileges and rewards. The presence of *chakari* is, for Bista, an indication that Nepal not only needs to learn new things in order to progress, but must also unlearn old things (1991: 5). Despite their requirement of active management and pursuit, these traditional and "corrupt" practices foster the assumption that one's life is under the rule of the collective.

Bista identifies a host of other behavioral norms associated with Brahminism, which he assumes that all Nepalis aspire to. Education, he argues, is treated as a hallmark of status, rather than a means of developing skills. The Brahminical goal is a salaried job that enables one to delegate work and diffuses responsibility for productivity. The idea that the gods are behind it all enables one to blame others for not doing the work one shamelessly refuses to do. With its cyclical apprehension of time and its endless cycles of rebirth, Brahminism makes it hard to be deadline-conscious or concerned with planning for the future. The addition of bureaucratic culture to this fatal nexus leads, he says, to absolute inefficiency. The system of dependencies upon collective social action that Bista describes produces a high degree of stability but, he argues, it also stifles "progress." Those who aspire to and hold important offices seek modernization for Nepal but are largely foreign-educated and remain out of touch with the needs of the people. Their desire to succeed forces them to adopt and aspire to Brahminism, which, in turn, translates to defeatism within their own system. Consequently, they look to the outside world as a source of sophistication and culture – a direction that Bista considers problematic. He sees the salvation of Nepal in the ethics of equality found among its various ethnic groups but abandoned in favor of fatalism by their elites. Finally, he suggests that despite the fact that in his view colonialism "left a positive legacy of development" in India and that Nepal, not having been colonized, lacks infrastructure that many developing countries have (Bista 1991: 28), he feels that Nepalis ought to look to their own traditions as models for their future. His dénouement that rejects Western hegemony notwithstanding, Bista has clearly drawn from development rhetorics which have also blamed development's failures on specific kinds of Nepali culture, although in his case this culture is not truly Nepali but a holdover from another era of colonialism by plains Hindu elites. Suggesting that neither Indian nor Western hegemony will suffice, Bista brackets "culture" as that which will provide Nepali nationalism a distinction of its own but does not require practices of caste inequality, Brahminism, favoritism, *chakari*, and patrimonialism – the reasons for Nepal's failure to develop. Just like the development view which holds that traditional culture is both a nemesis and resource for Nepal's modern future, this argument has served to justify calls for a society organized around objective principles of science, equality, and democracy while still remaining distinctively Nepali in culture and national character.

It might be argued that Bista's views are peculiar to the social position from which he speaks; he is a high-caste Chettri and an anthropologist alert to the political sensitivities of ethnic groups that view the king's Hinduism as a form of hegemony. But it might also be suggested that the behaviors he identifies as corrupt are, in fact, traditional ways of being "Nepali" precisely because the king engaged in them and because these relationships have for many years been the means by which moral responsibility has been operationalized in everyday Nepali social life. I am not then suggesting that the sorts of behaviors he identifies as problematic are thus something to be either glorified or targeted as true obstacles to development; rather, I am interested in examining the forces that compelled Bista to articulate his country's problems in this particular way. I am also interested in how the many persons who shared his views negotiated this sort of self-criticism before, during, and after the revolution by juxtaposing it to something different – an impartial system. In any case, his sentiments capture the mood of many Nepalis at the time of the revolution, when the cultural pattern which put family and social affiliations first was called corruption and identified as the reason for all Nepalis' troubles, whether in terms of bahunism, political representation, economic opportunity, or otherwise. Given the widespread internalization of the idea that certain traditional ways of doing things were corrupt, and that the king epitomized these ways of doing things, the revolution made sense. Gellner (1993: 228) points to its inevitability, under the circumstances:

> Increasingly . . . the Panchayat system came to be seen as corrupt. Since there were no parties, the National Assembly became divided into factions owing allegiance to different personalities, with links to different people in the royal palace. The example of India, a secular republic where political parties and trade unions could operate freely, was continually before the people. Finally, and perhaps most crucially, the Panchayat system became associated with economic failures, which ironically the governments in question could probably do little about. This, very briefly, is the background to the unrest of 1990 which led to the downfall of the Panchayat regime.

Corruption became perhaps the most salient motivating factor in the revolution, for even economic failures were blamed on corrupt use of foreign aid, misappropriation of government funds and resources, and exclusive access to economic opportunities. Even the lack of political freedom was tied to corruption, since it was believed that the reason political opposition was punished was that elites' corrupt hold on privilege and power would be undermined by it. In the end, the king and queen themselves came to represent everything that was wrong with panchayati Nepal, because the panchayat system was seen as the king's own system. The king held the unenviable position of being chief arbiter of socially based distributions of development's rewards and privileges. People came to see that the panchayat system used a rhetoric of development to preserve the nexus of power on which the king and his family relied for maintaining social order and for protecting their personal financial and social security. Additionally, this system's ability to ensure rewards for the average Nepali had begun to be seen as ineffective because the development promises it had promulgated to them remained unfulfilled.

If the system failed, it was because it was corrupt; and if the system was corrupt, they reasoned, then the king and queen must themselves be corrupt. The significance of this was stressed by Dr. M. D., an organizer of the People's Movement:

It was difficult for the Panchayatis to deliver the goods and "be straight from" [avoid] corruption for up to thirty years, cumulatively. The King and Queen came to stand for the very idea of corruption. "Pampha devi" the protestors yelled. I mean, this was a breakthrough. It had never before occurred in Nepal. That kind of anger accumulated and they even brought out his [the king's] name and spoke like that against him. You have to understand about the monarch; you have to keep in mind that he is considered an incarnation of a revered god. So [the people] were ready to change their way of looking and rethinking the religious aspect of their society. Because . . . the religious aspect . . . the movement's hatred borne by the movement and the mass killing, suffering was so much. . . . I think there was a breaking point at which they did not hesitate to come out against him and call his name. So they were not only challenging the "source-force," they were challenging the whole thing. In the heat of the moment, they were saying to go out of the country. . . . That was the slogan. *Birechor* – Bir is the Birendra, Birechor [*bire cor des chod*] means thief – country thief, leave the country. . . . So even the pro-panchayat people were literally demoralized, and when the critical mass of politically conscious physicians set the ball rolling and assumed the responsibility of leadership in the professional sphere . . . at that time, the movement was successful.

When doctors articulated their demands for democracy their calls were for impartial principles of science and morality – principles which they believed transcended structures of partiality that plagued Nepal. For many, there was a belief that the medical profession provided them with the truths around which not only government but the whole of social life could be organized – that is what a democracy represented. But, the ideal democracy many of them aspired to was supposed to resemble Western society only in some ways. The shift from panchayat to constitutional monarchy and multiparty democracy was perceived to entail a shift both in the ways in which privilege was distributed and the ways in which politics were conducted. The politics of reciprocity, patronage and flattery would give way to profession, political parties, and truth. Most important, the new system of government would treat all citizens as individuals with the same rights and duties, privileges and responsibilities. This vision of a democratic politics was, however, also articulated through very specific notions of Nepali national identity.

    The text to which Dr. M. Maskey referred me above, by Debiprasad Chattopadhyaya, proved to contain a materialist critique of Indian philosophical idealism (both Hindu and Buddhist), in favor of a heterodox pre-Gupta philosophy that opposed Brahminism called Lokayata.

Like Bista, Chattopadhyaya would have his countrymen return to the philosophies already present in South Asia to promote science and the principles of materialism. In doing so, he sought not so much a South Asian science as principles upon which universalist science was formulated in the South Asian historical context. His argument for a materialist view of consciousness helps to clarify his point (Chattopadhyaya 1976: 610; see also Samkhya, cited in Chattopadhyaya 1976: 422):

> If there is anything in traditional Indian philosophy that has successfully stood the test of advanced scientific knowledge, it is this proposition of the Lokayatas, viz that consciousness – ordinarily understood as the differentia of spirit or soul – is only a product of matter. Rejecting the conception of the soul, the Lokayatas talk of enjoying life rather than evading it. While the others view life as only a painful prelude to eternity, the Lokayatas are the only Indian philosophers to insist on making "the most of our brief lives as human animals." There is no sense, according to them, in taking such a gloomy view of human existence as to imagine that the only way of avoiding suffering is to negate life altogether.

Chattopadhyaya searches the Indic traditions for a dialectical materialism, but ultimately he finds most of them lacking in support for the sort of materialist freedom he would advocate.[19] Perhaps ironically, he ends up with a dialectical materialism which can undermine Brahminism but in the spirit of both the Lokayatas and the Western philosopher Jean-Paul Sartre.[20] Later he advocated support for the medical science of India, Ayurveda, as truly South Asian in origin, envisioning its materialism and efficacy as transcending culture and ideology while remaining philosophically Indic. This valorization of an ethnoscience, even at the risk of legitimating it in terms of a hybrid set of philosophical positions, clearly influenced at least some Nepali intellectuals.

Although I encountered no biomedical practitioners who envisioned a return to Ayurveda, echoes of Chattopadhyaya's materialist, dialectical, and "indigenized" agenda for liberation are found in the work of various Nepali intellectuals and literati today. One of these, Pramod Parajuli (1992), suggests that the real threat to Nepal's civil society is the ongoing failure of the elites to recognize and attend to resistance among the subordinated masses. Parajuli argues for a dialectical materialism which would allow the masses a more participatory role in governmental and development decision-making and greater attentiveness to the ways in which the masses resist domination by elites. He sees Nepal as having experienced three distinct eras of "partially successful" hegemony: a pre-unification (pre-1768) era which effected hegemony through notions of dharma; a post-unification era in which the hegemonic principle was national integration; and a contemporary era (beginning in 1951) organized around the hegemonic principle of development.[21]

To the extent that Parajuli sees development as itself a subordinating discourse, he is more critical than many of the revolutionaries in the health professions I met. At the same time, he notes, as do other revolutionaries in Nepal, that the development rhetorics can be used either to attend to the needs of the majorities or to oppress them. He shares with many medical professionals the idea that development can be attained through "struggles for democracy" expressing the interests of the subordinated masses and attending to their needs. Like them, Parajuli believes development can be derailed when funds and agendas are misappropriated with the consent of the masses who are unaware of their own exploitation. Thus, democracy struggles embody resistance to the use of development aid for personal enrichment at the expense of the masses for whom it is intended. Parajuli restates for Nepalis the goals of development which have been recognized since the 1950s; he wants this development both to serve the interests of social equality and to preserve a way of life that is distinctively Nepali. In the end, however, he confronts the fundamental dilemma articulated in terms of Nepali identity structures: whether to cultivate collectivism that fosters social equality or to resist the collectivist social relations which lead to practices of familism, favoritism, and *aphno manche*. The final goal, he notes, is "democratization of political culture," which "entails respect for the knowledge and traditions of the oppressed . . . . Justification for more egalitarian and collective forms of livelihood in Nepal *do not have to be imported from abroad. They are present in the remnants of our own collectivity*" (Parajuli 1992: 4, my emphasis).

Bista, Parajuli, and Maskey all attempt to recuperate something distinctively Nepali in their calls for revolutionary yet nostalgic action, but their proposals also presuppose a forged hybridity with Western interests in the practical use of specific politics and knowledge imported from abroad. Here, concerns over what could be shed and what should be retained in Nepali culture – acts of selective recuperation – become important expressions of this hybridity. "We don't have to hang onto *sati* (widow burning) or child marriage in order to remain Hindu," one of these authors told me, making the analogous point that Nepalis do not have to hang onto *chakari* and favoritism in order to remain a nation that values religious and ethnic pluralism, peace, and natural beauty, or a sense of sacred duty and the collectivism this sort of desire engenders. For me, however, the paradoxes of this stance are many, among them thinking of democracy as largely an outgrowth of rational and objective *rather than* cultural principles, desiring a political engagement which rejects traditions in order to recuperate versions of it that are deemed undisruptive to modernity yet not modern themselves, calling for an end to corruption without undermining the institutions of family, caste, reciprocity, and the sentiments of sacred and moral duty to care for one's own people – again, institutions from which ideas of collectivism emerge. That Nepal was never colonized has perhaps contributed to the adoption of the belief that development and democracy are acultural, neutral, and technical instruments that can bring about liberation, wealth, and equality, but this fact cannot explain it all. This belief held by many Nepalis also derives from the history of development discourse in the country which has taught Nepalis to see much of their culture as an obstacle to development. This untenable proposition thus forged the contradiction – the need for oscillating value judgements that at once indict traditional behaviors as corrupt yet try to salvage tradition for the sake of indigenous pride and national identity. Such is one dilemma faced by even those who have not been colonized, but who have post-colonially internalized a rhetoric of modernization. Such is one outcome of the development rhetoric offered Nepalis by panchayat governance. The more the panchayat regime advocated development, the more it would undermine its own mode of power by enabling it to be identified as an obstacle to the development the regime promised. At the same time, the more development came to be characterized in terms which rejected traditional ways of doing things, and called them corrupt, the more Nepalis sought ways to retain a sense of culture that they could be proud of – a culture which could both stand outside science and democracy and shape their expression in Nepal.

Movement towards democracy

As you know, we want democracy because this country has always been ruled by our own people, not by outsiders. You know that is the history of Nepal. The Ranas ruled for 104 years, and then there was a movement to change that system and then by 2016 (1959) we had elected our own government. But by 2017, again there was a problem . . . Maybe King Mahendra wanted something new to introduce again. Everybody wanted their own name and their own power. It is this way all over the world. Look at Moscow right now [Yeltsin's challenge to Gorbachev]. The same thing is happening. So, Mahendra dissolved the elected government and started the partyless panchayat system. The panchayat system philosophy was good, but the people in the government became bad. The partyless system means there was no room for criticism. Without party means 125 people were under one umbrella (national panchayat). That umbrella was the king and he was very powerful. (*B. U.*, Nursing Education)

Many Nepalis consider the first democratic movement of Nepal to have been the restoration of King Tribhuvan to the throne in 1950–51. In the sense that this movement was inaugurated largely by the actions of the Nepali Congress party (organizing in India) and that it removed from absolute power a ruling elite, it was a significant step towards democracy. But for many revolutionary Nepalis in the years after 1960, the label of this movement as a democracy movement was precisely the sort of monarchical tactic that they disagreed with. In fact it was not until King Tribhuvan's son, Mahendra, came to the throne that Nepal saw its first truly elected government. This democratic movement (the second according to official sources) produced the nation's first elected prime minister, B. P. Koirala (Joshi and Rose 1966). Despite the success of the elections and the support of the king for this elected government, economic and political turmoil in Nepal led Mahendra to dissolve it after only a brief existence on December 15, 1960. The outcome of this political upheaval was the creation of the panchayat system, designed to provide a partyless, partially elected government that was as representative as possible geographically and demographically.

Members of the Nepali Congress considered the creation of the panchayat system a betrayal of democracy, for it outlawed political parties and governing powers were still held almost absolutely by the king. Opposition activists did not give up their demands, but they retreated from public view in order to avoid persecution (in many cases returning to India, where they continued to organize and plan for a democracy). The more than forty years of development aid from Western capitalist nations and from socialist countries (the USSR and the PRC) helped spawn political activism throughout the countryside of Nepal. In particular, various factions of leftists emerged within rural Nepal (see Rose 1965; Whelpton 1995; Gellner 1993), hearing dissent that was shared by urban student activists and tapping into the increasing frustration over poverty and disempowerment among rural villagers. Efforts on the part of the panchayat government to silence the emerging communist parties included expelling activists from the urban centers of power to the countryside and an ironic result of this strategy was the increasing support for Marxist/communist ideology among the nation's poorest rural populations (particularly in the east and terai areas). By the late 1970s two major leftist political parties, alongside the more popular Nepali Congress, were already large and "illegally" operating within the panchayat system (Rose 1965; Gellner 1993; Whelpton 1995).[22] The 1970s saw a great deal of covert political and party organizing and activism. In fact, some of the main colleges in Kathmandu became unofficially known for their party activities, including Amrit Science College, which was a main educational passage point for many doctors-to-be and Trichandra College, along with others.

By 1979, pressure for a multiparty democracy had reached fever pitch. Added to the long-standing activities of political party leaders, were more and more vocal and violent student protests of the panchayat system. Repressive measures against student protestors ignited a flurry of political activity, including the arrest of B. P. Koirala, the former prime minister. King Birendra, the Harvard-educated son of King Mahendra (enthroned in 1972), acquiesced to public demands for a referendum. After a year of planning but according to Shaha (1993) without any serious national debate on the issue, the public was allowed to vote to continue with the panchayat system with "timely" reforms or replace it with a multiparty system. The referendum was held in May 1980 and resulted in a narrow majority in favor of sustaining the partyless system. The election commission revealed that nearly half of the population voted. Delays in announcing the results, however, led to widespread rumors of election fraud, which only fueled popular support for the outlawed political parties (Shaha 1993). Nothing was immediately implemented to promote a freely elected multiparty government, but the resolve of the opposition was hardened and the public in general gained confidence that such a narrow margin of success boded well for a more revolutionary democratic movement that would take only ten more years.

In the succeeding decade political parties continued to gain support, given the increase in numbers of literate and educated Nepalis and the expectations raised by the referendum. Even illiterate rural Nepalis were by the 1980 referendum thoroughly engaged in discussions of political parties. Although parties were still outlawed, political organizing was a legal right as long as no demonstrations or public meetings were held and no candidates openly campaigned on the basis of their party affiliation. Thus Nepali Congress witnessed the rise to leadership positions of two figures who by the late 1980s had become spokespersons for the revolution: Ganesh Man Singh and Krishna Prasad Bhattarai. Among the most important of the leftist leaders was Man Mohan Adikhari, leader of the coalition United Left Front. Innumerable opposition party members participated in an elaborate underground activist network throughout the country. By 1990 many educated Nepalis from cities and towns were already actively voting with party affiliations in mind. Political parties became one of the main means by which people voiced opposition to governmental failures. Opposition newspapers emerged along with occasional violent rallies and protests on campuses throughout the Kathmandu Valley. Another form of protest was even more violent: although much more seldom, there were direct bomb attacks on palace-owned businesses. In response, the government meted out efforts to control the opposition, often ending in repression.

Government repression including imprisonment, disappearances, torture, and alleged assassinations of opposition figures and the less violent but equally repressive abuse of a system of reciprocal rewards and punishments led to the creation of Nepal's first human rights organization in 1988. The Human Rights Organization of Nepal (HURON) was founded by the scholar and historian Rishikesh Shaha and a group of urban professionals (Shaha 1993: 158).[23] A second organization, the Forum for the Protection of Human Rights (FOPHUR), was formed under the direction of the physician and professor Mathura Shrestha. These organizations came to be a central force for the revolution.

Nepal's revolutionary movement was thus aimed not at eliminating a colonial "Other" but rather at eliminating what came to be thought of as a repressive system of its own making. The single party panchayat form of government came to be seen as an instrument for protecting the monarchy and its hold on control over resources, privileges, and even basic freedoms. At the same time, it was panchayat development that gave Nepalis far and wide a language with which to articulate their critique of the government and a vision of alternatives to it. "Corruption" epitomized by the palace's hold on power and privilege was juxtaposed to democracy which was seen as being the primary means of undermining that hold. The solution to corruption was, for activists, development and progress. Development was thought to be the impartial system that would bring about an impartial government; true development was only possible with true democracy. The symbol of the state, the king, and his panchayat system were seen as "deviant" within the universalist jargon of modernity which development offered. The power of the king came to be seen as the enemy of democracy, the enemy of development. The power of modern professionals became aligned with democracy through idioms of science, meritocracy, development, and progress.

Medical professionals in politics

Along with the growth of political parties, over the past half-century Nepal has witnessed the development of other modern institutions within the context of the panchayat system (Adhikary 1995), and union-like professional organizations have been allowed to organize, hold meetings, collect dues, and express their professional and political views so long as they did not directly attack the panchayat system. Although similar ethnic organizations (*kendra*) were to make a difference in terms of the expressions of politics in the new democracy, the more important of these organizations in terms of the growth of the revolution in 1990 were the professional groups. Professional organizations such as the Nepal Medical Association, the Nepal Nurses' Association, and the Nepal Paramedical Organization (not to mention those of lawyers, teachers, engineers, etc.) emerged within a larger infrastructural field of medical development put in place through development aid. These emerged over roughly four decades of medical development. Modern medical institutions in Nepal began with missionary hospitals which allowed Christian groups to demonstrate their religious values through medical and educational programs supported by the government, in lieu of proselytizing, which was illegal. Soon after these early arrivals, health development efforts by multinational, bilateral, and other non-governmental organizations augmented the government's efforts to develop a biomedical health infrastructure. There were hospitals in Kathmandu and other major urban areas of the country and an elaborate rural health network to provide both auxiliary services in the most remote villages and referral to better-equipped health centers and hospitals located at district headquarters. The biomedical health infrastructure not funded by the government includes numerous private clinics run by physicians and a retail pharmaceutical industry.

Nepal's premier medical institution was and is its Teaching Hospital, a branch of Tribhuvan University, located in Maharajgung, in the north of Kathmandu. Nearly all of the local national physicians working at Teaching Hospital in 1990 had been trained outside Nepal, most of them in India and the remainder either in the Soviet-bloc cities (especially Moscow) or in the English-speaking Western countries. The first MBBS (Bachelor of Medicine, Bachelor of Surgery) degree holders (physicians with two years' less training than US physicians) graduated from Nepal's academies only in the late 1980s, and those physicians usually went on to specialty training outside Nepal. Most other health professionals, including most nurses and paramedicals, received their training in Nepal. Together, health professionals became, among others, critical purveyors of modernity and development to the Nepali public.

Both government and foreign aid agencies conducted rural health programs in Nepal for over thirty years, but most of these programs were limited by lack of supplies, poor communications, and rapid changes in policy. Development money was poured into the creation of a rural infrastructure for health via the Ministry of Health, but plans and progress in this area were slow for a variety of reasons (see Justice 1987). The very apparatus which intended to deliver biomedicine to Nepalis had in some cases failed to earn the confidence of recipients, particularly in rural areas. Mistrust was aroused by its failure to provide appropriate services (Stone 1986), and by practitioners' occasional exploitation of patients by, for example, charging for medicines intended to be delivered free. Early on, Justice (1983) offered yet another reason for villagers' suspicions: in a tour of rural village health clinics which were meant to be equipped with basic pharmaceutical supplies, regular visits from auxiliary health personnel, and a permanent trained village health worker (VHW), she found that in most instances the only person ever present at the clinic was the "peon," a multipurpose watchman, water carrier, and janitor. To her surprise, she found that it was often the peon himself who gave injections, medicines, and medical advice, using what knowledge he had acquired by watching the health worker, and that villagers usually trusted him more than the latter because he was from the local community. In some clinics, things had not greatly improved by 1990. Again, corruption was blamed.

Structural inequalities between practitioners and patients in many rural areas produced a demand for biomedical services simply because they represented a form of power and privilege associated with development and elite status (Pigg 1992). Knowledge and confidence in biomedical efficacy cannot entirely explain villagers' desires for better biomedical services, or their mistrust of them. Structural inequalities between elite practitioners and rural patients ran the risk of also producing mistrust among villagers. This, coupled with the fact that panchayat politicians often used promises about biomedical services to gain popularity meant that some villagers thought of medical services as no more than political instruments.[24] When they interacted with health workers recording immunization acceptance rates, fertility control measures, parity, or HIV seropositivity, for example, villagers were often quick to realize that the information generated from their bodies was of more use to others than to themselves. In the process, immediate health needs were often neglected. Stone (1986) offers a poignant case from fieldwork in the 1970s. She describes the experiences of one VHW whose duties aimed at improving local health conditions included measuring the size and growth rates of children among villagers who regularly did not have enough to feed themselves. The worker told her about one encounter: "Sometimes they get angry. One woman, when I measured her child's arm with the tape, we saw the child was too thin. She got angry and said 'Then why don't you do something? You come to show me my child is not good like this and then you do nothing!' " (Stone 1986: 297).

In fact, one can find among rural Nepalis both high levels of belief in the inherent efficacy of biomedicine (the same sort of efficacy which they attribute to other healers, such as shamans) (Pigg 1996), and a great deal of skepticism about biomedical practitioners. A contrasting example of the way villagers internalized ideas about the objective nature of biomedicine versus the social nature of traditional practitioners is offered in a compelling case from Pigg (1990): some people said that one advantage of biomedicine is that it could be used as a way to escape from the cycles of obligations to local spirits and deities. Thus, while many villagers recognized and identified with the various truth claims about impartial disease agents, nutritional requirements, and hygiene, for example, as promoted through health education campaigns under panchayat democracy, many villagers used biomedical services for reasons that were unrelated to this knowledge system.

Ambivalence towards biomedicine was also related to the uneven distributions of biomedicine's benefits and damages, and to a widespread recognition of the political corruption of its truths. Villagers who I visited in one community several hours from Kathmandu, for example, doubted the existence of HIV and questioned the need for regular gynecological examinations to prevent sexually transmitted diseases. Some considered the claims of biomedical professionals no more than self-serving political statements – like *hawa ko kura* (things in the wind) – and interpreted them in terms of a complicated set of assumptions about the political intentions, social class, and caste background of those who delivered them. At the same time, many villagers aimed their skepticism towards individual practitioners rather than the biomedical system as a whole, being angry about the lack of adequate biomedical services in villages rather than decrying them as uniformly useless. Many saw the medical system as being the sort of thing modernity represented – a solution to their major sources of suffering. If only the corruption of modern purveyors of development could be eliminated, then the system could flourish and bring about its proper, and inevitable, ends.

The incessant search for the most competent and often what Nepalis call the least politically motivated biomedical practitioner is evidence of many Nepalis' confidence in biomedicine whatever their criticism of any one practitioner or clinical arrangement. It is worth noting in this regard that rural educational systems developed under the panchayat system made basic biomedical knowledge of the germ theory, reproductive health, hygiene, immunizations, and the need for hospital visits even as common as literacy. Thus, although most Nepalis always had access to a wide variety of healing experts (from shamans to Ayurvedic practitioners and Buddhist lamas) and nearly all continued to use these healers, it was just as often to biomedical knowledge providers and producers, when available, that much of the consuming public turned for advice about health care by 1990. The believability of biomedical practitioners and to some extent even of biomedical truth claims was largely configured by the apparatus through which biomedicine was delivered, and that was dependent upon panchayati forms of development. Since the apparatus was unevenly organized throughout the country, so too, it was believed, was the distribution of biomedical benefits and their believability.

Some of the variation in belief in biomedical truth claims reflects the uneven distribution of what I would call biomedical objectivist consciousness, transmitted through educational institutions and clinical practices. Biomedical objectivist consciousness among Nepalis was linked to the spread of language and beliefs associated with both science and development (Adams 1996) and while it did not necessarily replace other beliefs and knowledge systems already in place (see also Stone 1986; Pigg 1995a), it came to stand in opposition to traditional beliefs. Traditional medical ways were seen as obstacles to development's successful implementation. In this sense, this consciousness refers, again, to what Nandy (1983) called a "second form of colonialism" in which the neo-colonized come to think of themselves through the objectifications of native subjectivity created by "the colonizer." In the case of biomedicine, this refers to the way that Nepalis have been offered the opportunity to internalize the idea that their bodies are objective entities that can stand free of their social constitution and social contingencies, susceptible to effects of universalist knowledge. It refers to the way they accept the possibility of an objective and value-free science, beyond politics and culture, which can not only reveal the body's truths but also attend most effectively to its needs. Not all advocates of democracy adopted an objectivist position, but few indigenous knowledges or epistemologies were constituted around the particular notions of objectivist truth, individual responsibility, and political neutrality found in twentieth-century biomedicine, and delivered through a scientific, universalist rhetoric of development. It was partially because not enough Nepalis had adopted this view that some medical professionals felt it was necessary to have a revolution.

Again, not all Nepalis who resorted to biomedical practitioners did so because they held the same beliefs about the body and its biological facts (and disorders) as biomedical practitioners. On the contrary, belief in the efficacy of biomedical practitioners can be as much a result of how socially connected the patients feel to the doctor, whether the doctor will be compelled to feel socially obligated to the patient hence providing them with "better" care than others less closely connected to them, and whether or not the doctor has a reputation for successful outcomes, as transmitted by word of mouth rather than established credentials attesting to the doctor's competence and knowledge. Shared explanatory models regarding the cause and nature of disorders are not the only motivation for belief in a physician, or for efficacy. Thus, biomedical practitioners who recognized this were troubled by it. In contrast to the case found by Pigg (1995b) in which patients used doctors to avoid the cost of shamans (in sacrifices etc.) or risks of stirring up social tensions, one rural Nepali doctor told me that he was deeply troubled by patients who brought him gifts of food or other valued items before receiving treatment because he recognized these as being the same sorts of offerings made to spirits and deities when they were enlisted to help cure patients. When offered to supernatural beings, he knew, Nepalis believed that they would obtain good results (i.e. a cure); that they believed the supernatural being would feel more obligated to provide a cure to the patient. This physician felt troubled both by the idea that some patients thought his medicine's efficacy was based on a social obligation like that engendered in offerings to gods, and by the fact that they thought he, as a physician, would be swayed to change his caregiving strategies because of this gift exchange and the social bond it was intended to generate. He told me he cared for each patient as best he could, but that in any case it would be according to prescribed, scientific protocols, not because of his sense of obligation unevenly distributed to different patients. Even with the best of care some patients would die anyway and he didn't want patients to think the outcome was because he was personally unpleased with their offering. His concern was thus that patients would interpret his scientific and professional actions in terms of a non-scientific moral discourse about one's social obligations to those from whom one has accepted a gift. "If they bring gifts after the treatment is successful, to thank me" he noted, "this is not a problem". Before the treatment, however, gifts had the untoward effect of transforming the clinic into a shrine wherein the laws of a socio-moral universe reigned over those of the objectivist and scientific world. If the medicine failed to cure a patient in a family which had brought such gifts, then they interpreted the failure as one that was related to the physician's will rather than to the objective facts of the case. Overall, he noted, this leads to an undermining of the legitimacy of the biomedical system, especially in rural Nepal. So, while many Nepalis already shared his scientific view of the body and its health needs, too many, he felt, still needed to be taught this knowledge.

This sort of problem, familiar to many physicians and medical professionals, was thought to be one example of the failure of the biomedical infrastructure of the country. Many health professionals saw the sort of traditional logic that misunderstood or remained ignorant of biomedicine as non-modern and in need of eradication. Traditional consciousness, seen as an obstacle to health development, was why it was believed there was a need to establish uniform health resources in the country. Recognizing the uneven distribution of biomedicine and its benefits, a handful of physicians trained in community health at Tribhuvan University aimed to fulfill the development promise to make medicine more attentive to villagers' needs. This meant teaching people about the objective medical truths a biomedical system made clear. Adequate health care, they suggested, was most lacking among villagers, and villagers were those who could benefit from it the most because adequate access to good quality medical care would establish a basis for improving Nepali popular biomedical knowledge. Ensuring adequate resources would, they envisioned, lead to an eradication of backward health traditions. This, many of these doctors felt, aligned their interests, as persons whose training in a scientific field gave them privileged insights about the truth of village suffering and the most effective solutions to it, with village political concerns. Both concerns became aligned through a rhetoric about eradicating corruption. Corruption caused inadequate rural care and was the inevitable outcome of adhering to traditional ways of life and traditional beliefs about responsibility to gods, patrons, and even politicians.

Although expanding knowledge of basic health and hygiene among all Nepalis was considered critical by most medical professionals, it was a concern for the latter – village political concerns – that was often missed by urban physicians and caregivers. It was this gap between rural-based politically oriented health professionals and urban professionals that was filled by the community medicine programs at Tribhuvan University. In many developing countries, health ministries often find themselves in conflict with urban physicians who prefer to see investments in the development of high-technology, hospital-based services. In Nepal, this tension was somewhat mitigated by the presence of the Department of Community Medicine and by the requirements that all medical students attend courses in community medicine (a village-oriented program) and that all graduates in the health professions serve a minimum mandatory period of time in a rural area of the country. Physicians here, some of whom received training in public health abroad, were the most vocal about rural medical needs. The department trained rural health auxiliaries who were also a constant source of feedback and insight about the health problems of rural Nepalis. The strong case made by Nepali physicians from this department was for a health-care focus that could encompass social and political concerns as economic inequality. For them, health interventions should begin with social interventions, as was clear even after the revolution in this appeal to international donors:

> We don't need to acquaint you with a detailed description of the miserable state of health and health care in Nepal. Despite the continued efforts of governmental and non-governmental sectors the fundamental health scenario does not seem to have changed much, at least for the average Nepali citizen living in Nepal today. Each year, hundreds of thousands of Nepali people, especially the women and children, not only unnecessarily suffer but lose their lives due to the lack of very basic medical treatment. The status of health of the people basically reflects the quality of life they enjoy in a given society or country. Sustained improvements in the health status of the Nepali people, therefore, will not be possible without resolving broader issues such as poverty, social injustice, social inequality, and human rights abuse. Since it will take time to resolve these problems, we cannot afford to wait until progress is made in these areas. While we must aim for and learn to optimally utilize our existing resources and talents to tackle our problems, we must explore potential resources and seek new allies to supplement our efforts in this regard. We believe that one of the ways to improve the health of the Nepali people is by enhancing the standard of medical care in Nepal. In order to do this we have to augment the technical capabilities of our medical institutions in general and academic medical institutions in particular. Continued educational and research efforts are essential aspects in building and upgrading such technical capabilities.[25]

The goal of medical professionals in the years leading up to the revolution was to bridge the gap between village perceptions of need and universalist truths about health and disease found in biomedical orientations. They advanced their scientific views of villagers' health problems by becoming political spokespersons for what they believed the majority population wanted – transforming poverty, reduction in mortality and morbidity, and the political and economic security and freedom that could bring these about into factual not partisan matters. Popular support for physicians and belief in universal objective truth claims were merged for physicians with making village needs heard. This was merged with perceptions of their own political need for freedom, accomplished only by eradicating corruption as an obstacle to a system built on truth. This merging of interests aimed to eliminate local traditional cultural conceptions of the nature of healing and the socio-moral contexts within which efficacy was made possible. To the extent that not enough people sought ways to avoid this traditional behavior already, revolutionary activities might speed up this process.

Village needs, professionals argued, were not only objective truths but also the most significant because they were the majority's needs and because they articulated with their own demands for freedom of political expression. Poverty caused ill health and even villagers knew this. But poverty for physicians and other medical professionals was often distilled to an objective category, related in important ways to social inequality and corruption, and so related to the moral universe which established this inequality as a necessary and important requirement for the good life – for example, as found in the more widespread Nepali notions of sacred duty emergent from such hierarchy. Bringing villagers to a state of health was possible only by attending to political reform – reform that could eliminate social inequality by naming it in an objectified knowledge system – one that objectified conditions within their socio-moral contexts. The social contexts within which such things as poverty emerged came to be identified as problems of backward practices, and in being backward they became linked to corruption. By being packaged as obstacles to technological development solutions, they themselves came to be identified as technical problems. At the same time, these ways of doing things were tied to ideas about morality and social responsibility. The medical professionals thus had to undo the link between morality and traditional culture, by turning traditional culture into an immoral set of social practices. Poverty was an objective thing; what brought it about was a corrupt system based on backward cultural practices that tied people together in networks of reciprocity, favoritism and *aphno manche*. Objectified as a technical problem, not a moral conflict, a new notion of morality could be attached to their ideas about ending poverty. Thus eradicating these networks and the belief in them was seen as a necessary step towards finding solutions to poverty and finding solutions to these problems became the only way to be morally responsible.

This belief in eradicating corruption by eradicating the belief in the power of social affiliations (tied in many instances to the belief in the sacred power of the office-holder, like the deity), was a primary motivation for the revolution. Of course, many physicians were aware that even medical practitioners could succumb to corruption. This occurred in a number of ways when the old beliefs in the power of social affiliations seeped into the practices of medicine in the form of unreliable knowledge production and in the form of using source-force to evade professional and objectively established job responsibilities. For example, having a ministry that produced reliable health statistics about Nepal's populations was critical for effective medicine, but even that could be corrupted. The use of "source-force" would result in the production of data which were politically tainted. Awareness of this problem was articulated well by

S. P., a member of the Ministry of Health, with regard to a former Minister of Health:

She was always ambitious. She was able to provide the good rates of success, you know. If other sectors had success rates that were only forty percent, like that, then she had one hundred percent success. That is not true, though. She looked like a great success, like her programs were more successful, but actually, she was only making up those figures. There was no one to check her results. She only knew that the palace wanted to have high rates, so she gave them. But other sectors did better work, only they told the truth. Those people were fired for telling the truth. That is why we needed a real revolution.

In another case, one Nepal Medical Association officer attested:

Many doctors were supposed to go to work in remote areas and they never went because they wanted to be here in the capital. Because they all had their own *aphno manche*; they had their own minister to help them. They had their Panchayat member and connection to the King and palace. So naturally, the discipline was not there. Discipline should have been maintained from that time. Nobody should get privileges through the back door, not even my own son. Everybody has to follow the rules.

Most health professionals expressed frustration over the fact that "corruption" undermined their ability to perform according to the rules and procedures of their profession. One significant aspect of their role in the revolution was that their actions suggested the need for a shift of authority from the monarch-as-deity figure to the educated professionals who provided rational knowledge about the health and welfare of the citizenry, the economy, public needs, or the polity on the basis of "objective" criteria. Thus, when physicians associated with the Department of Community Medicine got involved, their message was that politicizing medicine would not corrupt its truths in the way that using social affiliations would. On the contrary. The political efforts required to establish a rural community health infrastructure were part of their professional responsibility and could therefore be seen as objective facts. Politics would be put in service to health because political facts were objective truths. This would rout out even corruption within.

Most professionals recognized that an infrastructure that could promote objectivist consciousness and eradicate its opposite in beliefs in the power of the social bond was essential for the survival of the democratic state envisioned by the Nepali people. This strategy meant teaching Nepalis to internalize a sense of responsibility and reliance on themselves as opposed to relying on others, and relying on the facts as provided by outsiders rather than on the sacred security that emerged from their social resources in family, obligated friends, and supernatural beings. Effective rural health programs which could generate self-responsible scientific citizens would not simply save lives, they would make possible the institutions of social discipline – the internalization of notions of impartial and objective truth that enabled people to avoid corruption – that the new democracy needed for survival.

Doctors, nurses, and paramedicals promoted their agenda while keeping in mind the need to purge their own ranks of the corruption that came from relying on social affiliations rather than objective measures of truth. Saul Weiner wrote in 1989 that the Nepali medical profession was characterized by the patrimonialist institutions of "source-force" which, I have suggested, the majority of professionals opposed during the revolution. He noted a great divide among doctors between an older generation of elite, urban doctors who had received their educations abroad and younger generations trained within Nepal's own medical infrastructure and sometimes originating in rural areas and ethnic minority groups. The former tended to benefit from the use of "source-force" for a variety of benefits (the most significant being the ability to evade serving in a rural health post, the opportunity for government-sponsored postgraduate study abroad, and permission to operate private (for-profit) clinics in Kathmandu, and promotions). The latter, lacking access to "source-force" were often assigned to one hardship rural health post after another and denied most of these benefits. "In some cases," he writes, "the performance of an officer on written examinations, his or her level of seniority, and performance in earlier posts are considered; in most cases, appointments are based on a person's connections with key decision-makers." His main informant described the situation as follows: There are three categories of doctors in Nepal. The first category is more powerful than the Minister of Health and can exert influence wherever it wishes. The second category is on a par with the Minister, so he leaves its doctors alone and they leave him alone. Sometimes they exchange favors. The third category comprises about 40 percent of the doctors, and they are below the Minister and lack all "source-force" (Weiner 1989: 672). This last group, Weiner notes, actively resisted those in a position to mobilize "source-force," petitioning the government to regulate the profession in terms of more equitable measures of rewards and privileges.

It is interesting to note that Weiner's work contrasts sharply with the ethnography written by Justice in 1987, based on fieldwork carried out over a decade before him. Justice showed that Nepali bureaucratic health cultures operated according to principles fundamentally at odds with those of foreign health development bureaucracies (notably USAID, WHO, and UNICEF). Then, Nepalis placed a greater emphasis on patronage and social reciprocity in evaluating their work performance and promotion opportunities than on standard or objective criteria of efficacy and productivity. Although she suggests that greater efficiency would be possible if Nepali health workers behaved more like foreign ones and if foreign planners paid more attention to the cultural practices of Nepalis, she is careful to reveal how few Nepalis at the time would have considered patronage, "source-force," and *chakari* "corrupt." Rather than taking the position that foreign bureaucratic procedures were the only correct and effective ones, she held that foreigners should "play" by, or at least be attentive to, the Nepalis' culturally distinctive bureaucratic "rules."

If we can read these accounts as offering ethnographically reliable perspectives, between the time of Justice's work and that of Weiner a major transformation occurred in the ways in which Nepali health professionals articulated the problems of health development. What are taken to be conventional norms for bureaucratic practice in the 1970s are two decades later viewed as "corruption." To the extent that Justice's book was read by some Nepali health professionals as an indictment of indigenous cultural practices for impeding development even at the time it was written, we can also note that by the late 1980s this perspective had become the norm in their own professional culture.

By 1993 I found that a large number of the younger graduates identified by Weiner had become members of a privileged medical elite able to travel abroad. Alongside them, many older generation physicians were the most active in the revolutionary activities aimed at eliminating all forms of "source-force." I found greater uniformity than Weiner, among those in power in the Nepal Medical Association, in support of the elimination of various forms of "source-force" from the medical profession, along with greater privatization and deregulation by government. Their professional interest in having the government less involved in their profession was based on their assumption that the government itself was the source of corruption and that they, as scientific experts, were more capable than the government of regulating themselves. Judging from the statements of doctors reflecting on their motivations for involvement in the revolution, the desires and dreams of what Weiner identified as some 40 percent of the doctors in 1989 had become by 1993 the status quo.

The majority of physicians in particular perceived themselves as having created an institution that was capable of being immune to favoritism, *chakari, aphno manche,* etc., but they believed that the accomplishment of this would require a democratic society built on meritocratic principles. When physicians spoke about their involvement with the revolution, many did so with reference to what they saw as their occupational mandate: to tell the truth as opposed to lying or inventing truth in order to gain political or social patronage. The words of D. S. M., an elderly Kathmandu physician, are exemplary here:

You see, as health professionals, we are confronted with the intimate facts of life and the conditions of the people. I feel the pulse of the people, literally and figuratively. In my place, sometimes even royalty visit here only half an hour after the lowest, poorest person comes in here. Then the politician comes here, then the engineer comes, then the teacher comes in, and I get the whole story. And, you see, naturally we see that there is something to do. We ask what is happening in their place, we ask them "How are you?" and we feel the pulse of the people this way. I said this to other doctors, and I said this to the present government. I told them all: "I feel the pulse of the people, literally and figuratively. I am telling you the truth. I tell you what people are feeling." What I have always said is that doctors in Nepal, as well as all over the world, have a tremendous role to play whenever they reach the high power. The point is: they feel the pulse of the people. Tell me when you've got a person naked on your bed he doesn't usually tell you false things. So, all over the world you find doctors close to power have always got a lot to say. They can mould a person. When I started my practice here once upon a time, one politician had come to me and he is a very nice man who is quite powerful in the palace, and I said to him, "What is my duty to the country?" So he says, "Doctor, I will tell you one thing. You as a doctor will be reaching very high places. Try to tell the people the truth of what is happening." That was quite a gift to me. He told me, "Tell them because you will be telling the truth, whereas others may not be." He said, "Your job is to tell people what is the truth. If you do this you will be doing your nation a great service."

How could this member of the palace elite have known that the truth this doctor would tell would be that his own palace had failed to uphold these truths, preferring instead to let truth bend to the political will and whim of those, and only those, already in power? The physicians' revolutionary activities reveal how committed they were to the idea that *truth was on their side*. It was a motto of sorts. This was ironic in that doctors in particular were among the privileged elite who had perhaps the most to gain from the political status quo – a system which enabled "truth" to be bent to the will of personal interest (again, leaning towards the palace). Initially, indeed, some physicians watched safely from the sidelines while the politically committed became involved in politics. But others felt that even at the risk of their privilege, they would have to stand up for their professional interests, that ultimately this was for the good of the people. The aim of the latter was to politicize medicine as part of good medical practice, and eventually organize their peers around the related ideas that science equals truth and that good medical science will tell the truth about both social inequality and what can be done to eradicate it. For them, the human rights rubric was a means of involving themselves in political action without compromising their truths, for this was a rubric which attended to their own ideas about neutral, objective truth, but it did so through a rhetoric of morality. Human rights were after all about objective and universal limits to moral tolerance. In the course of developing a discourse about human rights, medical professionals also accomplished a feat of modernization: they created a domain for the exercise of moral culpability and responsibility that was outside the sphere of the sacred and religious in Nepal. Morality could now more than ever be pursued as a secular activity.

4 Revolutionary medicine: scientists for democracy

A politically active physician described the major events catalyzing the People's Movement of 1990 as follows:

Before this Andolan, things were smoldering. There was a smoldering fire which was kept alive by the leaders who had been to jail. Because of the jail terms they went through and the torture many of our [political party] leaders went through, the fire was kept smoldering. The leaders, they had the fire smoldering but they themselves would have never been able to get this thing done. It was this fertile field – the king not knowing what was happening (which I am convinced about today). And, then the Indian leaders coming here and giving us the go-ahead saying, "It is your problem, and you have to solve it yourselves." . . .

"Yes, you solve that," they said, and suddenly this gave the intellectuals the inspiration, because it was mainly the intellectuals who were there – the middle class intellectuals. It suddenly gave them the thought, "My God, what are we doing this time?" and then suddenly everything went haywire. So, professionals like me, for example, I was not concerned at all in the sense that I was doing my work. I was doing my work in the Bir Hospital, I was working as usual as everybody does, doing my clinic and I had no time to think on these things, frankly. But when we saw the people in line when they were not getting their food [because of a year-long blockade of Nepal's borders by India], this terrible problem with India. At that time, we said, "Who is to blame? Is it India, or our government?" And I was convinced our government was more to blame than India. I came to realize at that point that the treaties should have been renewed and were not renewed, God knows for what purpose, and I was convinced that our government was more to blame and India took this opportunity to squeeze us. There's no doubt about that. But I suppose everyone has a right to think the best for his own nation. But why didn't my people think the best for our nation? Why didn't the people in power think for the best of my nation – for my common people?

So these things started preying on us and it was going on like this, but we were still working. And I suppose the politics at that time were already working. Politicians were working and the cadres were working, but even at that moment we were not aware of this. We knew that things were not good. We were unhappy. In my personal case, I was working in Bir Hospital and what I found was that petty things were taking place, but they were important because they were part of a larger problem of corruption. The Health Minister for the Chief of Parliament, the Panchayat, for petty health problems would take a trip to America or England or Bangkok, for simple things like diabetes, spondylosis, accompanied by Nepali doctors. Mind you, this was all at the government's expense! Meanwhile, in the hospital, I was finding that I was not able to give one paracetamol or Tylenol tablet to my patient because the government hospital had no stocks of any medicines, because of negligence on the part of the government. So, you see, it was that day when it hit me very hard. I was on my rounds in the hospital and I was very disturbed with what was happening. . . . I was no longer prepared to go along with a government which is so insensitive to the problems of the common people, you see, because it was building up. I had no intravenous drips to be given, I had no drugs. OK, intravenous drips cost a little bit more, but a simple paracetamol tablet?

You see what was happening in the hospital? My feeling is that a health minister or a prime minister must never go abroad for care simply for the reason that they were instrumental in not getting the services done when they were in power. They have no right to go. . . . I made a statement, and I said that if these people are to die, they must die in the hospital. I said, "If they want to die they must die on our soil." And politicians cannot go abroad unless the politician has nothing to do with this sort of insensitive attitude and the people generally love him. And here the question of human rights arises – OK, there is such a thing as human rights, and a politician has a right to go abroad, but if that politician was instrumental in shaping the health services and has done nothing and has made my people suffer more and more, he has no right to go at that particular point in time. I resigned from the hospital then and there, and then later, this is why I joined the Andolan.

Along with generalized dissatisfaction with corruption in politics, development, and society, there were a number of immediate, external factors that served as catalysts to the revolution. Perhaps the most important of these was the lapse of Nepal's trade and transit treaty with India. When the treaty was not renewed in 1989, the result was a virtual blockade of Nepal; only the difficult Himalayan routes into China at Tibet remained open. Rishikesh Shaha attributes the lapse to greed on the part of the then prime minister, Marich Man Singh, and his finance minister, Bharat Bahadur Pradhan, who were interested in serving the needs of Nepali commission agents for Japan- and South Korea-based manufacturing and construction companies (with whom it is presumed they had financial interests) rather than those of the Nepali people.[1] He writes (1992: 157) that these government officials therefore

> embarked on a policy of pursuing trade with India on the terms of the Most-Favoured-Nation-Treatment as with other countries. This involved considerable depletion of Nepal's scarce convertible currency reserves and also put obstacles in the way of Nepal's exports to India. Such a policy resulted in high prices and shortages of essential commodities in Nepal causing immense hardship and suffering to the common people. Marich Man Singh's government had tried in vain to divert popular attention away from its own failures and shortcomings by whipping up anti-Indian feeling on the pretext that shortages of essential

commodities and hardships for the common people were a result of India's abrupt and unilateral termination of the existing trade and transit treaties with Nepal.

The widespread discomfort spawned by the blockade served as an important motivating factor for a Nepali revolution. In addition to successfully arousing anti-Indian sentiment, it stimulated a great deal of opposition towards the Nepali elites who prompted it: those who seemed to remain untouched by daily shortages of basic commodities. The need to wait in endless lines to receive rationed supplies of sugar, foods, material goods, kerosene, and petrol, and the depletion of fuelwood resources brought in from the countryside to replace gas and kerosene for cooking contrasted sharply with the visible privileges of palace elites and foreign diplomats. The wealthy and well-connected continued to drive in chauffered limousines with seemingly unlimited supplies of petrol; they appeared to have no shortages, and they even seemed to be profiting from the blockade. The visible distance between have-nots and haves and the widespread belief that the Nepali government might be deliberately creating shortages hardened the resolve of the average Nepali to work for social change.

A second catalyst was the fall of communism elsewhere in the world (Shaha 1993). Fear that their agenda had been discredited brought the left to the bargaining table with the more popular Nepali Congress party to discuss the possibilities of a joint movement for democracy. The leadership of the political opposition presented King Birendra with an ultimatum demanding a free multiparty system by January 18, 1990. When he failed to meet their deadline, the Nepali Congress party began a convention in flagrant disregard of the king at the home of Congress leader Ganesh Man Singh in downtown Kathmandu. At this historic joint meeting between opposition parties, a delegation led by Chandra Shekhar of India's Janata Dal[2] was invited to offer advice to Nepal's opposition movement. The outcome of this meeting was a renewed and, for the first time, unified agenda for a popular movement among parties which had historically opposed one another.

Still another factor was the increase in international attention to human rights. The growth of organizations like Amnesty International, Asiawatch, and others was increasingly visible in Nepal. The 1986 movement against Marcos in the Philippines and the Tiananmen events of 1989 in the People's Republic of China helped build Nepali confidence not only that widespread protests against oppressive regimes were possible (Raeper and Hoftun 1992: 86) but also that one way to create international pressure on one's government was by combining human rights rhetoric with calls for democracy. Medical professionals who were already advocating radical political and social change were able to arouse support of other physicians, nurses, and paramedicals under the banner of human rights to produce a fully-fledged and successful People's Movement for Democracy.

Democracy day

Respected Revolutionary Doctors – Lal Salam (red salute). The history of Nepal will preserve for everlasting your names in golden letters. The end of this fascist dictator Panchayat system (a 20th century Ravana[3]) will bring your victory! Lastly, Nepali people will never forget your voice raised for the sake of human salvation. (Message supporting the doctors on strike, written in the medical register by a citizen during the final days of the Andolan.)

Democracy Day, February 18, 1990, had been designated by the government to celebrate the fortieth anniversary of the restoration to power of the king's grandfather after 104 years of rule by the oppressive Rana prime ministers. By 1990, however, rather than being a symbol of democracy, for many the king and palace had come to stand for all that was wrong with panchayati Nepal. The Nepali Congress party and the United Left Front called for a peaceful demonstration for multiparty democracy on that day in a press release issued by Rishikesh Shaha on February 17 (1993: 187). Among the organizers of the demonstration were a number of politically active doctors, most affiliated with the Department of Community Medicine. It was these physicians who had also been involved in establishing the Human Rights Organization of Nepal (HURON). Aside from articulating human rights in terms of basic needs (including health, social equality, and political freedom), these doctors were interested in documenting and helping political prisoners. Of particular concern was not only the torture of the prisoners who had been arrested for what they considered were illegitimate reasons, but also the welfare of the families whose primary breadwinners had been imprisoned for many years. They found that as doctors they were able to visit prisoners who were otherwise denied access to any other than immediate family. Dr. Mathura Shrestha told me about the conditions he observed:

I went as a doctor, because the prisoners were asking for medical personnel. So I influenced the jailers, and they let me go. Most of these prisoners were put in jail with no trial, and many were in security so no one could visit. But medical persons and relatives were able to meet them. One very famous leftist leader who was in jail, who was worshipped as a leader, was Kamal Raj Regmi. He capitulated [to the system]. He later became a major supporter of the panchayat system. He was a popular communist leader, and everybody thought that he was a role model. But suddenly he capitulated. And the answers he gave [to why he did] were very shocking. It seems that everybody had forgotten. His wife and children were forced to beg. That was what he said. Because nobody took care of them. He said, "I sacrificed my life, but the interests of my children were sacrificed by the people, and that is another thing."

There was no party to take care of them, nobody to think of them. And that forced us to consider, "Is it true? How can it be true that something like that can happen?" We thought, "Maybe he was only rationalizing his capitulation," but we thought, "What if it is true?" So we investigated. We studied the children and wives of the many people who were in prison, and we found out that they were in very bad condition. This was during a very repressive period, and these wives of political prisoners were in social isolation. Everyone – even relatives were afraid to talk to them because they felt it might put them in jeopardy. So they were extremely isolated.

The prisoners were also in isolation. They did not receive any visitors, any papers, news . . . nothing. And they were tortured, all types of torture, very cruel. Sometimes they were isolated. They were put in one room, isolated from everybody. So they were very depressed. Before we found that, we said that we did not think our committee was very important, but when we saw that we knew that we needed to develop a system. First of all, we didn't have any statistics. We needed to update statistics of political prisoners or those implicated as political prisoners. How many of them were prisoners with charges or prisoners without charges? How many were real political prisoners, versus charged with some murders, or anything else? That sort of statistic was necessary. We would try to make those. And second in importance was how to contact them.

We went in as doctors, and they let us visit the prisoners, but they were in such bad condition. They were very depressed. There were some political prisoners, they said to me, "Doctor, can I get a drink?". . . I asked why they did not take a drink because there is no question of getting a drink in jail [they were not deprived of water]. "Are you addicted?" I asked them. They said, "If you prescribe some drink [alcohol] I think my mental torture, my mental torture will subside." They were talking like that.

The condition of the jails was very serious. Some jailers were cooperative. They took me inside and they allowed me to talk freely with the prisoners. As a doctor and as a medical officer, it was easier. In other jails it was not so easy. But going back to my point. We needed to improve the statistics and to boost their morale. They were not even allowed to write. They weren't given any paper. So we began to smuggle those things to them for writing and we smuggled them back out for printing, for outside publication. We also started visiting the families of political prisoners and talking to their wives and children and devising ways to help them. We also tried to improve the morale of the prisoners by giving them a sense of belonging or a sense of doing something. We encouraged them to write their stories. Although there were some papers which are critical to the government, they could not write much, but, we told them that we would publish them outside. It was quite amazing. Even some jail guards risked their lives by serving as couriers of the letters, secretly carrying the letters and papers, books, etc. And this was very good for the prisoners. It gave them hope and the will to survive.

As for the families of the prisoners, they were suffering. The children of these prisoners and even the martyrs were so neglected. Their children were not in school, and they were very poor. After we began to show interest in them and help them, then even the relatives and neighbors became concerned. We could not do much financially, but in social terms we did much. We turned around the feeling towards them. You see, they were afraid of effects by incrimination . . . they were afraid because it was total . . . we used to say an environment of suspicion, suspicion and fear – terror, because there was terror – an environment of terror. So that created a chance for us to learn and then we learned there was Amnesty International, and we formed a branch in Nepal.

The exposure of these doctors to the various forms of violence as a result of opposition to the political system motivated them to direct involvement in the People's Movement through human rights initiatives. For them, political imprisonment was a direct result of the sort of power they rejected – the king's ability under law to repress those who opposed him. This repression was the most heinous form of corruption that could, they believed, be overcome by a modern regime that replaced relationships between king and subject with those between impartial rules of law and citizen.

Many health professionals were involved in politics for years before the 1990 democracy movement. Many nurses, students at Teaching Hospital, and paramedics had a long history of vocal political opposition. Even rural health workers were involved in illegal organizing for political parties. In February 1990, then, doctors, medical students, and other paramedics, immediately sought a way to make use of their medical expertise to facilitate the demonstration called for in opposition to the official Democracy Day celebrations. A group of medical students and professors from the Department of Community Medicine at Teaching Hospital had begun to hold meetings about the political situation, and they predicted that the call for a demonstration would produce a clash with the police. They reasoned that this time when issues of social inequality were more visible than ever they should promote more overt resistance.

These organizers were in contact with non-medical activists and together they prepared for Democracy Day protests. They devised methods of transport and care of the injured and wounded that would prevent the police from arresting them. Emergency clinics were planned that would operate outside of the premises of the hospital. Elaborate code systems were developed for telecommunications. An ambulance driver was recruited for use in transporting victims. Finally, training programs were set up to teach activists first aid.

Almost all of these plans were made on the assumption that if violence began demonstrators would be injured by *lathi* (baton) charges and physical combat with thrown stones or bricks. Although prisoners had been killed by police brutality in secret or had died of medical complications

Plate 1 Armed forces deployed to Kathmandu's neighborhoods in the days before Democracy Day.

associated with incarceration, the doctors and nurses were not prepared for police gunfire in the streets. Several people had, however, been killed outside Kathmandu in the hills and in Chitwan, in the terai, for protesting against the panchayat system just days before. As it turned out, the peaceful protest turned more violent than expected. As government officials' motorcades proceeded down the main streets near New Road – one of the first two roads paved in the city only twenty years before – bricks and stones were hurled. People scrambled for safety, or for ammunition, as the case may be. Gunfire was heard. The center of the Democracy Day celebration had suddenly turned violent just in front of Bir Hospital. During the clashes protestors ran to take shelter in the hospital. People took refuge in the hospital courtyard and entryway. Several doctors began to photograph the events and the wounded as they arrived. One physician even snapped photos of the health minister and the home minister on the street, jarred from their positions in the formal procession and resorting to throwing bricks and stones at the protestors. Eventually, even these officials took refuge in the hospital from flying stones, bricks, and bullets.

The outcome of the protest in the city was that the government's Democracy Day celebrations were derailed, and instead there were over 1,000 arrests (added to the already 5,000 or more over the preceding months). The emergency clinics were not, in fact, used as had been planned; by the time the organizers were able to get emergency vehicles to the scenes of the violence, the patients were gone. Instead the injured were brought by protestors to Bir Hospital and doctors and nurses treated them there. After that, the police received orders to follow even injured protestors into the hospitals in order to arrest them. One effect of this was that health personnel not already directly involved in political organizing had begun to get involved. Medical workers protected the injured by barring police from entry, and they helped protestors to escape through emergency and back exits. Doctors demanded that the hospital director remove the police from the premises on the grounds that it impaired their ability to do their job. When the police threatened them with guns, the doctors and nurses refused to yield, claiming that the police had no authority on the hospital grounds.

Throughout the next day, the hospital director and health minister pressured the hospital staff who were known to have been involved in protecting demonstrators. The hospital director demanded the names of doctors and nurses and paramedicals who had participated in opposition activities from the hospital physician-in-charge, Dr. Bharat Pradhan, who refused to cooperate. The director, joined by the health minister and the home minister, demanded the registration records of patients in order to identify the names of the injured agitators, and again Dr. Pradhan and others refused. Dr. Pradhan explained, "We refused to be used as tools for a repressive political tactic. We did not give in. There was a growing sentiment that if we were going to be compromised [as health care providers] in this way, we would refuse to give care. We would go on strike and close down the hospital." Eventually, that threat was carried out.

Deaths in Bhaktapur

The day after the Democracy Day demonstrations, the movement retained its momentum. A nationwide strike was called, and there were clashes with police throughout the country. In Bhaktapur, a sizable town about eight miles east of Kathmandu well-known for its communist sympathies (Gellner 1996b), police opened fire on a massive crowd of protestors; four people were killed by police fire, and many more were wounded. This tragedy marked the start of the high-profile involvement of doctors. Bodies of victims of police shootings were an embarrassment to the government, and so they were generally made to "disappear." They were often taken directly to the morgue for postmortem examination and from there disposed of on the pretext that no family could be located or that the victim could not be positively identified; alternatively, they were disposed of instead of being taken to the hospital or the morgue, forgoing any postmortem. At the time of the Bhaktapur protests, the bodies of the young protestors were taken to Bir Hospital and medical records of the postmortem made before entering them into the morgue. Once the bodies were entered into the morgue, they were no longer under the control of the doctors or the Health Ministry but rather under the control of the Home Ministry, and so the doctors involved in the examination of these bodies made great efforts to identify, photograph, and document the condition of the bodies for the opposition.

In the days that followed, protestors agitated outside Bir Hospital and the morgue attached to it, demanding that the bodies of the deceased be released to the families for proper funerals (Shaha 1993: 141). Dr. Mathura made inquiries about the bodies at this time and examined the postmortem reports and X-rays that were smuggled out of the hospital in order to determine what type of bullets the police had used. Many of the public had assumed that the police were firing blanks, because they could not believe their king would allow real bullets to be used against them. But Dr. Mathura determined that the police were using not only real bullets but bullets which had the same effect as the "dum dum" bullets outlawed by the Geneva Convention. They were hollow-points whose tips had been altered so that they would explode inside the victim's body (as dum dum bullets would), making surgical removal of the shards impossible. Even for survivors, he noted, the effects of lead poisoning on most victims of these wounds would be devastating. The only way for a bullet to lose its tip in this way was to be scraped against a hard surface such as cement. Immediately, Dr. Mathura began a publicity campaign to mobilize the entire medical profession against the government.

Already physicians organizing through the Department of Community Medicine at Teaching Hospital had been planning a general strike to protest against the killings of innocent people and to demand a multiparty system, but Dr. Mathura speeded things up after his discovery of the bullets. When he returned from Bir Hospital with the information about the government's blatant violation of human rights he gave an impromptu lecture in the assembly hall at Teaching Hospital, urging the hundreds of health employees (doctors, nurses, technicians, etc.) assembled to speak out, show support, and call for an end to the repressive panchayat system.

Black armband strikes

Doctors already involved in the movement made plans to mobilize other doctors at both Teaching and Bir Hospitals for a large public protest. Students at the Institute of Medicine had unfurled a black flag on top of

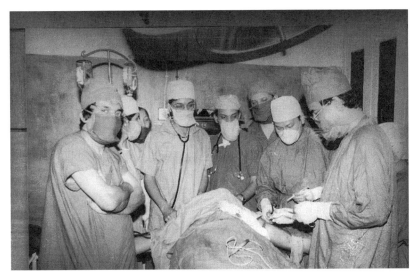

Plate 2 Physicians at work in the surgical ward during the protests, Bir
Hospital (reproduced with the permission of Dr. Bharat Pradhan).

the Department of Community Medicine building. This committed
activity of students, the doctors' feeling about the killings in Bhaktapur,
and their concern over the instances of abuses of human rights (in prisons
and now on the streets) led them to organize a black armband silent
protest strike of all hospital staff the day after Dr. Mathura's speech –
February 23. Doctors and nurses at Teaching Hospital urged their colleagues at Bir to do the same.[4]

> Press Coverage: *Samaj Daily* Falgun 14 [February 25, 1990]
> TEACHING HOSPITAL DOCTORS ON TOKEN STRIKE
> (Samaj Representative)
> Kathmandu, Falgun 13 [February 24, 1990], Yesterday, doctors
> and other staff of the Teaching Hospital launched a token strike
> for two hours, and the rest of the day they worked with black arm
> bands and badges. It is said the strike was launched as a protest
> against the gun firing by the government during the demonstra-
> tion on the date of Falgun 7–8 [February 18 and 19], which was
> conducted at the call of the banned Nepali Congress and the Left
> Front. The doctors did not hold conversation with the Press
> during the period of the strike.
>   Doctors claim that the protest program was conducted after
> gaining a clear understanding that the government used bullets

Plate 3   First black armband strike, Teaching Hospital (reproduced with the permission of Dr. Mathura Shrestha).

at the rally on the 7th and 8th, the use of which was prohibited by the Geneva Convention. These bullets were not allowed after the Second World War, according to sources of information. According to a doctor, the body of one of the persons hit by the government's bullet gets torn up and there is no way for the doctors to save the life of the victim. The doctor says, further, that if the government uses the bullets intentionally to kill people, why should it bring the victims to the hospital under the pretext of trying to save their lives. So, we have to protest, they said.

Yesterday, in the evening, students came out in a side demonstration at Sivaratri festival place, where they also distributed pamphlets.

During the two-hour strike, medical staff came out of the hospital in nearly full force. Emergency services were kept open and Out Patient Department victims who needed urgent care were shifted there; minimal staff remained on wards for critical-condition patients. After this, pro-democracy student organizers continued to hold meetings and spread information via the Department of Community Medicine.

Many felt that this initial strike was the most important catalyst for the revolution because it legitimized protest for the public at large. Dr. M. G. described the effect of the strike on his countrymen this way:

What happened was that people always felt they were so weak that if they came out in front and were identified [as protestors], then that would mean inviting death itself because they were so poor many were barely living at that point in time. With that scenario, if the head of a family got arrested and was deprived of his daily wages, that would mean the end for him and his family. But then they saw that more powerful people in society, people with more – stronger – the doctors, that they were coming out and dealing with the thing, then I think that gave them the courage to say that "Now, if these guys are coming out, and their number is small compared to the number of average men, if these guys are coming out and risking their lives, then together we are too many. The government will not be able to do anything to these guys, because they are strong, and we are too many. I don't think the government will do anything." So, I think that we gave them some sort of courage.

The doctors initiated – they had a role in initiating the development of the feeling for freedom and desires for a better society. They initiated the feeling among other professionals too. They were instrumental in that sort of building – of that feeling that pervaded most of the professional society at that time. There were some people in the medical profession in this country who had been politicized from the time of their youth – people who knew that the line between health and politics was very thin, and in order to really make a difference in health, they had to do something political. There were some very big participants in this, who really believed that, you know.

At Bir Hospital the doctors had more difficulty getting staff to go on strike than at Teaching Hospital. Unlike the Teaching Hospital staff, which functioned indirectly under the auspices of the government but directly as a branch of Tribhuvan University, the Bir Hospital staff members were all civil servants working under the direct supervision of the government and the Ministry of Health. More was at stake for these employees, for they could be fired for the sort of political expression tolerated at the teaching institution allowed under an umbrella of pedagogical freedom. By February 23, however, some eight physicians met with Dr. Bharat Pradhan to try to convince him that they should also go on strike. At first Dr. Pradhan was reluctant, claiming that even though he was politically supportive of the protest and had himself helped organize the emergency clinics, they were a government institution and needed above all to keep the hospital running for the public. Much was at stake. While for some physicians, especially those from the Department of Community Medicine, all of these political activities merely instantiated better medicine for the masses, for others, though they were sympathetic to democracy, a strike at the most central public hospital was initially seen as a step in the wrong direction. Bir Hospital had, after all, become a site of refuge during the first protests on Democracy Day. How would the public read a protest among physicians at one of the few institutions available to the country's poor and underserved? Clearly, a show of broad support for democracy among elite professionals would enhance the movement and motivate other professional groups to do the same. But it was feared that protests at the hospital might hurt more than help. Many doctors and nurses would be arrested and possibly imprisoned. Was it worth risking this?

Eventually even these health professionals also went on strike. The factor that finally persuaded many of them was that they began to see the conflict not in terms of politics but rather in terms of their need, as health professionals, to protect inviolable human rights associated with health status. S. L., an opthalmologist, explained:

I was not involved in politics because I am not a political person. I am a physician, and this is not political. But I became involved . . . there are a couple of things that come to my mind now. One is the sight of something which any normal person would not have accepted. I saw a Beetle car, a yellow car, that came at the front of the hospital, and a man came out of the driver's side shouting abuses of the panchayat system. I couldn't understand what he was doing. He seemed like a madman. And then I rushed there, and I knew something had happened. I looked and I saw him go into the back seat and he lifted out a seventeen-year-old boy with a bullet injury right through his chest. And, you feel so frustrated and you feel everything is terrible, every bit in you is revolting . . . you cannot imagine that scene. It is something that I had never seen in my life. That triggered factors. Many other patients came and saw that, and many doctors came too. In the mortuary, in the operation theater. Then, you ask, why are you there? Why are these people [the victims] there? What was their crime? Just that they shouted something – a few words – against King Birendra or a few words against the panchayat system (and I am quite sure it was more for words against the panchayat system rather than the king). And for that they get bullet injuries! And somehow, some way or the other, I could not comprehend or support that.

For the majority of physicians, the demand for a protest against the violation of basic human rights brought into full view by Dr. Mathura and their witnessing victims themselves reinforced their professional and personal commitments to reform. After some deliberation, Dr. Pradhan decided he had to show his support. Once he decided for the movement, he said, there was no going back. He and other physicians divided up responsibility for mobilizing a strike.

Before the strike occurred, Dr. Pradhan was called in for questioning by the hospital director and threatened. He was warned not to call for a strike. Then he was summoned by the royal physician and president of the Nepal Medical Association, who was at that time residing with the king and his court at Pokhara (a large resort city a day's drive west of Kathmandu). Dr. Pahari urged Pradhan to consider his position as a member of the NMA, his job, and his professional responsibility, again to no avail:

First, he was very polite and he asked about my family and how my kids were and all of that. Then he asked me what was happening there at Bir Hospital. I said, "Nothing, but we are going to organize a protest for the day after tomorrow." "For what?" he asked. I said, "This is against the violation of human rights, the killing of people, of arresting our medical personnel in the districts, and all." He asked, "Who is authorized to do this?" I said, "Everybody. We medicals are going to do this." And he challenged me, saying, "Don't touch the Association [NMA], Bharat." "Who am I to listen to these things?" I said to him. "The Association is not yours. You are only the president, but the Association is ours, all the members'. So, in your absence, if somebody calls a meeting and we sit together and decide what is best, then we will do that. We are doing this from Bir Hospital, on our own, but if needed we will seek help from the Association," I told him. Then he became very polite and said, "Bharat, don't do it." I said, "It is useless, you know. Who am I to block everybody else? I am just joining them. I am not the leader. And, you know, I have problems in my home also. My wife passed away recently." He said, "I know, that is why I am telling you, it's not good to involve yourself in these things at all." But I said, "I can't live alone. Our medical professionals are doing these things for a good cause, and I have to do it too. I have to join. Even if I die also, I want to die as a doctor on the streets."

The Minister of Health then called Dr. Pradhan from Pokhara with more advice:

She was telling me very politely that she had heard about my difficulties in my family. She said, "I know that you have not been able to go for further studies in MBBS, and you are quite senior. You could only ask me and I could help you. Whatever you want, I can send you for more education." But this did not work. I told her that when we are in this type of movement, doctors will be beaten and we are striking against that. A person who was beaten, for no reason is not able to use "source-force."

She said that it was against the law to strike, and it was only for politics. I told her that politics is not a reason behind the strike. I said, "I don't know what you are talking about. We are voicing . . . we are protesting against this arrest and treatment of our colleagues, against the killing of people. This is totally a non-political issue. This is against the killing of innocent people who have done nothing but were killed. We are talking about human rights violations, the brutality of the police who entered the hospital and did violent things inside the hospital." And she said, "No matter what, we have understood what you are saying and that you are doing all these things. Please know I will keep my word, I will do this and this. . . . Please convey this to your colleagues. Please don't do anything because the whole nation is in trouble. The doctors should not be involved." And I said that we will have to be involved.

Dr. Pradhan said that he would enjoy taking advantage of the post-doctoral opportunity but would not call off the protests in exchange for such an opportunity. She then turned to a different tactic – threatening that he would lose his job. And he said, "Fine, then, if you must, do your job, and I must do mine."

Three days after the Teaching Hospital strike, Bir Hospital had a walkout strike of nearly all of the staff. Dr. Pradhan walked through the empty halls of Bir Hospital during the protest and found a room with a locked door. Inside were four senior physicians who did not support the movement, and along with them was the hospital director. Once he had opened the door, Dr. Pradhan recalled, they were confronted with the political problem of opposition to their peers and professional colleagues. Fearful of the implications of not participating, they made excuses about being busy with something in that room and then drifted downstairs, where some of them hovered at the edges of the protest.

After the strike at Bir Hospital, the minister of health, as expected, forced participants to sign explanation letters, questionnaires designed to root out and document in writing any disloyalty to the king and his government. People were brought in one at a time to the director's office and forced to fill out forms attesting to their participation in the illegal activities and to sign them. The director had an individual file on each of the participants and began his interrogations in a manner that was meant as much to intimidate as to uncover information. Such records were one of the key bases for dismissals; if one had such a record on file with the government, all of one's activities were scrutinized and even one's family was harassed. Thus, physicians decided to place the NMA between the protestors and the government. Dr. Pradhan alerted the NMA of the events, and on March 1 the association, without its president, issued a press release:

> Press release from NMA 2046/12/11 [March 1, 1990]:
> Today, whilst the rest of the world is progressing at various stages of development; we the Nepali doctors in a situation to deal with different diseases afflicting their poor countrymen, have been shocked by the cruel government oppression of the unarmed citizens who had launched a peaceful movement from the 18th of February, 1990. Not content with the use of boots, sticks and teargas, the government has gone to the extent of using banned bullets on the unarmed and innocent Nepali citizens. As a result, a large number of Nepali have not only been seriously injured but have also lost their lives.
> The doctors, as conscious citizens aware of their professional responsibilities, expressed their concern over this sorrowful situation in a peaceful manner. In return, the government demanded clarifications and explanations from the doctors,

nurses and paramedical staff involved. Not content with this, they tried to create a situation of terror by threatening and even arresting some health workers. NMA condemns and denounces such acts and demands the immediate stoppage of such activities, restoration of peaceful environment and respect for the professional dignity of medical personnel.

Today, while there is worldwide movement for change, the Nepali government has been exposed by its brutal action against peace-loving Nepali demonstrators. As a result of this, the government has been disgraced not only in Nepal but also in the international community. For that reason, we, the doctors who are concerned with the health of the people, condemn the oppressive policies of the government.

Many innocent citizens have not only been arrested and detained, but reports have been brought to light regarding torture and inhuman behavior towards them. We doctors are very concerned and worried about the health of those detained. The government has not even given any information about the whereabouts and conditions of these citizens to their families. This is a clear violation of their human rights. We therefore demand that an independent judicial inquiry be instituted and that the findings of this commission be made public.

We want to make it clear that if the government resorts to further repression, threats and police or administrative interference in the day to day workings of the medical personnel, then the Nepali doctors will not take it lying down. There will be an open retaliation of such actions. If such a situation ensues, the total responsibility for the consequences will rest squarely with the government.

Hence, for the creation of an environment where the people can avail of their creativity for the overall development of the nation, the NMA appeals to the government and people to:
1. Stop the oppression of all professionals, including the medical personnel.
2. Put an end to violent suppression of peaceful demonstrations and slaughter of unarmed peaceful citizens.
3. Seek a political solution for the present political problems.
4. Seek a peaceful solution for the present state of unrest and deteriorating situation.

Partway through the interrogations at Bir Hospital, the NMA issued the statement that health professionals should not be forced to sign the questionnaires and threatened further action if all those already signed were not torn up. Eventually, it won; the letters already signed were torn up one at a time, in front of the person whose signature appeared on it, and no others were issued.

The arrest of Dr. Mathura

Dr. Mathura was perhaps the most prominent physician involved in the Movement, and his background is worth describing at some length because it sheds light not only on the historical social environment leading up to the revolution but also the motivations for political action shared by many health professionals. He was raised in the hillside village of Bandipur, about three hours' driving distance west of Kathmandu. Born to a Newar family in a village where Newars were dominant, he was involved in politics from childhood:

In 1942 at the age of nine years old, my father used to take me to India, and they used to stuff pamphlets inside our overcoats, inside our pillows, to bring back to Nepal. These were pamphlets against the Rana government. At that time, even the Nepali Congress was not formed. It was the Nepal National Congress. That was one party. And there was a rift. Even as a child I knew there was a rift between B. P. Koirala and Dilli Ram Regmi. After that, in the same year, the Bandipur Youth Club was formed in our village. You see, it was a secret organization. There were forty-two members, including three ladies. We had a membership system. They slit open their thumb with a blade and signed. That way, they started. Our job was to guard their shoes and report if anybody is moving around by our door, and we were to alert them, you see? I immediately after that became secretary of the library, which was a political library. We raised that library. We collected books from everybody. So I was the secretary of that and I read all the books, political books and other things.

The orientation of that library was political; all of it was for a social awakening. It was for the social awakening, and it contained a lot of political books. It contained a lot of Marxism and other things. One day, the government from Kathmandu sent the people to confiscate all the books which were political. So I was the secretary. Well, we had to submit. What to do? We were surrounded by the police. And you know, that was during the Rana regime. At that time, you see, the person who came to confiscate the books, he was half-literate. Politically he was illiterate and, you know, he seized all the books that contained the word Congress in it. So this included some from the Soviet Union – any books, if it had "Congress" written then it was seized. Any books, on Mahatma Gandhi or Nehru, all these books [that mentioned the Indian Congress]. But Marx, Lenin, he didn't know anything about it. He was ignorant about Marx, and he only asked what the book was about, and I said it was a book about religion. Mao Tse Tung, the same thing, you see? I said they were books about how to produce more brains! And most of the Indian books written by Indian leaders were confiscated and so a few books, especially about reports of the Soviet Congress, were confiscated, but no books written by Marx or Mao. These were not confiscated, and we could read these as young children.

When I was fifteen or sixteen years old, I participated in the Liberation movement against the Ranas, and after that I was a student leader here in Kathmandu. I studied in Kathmandu, but at that time we went to the village and I became a volunteer to overthrow the government. They recruited me as a volunteer – a guerrilla – what is called a "Liberation Army Volunteer." So, we were given training for twenty-three days. That training was nothing; we didn't even know what a grenade looked like! So we were asked to imagine one small stone to be a grenade and how to use the fuse and how to throw. But I never saw what a grenade looked like.

All this was supported by the Bandipur Youth Club. Most of them were Congress supporters, and there were non-Congress there also. There were both Congress and communists, half-half, you see, because that area of Bandipur was under the flag of Congress. The movement was carried out under the flag of Congress even if there were non-Congress people there. I myself didn't belong to any party, Congress or other, at that time. It was all voluntary. We raised a lot of volunteers, even women. For example, they had to grind [the grains, corn, etc.] to feed the volunteers. Young women used to beat the rice. For the whole day and whole night they used to take turns, four or five shifts and in batches. They used to do this every day and every night, even in villages which were captured even without firing a single bullet. The villages areas were already liberated. Only this military area [of Bandipur] was not liberated. The military and office government areas were not liberated. [Bandipur was a regional government seat.]

So we were supported by the villagers for our training. The military office [of the government] was only a few hundred meters away from the village. The one useful thing I learned was how to march in the dead of night. That was very interesting, you see, they were planning that some day we will get enough guns and we will attack the military compound. We were trained not actually near that village but a bit farther away – three or four kilometers away from that village, in the forest. But the village people were supporting us. It was surrounded by the Rana areas.

My own squad commander was one Lal Bahadur Sarki. He was an untouchable, but he was such a remarkable man. And he was my best teacher, not only as a military person, because he was also such a good person, although he belonged to the untouchable caste. And during those times, untouchable – sarki – was very low social status. You see, he was an ex-military from the Indian Army, so he knew everything. He was very good. We accepted him.

So at that time we were waiting, and we didn't get enough arms, of course. This is very interesting. We were awaiting that someday, somehow, arms will come and we will go and fight and capture that garrison [Rana army]. But that never happened. Then two Nepali Congress leaders came there, probably from India. And they said that, yes, we should capture that place but without fighting, only by demonstration. So there was voting, and the overwhelming majority voted for the Gandhian policy rather than the revolution. And it was very confusing; even as a child I could not digest this. You see, they had already started the revolution – the war of liberation in the southern part of the country, and here they were propagating Gandhian philosophy in the villages. And, of course, overwhelmingly people –

there were about ten thousand people gathered there from all over the neighboring villages, and when everybody showed up and they did a show of hands. Of course I was not eligible to vote, I was young only 15–16 years old. But the overwhelming majority voted for the peaceful demonstration. So we threw away all the – even the sticks – away. We were not allowed to use them. And we marched. But when we marched, they started firing and my commander, you know, that I loved so much. (Even now I dream of him very frequently. If he had been alive, he would have been the ideal person. He would be my teacher.) You know, he got himself shot. He was just by my side. He got himself shot in the chest. You know, during that peaceful demonstration – a peaceful demonstration – they shot. He himself got shot. Several other people were also shot.

There were two things that really affected me. He said to me, "Don't – go away, go away, escape," you see . "You cannot stay. Escape!" he said. And he lay down and he became unconscious. He had started convulsions. I saw so much blood. It might have been a hallucination, but I saw so much blood there. And there was the noise of the bullets! This sound, when it passes like that near your ears, it is very irritating. I cannot explain. It was very irritating. That bullets were like rain. I didn't even know I was spared. So I jumped. There was a way to go, and I jumped. Below there was a slope and I jumped there to save myself. Before that, when I looked back, I saw these leaders. There were on horseback, and they were running away from the field, and immediately I hated these leaders. One was Sri Bhadra Sharma, and one is Marwari or something. These two leaders came from India and said that we must capture [the garrison] peacefully. And, suddenly there was no use waiting for such useless buggers. So, I jumped below, onto the slope. I was wearing half-knicker, half-pants, even though it was winter. So I jumped and I landed right in the nettle grass. I will never forget . . . .

That event was a very strong disincentive, physical as well as psychological, to see the useless leaders who belonged to Nepali Congress. That is probably why I eventually went away from Nepali Congress. Even as they were waging war in the south, they were propagating a peaceful movement in Bandipur. I saw eight people die. To me, these leaders were inconsistent. After that, I became a political leader and I became a communist, when I was a student. This experience was what made me decide to be a doctor. . . . We went afterward to collect the body. I brought my commander, Sarki. He was still not dead. Only there was some substance coming out [of his body]. And, I was asked to put my hand there to prevent the blood from escaping from that hole on his chest. There was a traditional Vaidya, Kabi Raj [a fully qualified Ayurvedic doctor], and he said you must put your hand like that – that's why I put my hands like that [on his chest]. So, after three or four hours, if you put your hand like that continuously pressing, your hand becomes very painful. But I thought that if I take out my hand, he will die. So I had to bear a lot of pain, and I started weeping. Somebody came and gave me relief, but the bullet went into his lungs. And the next morning, I again came to put my hand there and I put my hand there, and after some time he died. Just like that, you see? And that was a tremendous influence on me. You see, I had some feeling that if I had been a doctor before he died. . . .

On that same day, the main commander, the commander in chief, Radha Magar, he had been struck by a bullet here [he shows where on his neck it went in and out the back]. In my house – in everybody's house – there was a medicine bag and fortunately there was some adhesive plaster. Nothing but adhesive plaster. His wife put her hand on his head and I went there and put plaster on him. I plastered him, but there was no injury inside, and he survived. He is still living. He is in Bharatpur today. So that, too, because he had a miraculous healing. I don't know. I did nothing but put the bandage and of course his bleeding had probably already stopped because of the pressure put on by his wife.

So these were the two incidents – because of the love for my squad commander Lal Bahadur Sarki – and I always said that if at all possible, I will become a doctor.

Dr. Mathura went on to complete his studies and eventually to study medicine in India. He was a political activist leader in Kathmandu during his time at one of the local college campuses (Tri Chandra), and after his return from Patna University in India was blacklisted by the government because of his activism. By that time, the panchayat system was already in place. Banned from privileged positions in Kathmandu, he volunteered for work in Bharatpur Hospital in Chitwan. The government sent him from one rural area to another, where he was a recurring source of trouble for local district officers. "They never put me in one place for more than one year, but that gave me the chance to see the country, the people," he said, laughing. He was in India when Koirala was elected to power and reports that both communists and Congress worked to support that government from there, despite its eventual disbanding by King Mahendra.

He continued to work in the countryside, "blacklisted" by the government as an insurgent, most of the time without pay:

Although I was victimized by the government, I was the best. They cheated in every aspect, in every way. They transferred me from one place to another. Most of the time they did not even pay any salary to me, but I never minded. That time, I never earned any money. I never cared, but academically, I was always right. Everybody saw that academically I was right. Finally, I never practiced privately. I created some kind of reputation among the people, as well as in the profession, in the profession because of my academic standing and in the people because of my simple living conditions. And I always worked and hoped for the people. You see, during the later phase, when the panchayat regime was not so harsh, I conducted several studies for the Institute of Medicine [Teaching Hospital] that were financed by IDRC [International Development Research Center of Canada]. And that, again, took me around Nepal, and I could see many people and I could learn. That gave me the opportunity to learn from the people and also to make the people understand me, you see. It was both ways.

In the late 1970s Dr. Mathura was invited to study in England, in the Liverpool School of Tropical Medicine, having received the highest university award for his research. Both at home and abroad he was influenced by politicized scientists, including the Pugwash Declaration against the atomic bomb, and the Alma Ata Declaration promoting primary health care. In the 1970s and early 1980s, he was joined by others in the All Nepal Medical Association as a professional interest group for doctors. He was influenced in this period by an intellectual leftist group called the Ralpha Club:

There was a kind of mood to question traditional thinking and to bring in a new way of thinking. And we thought that we should involve the people in general. So that gave us a new type of song, a new type of writing, a new type of poems, new types of painting, and new types of thinking. It gave some kind of stimulation to all sections of the population, but especially to doctors, lawyers, and artists. There were not many artists, but there were many journalists and other people. Although the Ralpha Club broke down soon after it was formed, it gave some kind of incentive to debate – underground debate. That process of debate became a way of life . . .
    Several groups were formed, but one common feature was that people started debating, talking to each other, and that was a very good, very important foundation for social and political interaction. I myself was caught up in that way, and we were debating several things – the legal aspect, about the human rights situation, and about the social responsibility of professionals, especially the doctors. What was our duty? What should we be doing, and what could we do? Unfortunately, at that time, we believed that we could do very little. We formed a study group in the village. We were influenced by Paolo Freire [who wrote *Pedagogy of the Oppressed*]. He was highly influential, because he had a strong way of convincing, with a Western way of debate. There were others, too. I forget their names – even Miller, Arthur Miller, wrote novels in ways where he didn't distinguish between scenes and off-scenes things, and even his way of debate became very influential. Also Kafka, Sartre . . . and all these types – ways of seeing things critically. And of course critical consciousness, critical education, critical literacy. All these came with Paolo Freire.

In 1976 Dr. Mathura helped form a doctors' group of Amnesty International to investigate the situation of political prisoners that eventually became the Doctors' Solidarity Group. In 1984 he and several others decided to form a splinter group of health professionals more directly concerned with politics than the Nepal Medical Association was at that time: Health Professionals for Social Responsibility (an affiliate of the international group of physicians called International Physicians for the Prevention of Nuclear War [IPPNW], later re-named Physicians for Social Responsibility). This group included many of the members of the original Doctors' Solidarity Group, and its goals were fourfold:

To oppose any kind of war and violence, and in that we could explain that even ill-health is a kind of violence. Second, we were also concerned to provide relief in case of disaster (like nuclear war). Third, was to work for the environmental betterment or to preserve, conserve the environment. Fourth, was to develop a people-oriented health care system. Although it was for physicians elsewhere, in Nepal, we accepted everybody – nurses, health assistants, and laboratory technicians, everyone.

In addition to addressing political repression, this group proposed political activism for the sake of improving the health care system. For Dr. Mathura, the ability for the common man to demand social equality and attain it was critical for health. He later told me:

In my understanding, health status includes educational status and is related to the level of political participation of the people. Political participation in their home towns, in the national, as well as international politics. The more people will participate in politics, the more they will become conscious of their health. Health is a part of living, so I say that the health status of a nation is related to three factors: One is political participation, and that is the most important – the level of political participation. Second is equity in income and distribution. Income as well as distribution. The third thing is what is called the attainment of quality of life in terms of basic needs. These needs are shelter, food, proteins, health education, and security (and this means political security as well as old age and employment security).

At the same time that he was involved in the doctors' groups, Dr. Mathura was also involved in activities that led to the founding of the Human Rights Organization of Nepal with Rishikesh Shaha. By 1990, a second organization, the Forum for the Protection of Human Rights (FOPHUR) was also in full operation, largely through the work of Dr. Mathura and his colleagues, and it would play an important role in the revolution. Under the coordinating efforts of Devendra Raj Pandey, HURON, FOPHUR and the Human Rights Committee of the Nepal Bar Association held a forum on human rights in Nepal and began to develop a list of demands to be presented to the prime minister, Marich Man Singh Shrestha, on the same day as the black armband strike, protesting the government's actions on Democracy Day.

The list was presented to the prime minister at his home on that afternoon in late February by five doctors and sixteen delegates from other professions. The meeting, Dr. Mathura recalled, was a heated one but the prime minister gave the delegates the impression that he was sympathetic to their demands. He said that in contrast to the doctors and professionals, who were from high-status families, he was from a poor schoolteacher's family. "I understand the issues better than you people," he said. "Why the unrest?"[5] Nevertheless, the delegates left with the feeling that they had truly educated him with regard to the problems of the nation. He assured them there would be no more violence against citizens. After the meeting, the delegates held an informal discussion and decided to form the Professional Solidarity Group, which would later play an important role in the revolution. That night Dr. Mathura, the spokesman for the group, was arrested and jailed.

The Nepal Medical Association again became vocally involved, despite the fact that its president, the king's personal physician, Dr. S. K. Pahari, was unavailable to attend the meetings or sign its press releases. Physicians were unsure whether the president of their association would support the movement; in fact, he was rumored to have said that Dr. Mathura deserved to be arrested. In contrast, the NMA membership demanded his immediate release, claiming that his arrest was a threat to the whole profession and that they would, as a professional group, take action unless he was set free. Messages were also sent to the international organizations to which he belonged – Amnesty International and the International Physicians for Social Responsibility. By this time, the Nepal Bar Association also became more visible in its involvement, calling for another black armband strike.

Already, health professionals were transforming the movement, making it less an issue of allowing political parties than an issue of human rights. This move proved crucial because it redefined the terms of the conflict. The struggle was no longer about Nepali party concerns but about universal injustice that could arouse the support of international sanctions and attention. This was important for citizens in Nepal and for foreign government and non-government development and diplomatic agencies located there which needed to avoid involvement in local politics but felt their involvement in upholding international standards of human dignity was a mandate. It is not surprising that the major impetus behind this shift came from doctors whose profession was built upon this ideal of universal standards. Doctors, along with nurses and paramedics had first-hand contact with the fatal outcomes of the denial of the free speech that they saw as part of democracy – they were working with the bodies of the injured and killed – and to them the objective truths found in international human rights discourse described their situation exactly.

By basing the movement on a human rights issue medical professionals were able to argue against their superiors – hospital administrators, ministry officials, and other professionals – on the ground that those who opposed the movement were not simply anti-democratic but anti-modern, anti-development, and anti-professional. Resistance to the movement could be equated with lack of professionalism and backwardness. Human rights had become the means by which a revolutionary politics could stand for all that was modern, objective, fair, democratic, and objectively just – like the sciences of medicine themselves. Thus, what had started for many physicians and other professionals as a political movement turned into a movement about human rights, and what had begun for others as a call for human rights later became a basis for demanding a complete overthrow of the political system. For others the projects were simultaneously pursued.

Dr. Mathura's arrest brought strike threats from Teaching Hospital and such a public outcry that he was released the next night. In prison he was interrogated repeatedly but not tortured. This was not unusual; all the health professionals I met who had been arrested told the same story and believed that they had escaped torture because they were health professionals. Other professionals also noted that those who were well known were not tortured in jail. The outspoken opposition leader, Padma Ratna Tuladhar, a well-known outspoken opposition leader, explained (quoted in Raeper and Hoftun 1992: 59): "In Kathmandu, all the arrested students and youth leaders were tortured in police custody, but not people like me, because of our status. I was not tortured in police custody or jail – though there was a kind of psychological torture. I was taken from place to place at night, even outside Kathmandu." Although this immunity no doubt held true for many popular figures because they were well known, health professionals told me time and time again that the potentially violent conditions of their imprisonment were mitigated by the fact that even their lowly jailers respected them as medical providers of care – that somehow their status placed their physical safety above that of other prisoners. This double standard was linked to the way that the public itself saw the doctors' protests as somehow more legitimate than others' whose actions were of questionable merit because associated with one political voice over another. The medical professionals were speaking universal truth, not political truth. Jailed doctors were even able to negotiate their early release on these grounds.

Several days after the Bir Hospital strike, the missionary-sponsored Patan Hospital also went on strike in a show of support organized by the NMA. On March 5, the Nepal Bar Association held a black armband strike to protest human rights violations, and petitions were presented to the government by Nepali writers and by the Nepali Paramedical Association (Raeper and Hoftun 1992: 60).

A lull and behind-the-scenes agitation

The subsequent weeks saw a lull in activities, and the organizers began to worry that the movement was going to fizzle out. There were sporadic strikes and demonstrations throughout the country, and graffiti proliferated on walls of government buildings and hospitals. Because protestors were still being arrested and detained by police, the public found ways of expressing discontent in devious ways – tying oppositional messages to pigeons and hanging photos of the king and queen on dogs – sometimes placing chilis in the rear-ends of these dogs to make them run wildly through the streets. (So long as the animals were decorated with photos of

His and Her Majesties, the police could not shoot them.) Similarly, people wrote oppositional graffiti on sacred cows, since no one could harm them in any way. They produced sketches, posters, and cartoons with slogans about the corruption of the palace targeting individual members of the government and distributed these surreptitiously and anonymously. Small outbursts occurred, and there were more and more arrests accompanied by rumors of deaths. Occasionally corpses would appear in the streets overnight, according to citizens the bodies of victims tortured to death by police but according to police those of victims of public beatings (Raeper and Hoftun 1992). Still, the momentum seemed to be slowing. It was at this point many said that the doctors took the ball and ran with it. As C.V., a health professional, explained:

In Nepal, doctors are highly respected. You know that. Much more than the United States. The doctors' authority was increased tremendously with their participation because they sided with the people. The doctors also gave credibility to the movement. Most of the time, the government tried to discredit the movement by saying that it was only some street urchins, uneducated people, or that it was outsiders trying to upset the country. But when the intellectuals like doctors participated en masse, then even the outside world was forced to look and see what was happening in Nepal and that it was a credible movement.

In the beginning it was not only a few doctors participating; there were certain issues which galvanized the whole doctors' community. It was a broad medical horizon that was first conceived by a few politically conscious persons within the medical community. It was those that had a good community vision and who had been arguing for a long time that politics is medicine after all. We were the first ones that had the perception that something was going on and that we should be ready to try to do our best to help. We started the ball rolling, and eventually there was a snowballing effect. It went to a certain critical point and then exploded and there was mass participation, and then our stand also became clear and so in that way the whole medical community became organized.

So I think the doctors' participation had a very, very important role in two ways: one was to raise the morale of the struggling people of the movement, because the doctors' participation was a new thing in Nepal and because doctors are also kind of like a second god in Nepal; doctors are like the king because of their rank as professionals – almost like gods because they deal with life and death. So it was participation by the doctors that gave a huge amount of moral support and credibility to the movement. It also helped to arouse other intellectual groups to support the movement. They said, "Doctors are doing this, so why can't we?"

So the doctors played a crucial role in coordinating the professional movement. You can see if you look in detail at the chronological order of the different events. You will see that the doctors were the most involved as professionals who brought out statements and participated in all the effective protests.

Medical organizers and political leaders devised various strategies for keeping things going, for just below the surface calm there was a great deal of public discontent.

Decisive strategies

Between the final days of February and the end of March, the physicians and other health professionals managed both to sustain the level of popular dissent and to instigate more radical actions for revolution. They used their professional resources, including their authority as "scientific"experts, to promote activities which propelled the movement forward.

Dissemination of political information

One of the most important things doctors were able to do was disseminate information about conditions in Nepal to their professional organizations both within and outside of Nepal. Paramedicals used night buses to carry messages to politically active health professionals throughout the country, even breaking curfew restrictions. They sent pamphlets and distributed NMA statements and calls for strikes to the many rural health worker cadres in the countryside, some of whom became very active in their villages and went on strike along with urban hospital employees. Rural health workers disseminated news about events in the city which the official radio stations said nothing about and incorporated political awareness messages in everyday patient care. They pointed out to people that poor nutrition, bad water, lack of medicinal resources, and high infant mortality were not simply a matter of their ignorance but also a result of political and social inequality about which they could do something. At rural health posts, health assistants allowed posters with political slogans to be placed on their walls, claiming when asked by policemen that they did not know who had put them there.

Doctors also alerted their international professional organizations and their relatives abroad. According to Dr. M. K. D., this was possible, among other reasons, because of the physicians' facility with new technologies which were not even available to the average Nepali activist:

This is why our Andolan in particular was a success. If you ask me, the few causes of the success of the Andolan – of our particular Jan Andolan was, number one, the Indian leaders who happened to come here at the right time to give us advice. . . . The second thing was the fax advantage – fax and telephone advantage. If it was not for that, we would have been a total failure. On the one hand, we could fax our information, and we had so many people. I mean, I shouldn't say that, but we had so many people working with international agencies, foreigners as well as Nepalis, who were helping us. Even if we had no fax ourselves, we could give them the fax and they would fax for our cause. And this spread information like wildfire throughout the world and the Nepalis in New York would pick it up, Nepalis in Washington would pick it up, and would spread it to the Congress bench when the

Senators met, or to the Members of Parliament in England, in Germany and Denmark and Sweden, everywhere. . . . So naturally, once the government here knew that it was exposed, they could not clamp down. They tried to clamp down but they could not. That was part of the cause of our success. The telecommunications helped us in another way, too. What happened was that the police were using a certain band frequency, you see. Luckily somebody or the other got to know of this and all people who had radios with FM . . . knew exactly where the police were moving and what bullets were being fired and where and that how many. This also worked in our favor.

Hospitalization of opposition leaders

Opposition leaders were at this time already under house arrest. Ganesh Man Singh and his wife, Mangala Devi, of the Congress party, and Man Mohan Adikhari, of the United Left Front were suddenly put under hospital bed rest by their physicians, who had up until then been visiting them at their homes. Doctors with whom I spoke confided that this strategy had a dual purpose. First of all, the health of Ganesh Man really was failing, and he needed more constant care by medical experts. Also important, however, was that the strikes at the hospitals (Bir in particular) had made it clear that the hospitals were becoming a refuge for the opposition. It was decided that the leaders would be safer in the hospitals under armed guards than in their homes. The doctors knew that the government would not dare to attempt assassinations or disappearances of these leaders if they were in the hospital because even the government was beholden to the public perception that the hospitals were part of the modernity they themselves promoted and supported; medicine was even for them an important site for which it deserved credit – a development achievement. Moreover, they were also beholden to the idea that medical truths were not in essence political, but scientific and impartial. Opposition leaders knew that even the soldiers guarding these patients would not be able to override the doctors' orders.

Once hospitalized, these leaders were able to receive visitors from all over Nepal – from diplomatic communities, from political organizations, from other opposition organizers. In cases where even the soldiers would have been able to recognize political activists among the visitors (journalists and others), doctors and nurses were able to disguise these persons with hospital attire (white coats, stethoscopes, and name tags).

The Kirtipur Conference

In a speech on March 16 that was expected to address the popular demands for a multiparty system, King Birendra only reiterated how out of touch he seemed to be with the interests of his subjects and how over-determined were his assumptions that panchayat government already constituted a democracy. Shaha (1993: 196–97) provides excerpts from the speech:

> Any political system by itself is not an end but a means by which people's rights, interests and potentials are realized. As is known to all, our political tradition relies on the popular will, and the mandate given by the national referendum is the basis for retaining the Panchayat polity. Basing itself on the popular will enriched by the experience of the past, the dynamism of the Panchayat system lies in its ability to effectively fulfill the aspirations of the people in the coming days. In the past three decades, we have instituted reforms as called for by the changing needs of time, and taking into account the Nepali aspirations this process will continue. Let us always remember that all those who believe in democracy should consider it their duty to abide by provisions and processes of the constitution while seeking solutions to problems. . . . Any unconstitutional activity that disturbs peace, tranquility, and security will hinder the exercise of democratic rights and developments in the country. Indeed this cannot be to anyone's interest. There can be no solution to a problem where there is irresponsible behaviour and undignified acts disregarding the interest of the country and the people.

In response to this speech and to further the movement towards what opposition political leaders considered real democracy, they called a People's Solidarity Day or National People's Unity Day for March 23, to demonstrate the huge public demand for social reform. On March 17 a black armband protest was held by writers and artists at the Royal Nepal Academy and Tri Chandra Campus, resulting in arrests. The Professional Solidarity Group then called for a conference to be held at Kirtipur Campus three days before People's Solidarity Day. This conference, perhaps more than any other public demonstration, proved to be a turning point for the movement.

The Professional Solidarity Group planned to have seven members speak at the conference: two health professionals, a former judge, a journalist, an engineer, a poet, and an English professor. The health professionals were Dr. Mathura and Meena Poudal, a trained nurse. The speeches were supposed to focus on the role of professionals in the contemporary political situation in Nepal. The group's statement was as follows:

> The nation-building procedure is normally directed by its culture, politics and government system which are again enhanced by progressive art, literature, science, and professional activities. These factors are augmented by the creative, discriminating, and free thinking society of the country. Therefore,

encouragement and inspiration to this type of society are vitally important for making a positive impact on the development of the nation. Where there is no political culture befitting the modern age; where there is no room for the creative and discriminating talent in the country's administration; where there is no liberty in scientific and technological persuasion, principle and discipline due to the prominence of selfish interference and control; in a system like this, it is only natural for those of us engaged in professional activities (be it individual, private or national) to be stifled, dissatisfied and displeased.

At present, doctors, engineers, writers, and journalists are not free to use scientific and conscientious methods in our professional fields so as to produce genuine, proper and truthful results. Professors and teachers are deprived of their freedom of intellectual exercise only because of their interest in human rights. The dignity of the legal service cannot be sustained in this country as the government itself moves against the norm of the Rule of Law. Furthermore, all the civil servants of the country are facing the common people's insult and wrath, through no fault of their own but rather because of the responsibility and insatiable greed of governing authorities.[6]

Under these circumstances in the country, we of all groups of various professions cannot just stand as silent observers. All of the aforesaid common experiences are the force that will bring us the democratic government we aspire to and we offer our stern decision to cooperate with the national movement for the establishment of the democratic system we look for.

The next equally important and indispensable point for us is that we are human beings, and we want to live as human beings. We firmly assert that Human Rights include such basic things as food and shelter for mankind, and that the democratic system is the only base for Human Rights to stand on. The simple demand for the implementation of the aforesaid system in the country is taken to be a crime by the present government. This kind of attitude and the activity of the government have encroached upon the common rights of all Nepali citizens, and have subjected so many innocent devotees of the nation to various kinds of torture, domination, and unusual death. The prisoners are shifted from one place to another in order to conceal their torture, and in doing so, the government not only inflicts physical torture to the victims but also mental torture to their family members. We cannot help condemning the state-run terrorism such as inhumane and cruel behavior, widespread arrest, suppression, and a situation of insecurity of the people, including those who are in the prisons.

The Constitution should always be capable of maintaining a democratic environment and Human Rights. A Constitution which cannot speak out the feeling of the people is bound to be thrown out by the people themselves. It has got to be understood that the Constitution of the country is not an end in itself; it is only a means. In view of the present situation, it is the inherited right of all Nepali citizens to demand for a change in the Constitution. Therefore:

1. all the people imprisoned in connection with the peaceful movement should be released immediately and unconditionally, and the prevailing activities of arrest, torture, and suppression should be discontinued;

2. the worldwide announcement on Human Rights and the articles concerning it should be followed perfectly;

3. the right to open and free conduct of all kinds of organizations, including political organizations, should be provided without any condition or restriction;

In order to have the aforesaid demands fulfilled, we cordially request all the people of the country to make our each and every program successful, including the "Unity Day of the People" [Solidarity Day], which is going to be organized on the 10th of Chaitra [March 23, 1990] alongside the national movement of the people which is currently running.

At this point, medical professionals contributed to the momentum of the revolution by making claims about the nature of truth in a democratic system. For them, truths were made visible through professionals whose expertise carried a certain authority about these issues, but the only system which could give legitimacy to this sort of authority was a democratic one. Truths used in a monarchical system always ran the risk of being obscurantist, constructed conveniently around personal relationships and status differentials in relation to the king himself. In the partyless panchayat system, those who felt stifled were those who were persistently made to compromise their professional interests in order to accommodate monarchical and patronage concerns. Thus professional expertise would have to count for more than the king's or any patron's wishes, and this would require the political environment of democracy. The rhetoric that took center stage with the involvement of medical and other modern professionals was that of letting "truth" – the objective facts – reign.

Exemplifying this perspective was Meena Poudel. Known for her outspoken stand on political issues as a student and later as a trained nurse, she was invited to be the sole female speaker at the conference to offer her views not only on behalf of her professional nurses' organization but also on behalf of women in general. Again, this concern revealed the way in which activists laid claim to modernity, effectively denying the panchayat regime's claims to ownership of that discourse. Her story conveys the view shared by professionals that under the monarchy their commitments to transcendent truths were persistently stifled by both patronage demands and a social system which discriminated against her on the basis of her gender and her class:

When I was born into my family, I was the first child. From the beginning, I had to face problems regarding economics, especially for schooling and for my survival. It was very difficult. I was from the terai, from a Brahmin family. I am from Brahmin, that is why it was very difficult for schooling, because for my parents, and for the society where I was born, they believe a girl child does not need an education. They believe, especially, that a girl child should be married before her menstruation begins. In my case, my grandparents and my mother's brother wanted me to get married. At times, they said they wanted to give me away to other people because I protested so much. They proposed that I should get married when I was just a little girl, and I rejected that. I wanted to study, I wanted to do something for my society, for my family. I felt I had some responsibility because I am the first child, that I had to do something for my sister or my brother. I finally decided that because they tried so hard to throw me out, and I protested, that I would have to leave this family if I wanted to get a higher education. I was already menstruating when I decided to go to Kathmandu to live with my auntie. She was in the same situation, and she encouraged me always. She said, "You should do something. You should fight against this discrimination."

I came in 1979 or '80 to Kathmandu. Actually, my interest was in studying to be an engineer. My school background was math and science, and I wanted to study at the engineering campus, but the problem was that there was no girls' hostel there. I could not afford to stay outside the hostel and rent a room for myself. I tried to look for a scholarship. But there was only one campus with a girls' hostel and that was the nursing campus. . . . So, I started to study nursing. That was in 1980. This was the first time that I became involved in the women's group. The nursing campus was all women. Teachers were women, administrators were women, campus was women, students were women. Before that, I was the only girl in school. . . . At the school I became the top student. I came from the village, I came from the poor family. The urban people always say that village people are ignorant, that they don't know anything – all this type of discrimination. . . . When I came to the campus, I faced that type of situation. So, I went back to the family in the village, and, again, they proposed to me: "You should get married. You should not go back to campus." Being in a Brahmin community, their demands were difficult to ignore. But I decided that I should go back to campus so that I could support my younger sister. I have supported her from grade seven. I support my brothers too. . . .

At that time, the students' movement was very popular. We didn't really have political parties, just a student movement. I became involved with politics, and I was elected as the president of the nursing campus. The agenda at that time was for a multiparty system and to stop the corruption. The main issue was against the panchayat system – for a change in the whole political system, against the *natabad, crypabad, aphno manche*, all these things. As president of the student union for two years, I made lots of demands against the administrators. I had to spend two months in the rural area before I completed my nursing degree, and I saw how bad it was for women there. I went to the Sindupalchowk area, where so many girls are sold by their families to work in brothels in India. At that time, I saw that even the Rastriya [National] Panchayat members – the backbone of the panchayat system – even they were involved in this trafficking of women. I even saw that [minister] of the Rastrya Panchayat hired a helicopter to that area to bring a girl to Bombay. They chartered it directly (and this is at a cost that is more than the combined incomes for a year for the whole village). These politicians sold the girls and got money from the middlemen agents, and they got votes from that locality (because the families wanted to earn money from the girls this way).

Anyway, I felt very bad having seen this, and I thought that at that time when I complete my degree, I will try to do something about it. And, I have a strong commitment. . . . I became strong to fight against the system. The system was not good. I got my degree and even after, in the hospital, I found the same situation. When poor people came into the hospital, they did not get any treatment. In the Teaching Hospital, or in any hospital, the same situation: they get refused, and the administrator's mentality toward the poor people was very bad. They would just say, "I cannot treat you. You cannot get any medicines. We cannot accept you in this hospital. We cannot provide free treatment for you." This was the attitude of the hospital administrator. I always tried to fight him, because I was in charge of the ward in that department. My boss was totally of this attitude. Every meeting we had a fight. I always encouraged poor people in the hospital. I told them, "You should get some medicines, and you should get food, too, when you stay in the hospital." And the administration always asked me for clarification. "Why are you always encouraging this type of people? Are you ready to give some money from your salary to pay for them?" And I said, "OK, I can give some money for these people from my salary. If you want to do that, you can cut some money from my salary, because you are the hospital administrator, you have a responsibility. You can decide. You have the decision-making power. Why are you promoting this type of hospital? What is your purpose? Isn't it to provide health services to the people?"

Always we fought. I asked my administrator to send me back to the rural area after my degree, but he would not send me. "Can you provide me with some project to do in the rural area?" I asked. "I want to work with the poor people, with the women," I said. But he said no. He told me I must work in the hospital. So after that, I started my bachelor's degree in public health. I wanted to do this because public health is mostly related to the grass-roots-level people. General nursing and general health related to the curative side; public health was the preventive side. Hospital nursing is curative, only in the hospital. But I wanted to work with the grass-roots level, not in the hospital, because at that time the political parties were preparing for a political movement. I immediately became involved in the movement, and my administrator said to me that I will lose my job if I do that work. And I said, "OK, then, I will lose my job."

Actually, I resigned from my job before they suspended me. I had taken all the keys to my department, and I gave it to them and I said, "This is your key, your department. I do not want to take responsibility from today. Being a citizen, is it my responsibility to treat bullet injury victims, all these people?" Actually I decided to get involved in the democratic movement when they started to kill people. In Bhaktapur, the second day of the movement, they killed four people. We received those dead bodies in our hospital. We sent our ambulances and our staff to Bhaktapur. We received those victims in our hospital [I believe some of them went to Bir and some to Teaching Hospital]. We did the operations to try to save them, the surgical procedures. We took out the pieces of bullets. From that day, we started to organize the nurses and doctors. We had a big meeting in the hospital [February 22, 1990]. "You see this bullet?" we said. "These are dead bodies. These are our people. We are ashamed. In this situation, this is our responsibility. Being a health person, being a citizen, being a human being. This is our responsibility to protest against this type of atrocity."

Meena finished her exams for the bachelor's in public health just before the movement began. She received the highest marks in the school and was to be awarded the Queen's Education Medal (Aishwarya Vidya Patak) for academic excellence, but she refused the award on grounds that (1) the queen had done nothing to help the cause of women; (2) she stood for everything that Meena rejected politically and had certainly done nothing to promote Meena's own educational efforts nor to earn the honor of benefiting from them; and (3) the money spent on the medal was the nation's money and in this fashion, for this award, grossly misspent. Few had ever so ostentatiously criticized the queen before. When the Professional Solidarity Group asked her to speak at the Kirtipur Conference, she agreed, and after the other speakers she was again out-spoken about the queen and about corruption in government. Serious critiques of the king or queen were an egregious violation of the law, and before she was able to finish the police surrounded the auditorium, which at that time contained some eight hundred to nine hundred persons. Meena finished her speech and was followed by Dr. Mathura, who also took a stand against the abuse of human rights.

During Dr. Mathura's speech the police entered the building and demanded that the speakers cease talking. Dr. Mathura warned the police not to interfere with the academic rights of the intellectuals and the chairperson of the occasion, Nar Hari Acharya, quickly interrupted, asking the crowd to observe a moment of silence in protest at the police intervention. Then, after a few more minutes, the speakers began again, and again they were cut off. The chairperson, seeing the use of force as imminent quickly read as much of the draft resolution of the Professional Solidarity Group as possible at gunpoint, and it was approved by applause. Then the meeting was closed down, the records of it were apparently destroyed by police and nearly 800 people, many of them medical professionals, were arrested. They were taken to the traffic police station near the main government offices (Singha Durbar) and were held overnight in the underpass near the station because there was not enough room for all of them in the custody office. Then many of those who were perceived to be leaders were put in jail.

Some of the physicians taken into custody managed to get released that night. One doctor told me that he had his beeper with him and had arranged with his staff beforehand to call him if he did not return. His beeper went off while in custody and was able to convince his jailers, on the basis of the urgent need for him back at the hospital that they should release him. The next day the government had decided which of the arrested were worth keeping in prison as leaders and which could be released. Fewer than a hundred were retained.

The NMA issued press releases which not only notified the local and international press about the arrests but also threatened a shutdown of the country's health services if those detained were not released:

Press release from NMA 24th March 1990 (2046/12/11)
We, the Doctors, are concerned about the health of the People. We want to stress our commitment towards improving the health of all Nepalis. This is possible only in a peaceful environment. It is a well known fact that repression, arrest and torture of peaceful demonstrators demanding basic human rights have created a feeling of insecurity and tension in the country. On March 20, 1990, intellectuals representing different sections of the society, held a symposium in the auditorium of Tribhuvan University (Kirtipur Campus) Kathmandu, after prior permission of the concerned authorities, with the aim of exchanging views and opinions on the topic "Present Situation in Nepal and Our Responsibilities." The police brutally intervened to stop this exchange of views and arrested all participants present en masse numbering about 800.

The Nepal Medical Association strongly condemns this arrogant action of the police on these people who represent the conscience, aspiration and hopes of the Nepali people. . . . [lists doctors and health professionals who are in jail or police custody] The NMA will not be a silent spectator to the suppressive action taken by the authorities towards individuals exercising basic human rights. We demand that our jailed and detained colleagues should be unconditionally and immediately released. NMA has called for the closure of all medical services except emergency services in all the hospitals and private clinics in Kathmandu Valley on 28th March 1990 if our demand is not met by then. If positive action is not taken by the authorities, NMA has resolved to take further actions in a stepwise manner. The Government alone will be fully responsible for the consequences arising from these actions.

Creating the appearance of palace conversion

By this time, the NMA was in direct contact with their president Dr. S. K. Pahari. He had returned from Pokhara and, once in Kathmandu, had decided to sign the association's press releases. Clearly, as he recalls, he was in a difficult position:

I had to act promptly, not because I was a senior physician for His Majesty but because I was a physician. Because when I was president of the Medical Association, then I had responsibility. I had to think differently than for myself. You know. Individuals, you know, might be communist or might be supporters of Congress. I was, naturally, a citizen of Nepal. But I had a different vision, not to take a stand like a communist or Congress, but as a professional for the liberaliza-tion of our society – that the people should be liberated and have basic rights to do certain things as human beings. So I was always a believer of those things for the people.

I was, in one sense, close to the king, because I was his physician. Normally, we don't talk politics as physicians, but we must adhere to our professional role. Because I had access to this professional position, I had to use it to tell something about the situation in the country. I was with the king when the movement started, so I could not move anything from there. I did not dictate anybody. Whatever the Medical Association wanted, you know . . .I was not in the position of real force. Actually, it was individuals not the institution which acted before I came back. There was no time to think. I came back on the 10th Chaitra [March 23] from Pokhara with the king and on the 11th I signed this paper and therefore ended my relationship with the king. That was the end of it – finished!

The people tell me now that this was so significant. Their reasoning was that even a king's physician could have been very well off without doing this. If he has done this, then there is a reason for all the people to believe that the system is wrong. But the reason I signed was that I felt I had a moral obligation as the presi-dent of the association. All of my colleagues, if they were going in one direction, I could not have gone in the other direction. In this sense, I would say that my pro-fessional commitment won out over my sense of obligation to the king. I had a choice. I could have remained the royal physician throughout my life, enjoy my life – OK, and ignore my professional people. I would have survived as I am surviving now. But you know, what I thought was that my position with the king was as a physician, not as an adviser or politician. If I had been an adviser, that would have been different. Our relationship would have gone in a different direction. But I had a different sense of obligation, being his doctor. I had no obligation in this

sense to the king. But as president of the Medical Association . . . being his doctor
. . . I had to be loyal to him as a doctor, first.

You know, I came back from Pokhara, and there were lots of people who
believed I would not go that way, because it was a risk to my life. If the panchayat
system was still active, they would have taken it very badly. But the people were
convinced that my signing would be the igniting point for the movement, and they
were right, because it was our effort which was followed by the rest of the civilians.

The arrival and signature of Dr. Pahari was, in fact, perceived by outsiders as a major event (Shaha 1992: 199); that the royal physician
would shift his allegiance indicated that the tide was turning, that
support of the movement was reaching to the inner circle of the palace.
Surely even the king and queen were at this point becoming more
aware of the full extent of public discontent, and of their need to
respond with real political compromise. Nevertheless, the king did
nothing overtly to offer a compromise or lighten the repression meted
out by the apparatus putatively in place for maintaining the public
peace. The protestors found ways to promote the movement under fear
of further repression.

Jail activities

In jail, activists devised techniques to smuggle out notes to other activists
about their plans and to encourage them to continue without them. Aside
from using euphemisms when speaking with their visitors, some of them
stuffed notes into the cuffs of shirts which they gave to visitors for laun-
dering. Return reports arrived in clean clothes brought by family and
friends. For many of the detainees, their prison stays reconfirmed human
rights abuses suffered by those in jail. Some of these people had been
involved in trying to help prisoners for years and so were able to deliver
fresh case materials to human rights organizations to bolster their
demands for international sanctions against Nepal's government. For
others, the scenes in prison were startling. They witnessed the victims of
beating, starvation, and various other forms of torture. Some of the prisoners, particularly in the women's ward, I was told, died before medical
help was ever sought.

In fact, the arrest and imprisonment of the professionals triggered a
whole set of new activities – it breathed life into the movement. Along
with strikes elsewhere in the city, the hospitals began to hold protests as
the NMA had threatened. Incidents were reported from all over the
country, and the death toll had risen to about forty by this time. For
the next two weeks, activity in the hospitals and on the streets
increased.

On-the-job resistance

Doctors all over the country were being pressured by police and the ministries to engage in what they thought were actions that compromised their professional standards. For example, the doctor on duty in Bhaktapur at the time of the movement was a supporter of the opposition. Ordered verbally to perform the postmortem examination on the bodies of victims of new police shootings, he refused; without proper papers, he reasoned, these bodies would disappear. The police pressed him to give in and the director of the hospital threatened him with the loss of his job. The health minister and then the prime minister himself called and tried to force him to do the postmortem, and steadfastly he refused. Finally the director agreed to call a committee of doctors to witness the making of the report, and he went forward with the postmortem.

An innovative strategy used by the doctors was the refusal to use government outpatient hospital registration and prescription tickets. Instead of registering through the government system, which would supply money to the government they were trying to overthrow, the NMA, via the hospital, made it appear that there were no clients – therefore no charges were levied. Instead of official outpatient tickets they used forms prepared by the NMA. On the front of the form was the normal set of questions seeking patient and diagnostic information, and on the back was a set of demands – what they called the "prescription for health":

Demands of the Nepal Medical Association
1. demands the immediate establishment and upholding of human rights in Nepal;
2. demands that all jailed medical personnel are released immediately and unconditionally, and that arrests and detainments for interrogation are stopped immediately;
3. demands that people of all class and professions imprisoned under the present movement for human rights activities be released immediately and unconditionally;
4. calls for the condemnation as baseless the accusations made by the so-called, self-declared representatives of the people called Panchas that Bir Hospital doctors deliberately refrained from the treatment of patients; and warns them to withdraw false accusations and stop such activities from here forward;
5. demands the granting of permission for the Medical Committee for Human Rights, organized by the Nepal Medical Association, to make health check-ups for all prisoners arrested under the movement for the establishment of human rights;
6. demands the actual information about Dr. Laxmi Narayan

Jha's present condition, who was under custody since 2042/3/16 (June 30, 1985), and his immediate and unconditional release;[7]

7. calls for severe condemnation of the works of mental and physical torture to children that is taking place against international regulations, and demands that such activities be stopped immediately;

8. demands that intruding and posting of the police in and around the hospital complex be stopped and that police obstacles to patient entry for treatment in the hospital be discontinued;

9. invites all brothers in the police service to stay away from suppressive acts by using arms and shooting at helpless people;

10. prays that all people, including our staff nurse, Vidya Joshi,[8] who got injured in the course of the people's movement, are soon recovered, and that the souls of those who have died rest in eternity;

11. demands that the local administrative activities of suppressing, attacking and terrorizing health workers outside of the capital city through the police and mandale [civilian dress police rabble rousers] terrorists are checked;

12. thanks all paramedical workers, nurses, and people in general who extended good wishes, maintained understanding and cooperated in the program of medical professionals;

13. apologises for the inconveniences to the people in general caused by the impudence of the government which left no way for us, the medical professionals, other than taking up a struggle with a full program of opposition.

The authority of these demands came not from their political clout as opposed to others, but from the way these claims were attached to and purveyed as a medical document carrying the weight and force of objective scientific truth.

Within the hospitals, doctors and nurses provided protection to political activists, wounded or not, by giving them white coats, name tags, sometimes equipment like stethoscopes to disguise them from police, including the plainclothes policemen (CID, Criminal Investigation Department). As we have seen, occasionally persons who were at risk of arrest were posted as employees in the hospital. Patients at Bir who were already under arrest were prescribed extended hospital care or given help in escaping. Those who arrived at the hospital dead as a result of police violence (beatings or gunfire) were photographed for fear that their deaths would go unrecorded and their bodies were smuggled out to families in the middle of the night.

Alienating police

Health professionals say that they sought to recruit the police for the movement, but in fact the effect of some of their actions was the opposite. Hospital staff demanded that all police be removed from the hospital, arguing that their presence undermined the professional capacity of the hospital. Doctors threatened to refuse to work if the police were allowed in. The police were physically barred from certain areas of the hospital, and despite their guns, their control was curtailed again and again by doctors and nurses who made decisions about where they should and should not be and what they could and could not do.

While these efforts often had the effect of reinforcing the belief that police and protestor alike had to respect the authority of the medical professionals, there were other actions which alienated the police. In Teaching Hospital I spoke with nurses who indicated that they had even refused treatment to injured police. Although this claim was disputed, one nurse said she had told the police in her ward, "This is how it feels. We are human beings. These other victims are human beings. We should be treated as such, as you wish to be treated. If you treat us as nonhumans, then we will treat you the same. You can see how it feels." Police responded by sending their wounded to the army hospital instead of the public hospitals. Some injured soldiers were even removed from the one hospital and placed in the other. Clearly, not all health professionals followed the same strategy here, but the general climate of alienation felt by police was high enough to warrant a threat from some disgruntled persons in the government:

> Press Dispatch: *Inap Daily*, Chaitra 8 (March 21, 1990)
> Will the Teaching Hospital Burn?
> Kathmandu, The way doctors, nurse students, and administrative staff of Tribhuvan University Teaching Hospital are showing their support to the current People's Movement of the nation, and the way they are moving on the front line of the movement, are becoming matters of bewildering agony for the government.
>
> Blinded by anguish, the government is planning to create chaos in the Teaching Hospital by setting fire to it, according to the information received.
>
> Activities, such as rallies, demonstrations, strikes, general meetings, and the writing of slogans on the walls against the system and the government have been taking place in the hospital for some time now. The hospital administrators received telephone calls a few days ago regarding those activities. The person making the telephone call introduced himself as the Prime

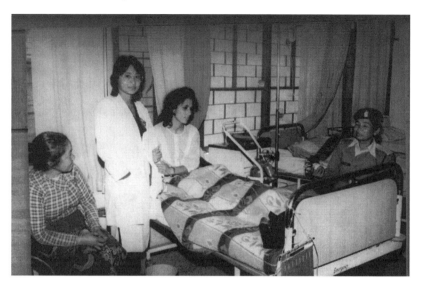

Plate 4 Police guard with a student activist under custody while in the
hospital (reproduced with the permission of Dr. Bharat Pradhan).

Minister, or a person from that office of the Prime Minister.
Then, the caller said, in an intimidating voice, "There are
slogans, demonstrations, and general meetings in your hospital
everyday. The hospital walls are full of undesirable slogans. You
better stop these activities or our commandos will be sent there,
as they were sent to other campuses."

After this threat, all the staff discussed the issue and decided
that all of them would resign from service immediately if the
commandos entered into the hospital. The commandos were not
sent there, after the discussion became known, and it may be
because the Prime Minister has had a bit of cool thinking about it
or because he was scared of the consequences.

The fact is still fresh in our memory that the government
administration shamelessly sent the commandos to Kirtipur
Campus, Pulchowk Campus, and Patan Campus where they
beat students and created havoc.

With more and more support from within the hospitals, people began to
liken the hospitals to the Golden Temple of Amritsar – the besieged Sikh
temple in North India which had served initially as a refuge during
Sikh–Hindu riots of several years before. Although the ability to claim
medical neutrality had early on become an instrument for arousing

support by both sides, it was becoming clear that in a political battle, the appearance of such neutrality was difficult to sustain. This problem of the difference between neutrality and objectivity became the most important factor in the health professionals' role in the debate: they wanted to hang on to the latter but not the former, all for the sake of the latter. One could not remain neutral when truth needed to be defended. From this point on, health professionals gained the ability to say that they were defenders of truth against those who would deny it for the sake of the king or the corrupt government regime. The armed forces from now on would not trust them. The reference to the Golden Temple was in fact more appropriate than ever since just as at that temple, its holiness and the hospital's neutrality were not enough to keep the military at bay (and in both cases the attacks provoked events that would bring the downfall of the nation's leader).

Throughout March the NMA issued repeated demands for an end to repression. Strikes continued throughout the city, now beginning to include other professional groups that were critical to the infrastructure of the country – the pilots and the telecommunications civil servants. Other civil servants at ministries, including the health ministries, also came out into the streets wearing the symbolic black armbands. On March 23, the police mounted a lathi charge on the Teaching Hospital, coming right up to its main and emergency entrances. The medical students erected obstacles and threw stones at the police. Graffiti calling for the complete overthrow of the government covered the walls. The publicity generated by this event was extremely favorable for the health professionals and lent credence to their claims that the police did not belong in the hospital area. One child was seriously wounded by police in the incident on the hospital grounds.

Press Dispatch: *Bishwabhumi Daily*, March 24, 1990
Terror in Teaching Hospital
Kathmandu, His Majesty's Government had its uniformed commandos force raid the Maharajganj Teaching Hospital yesterday. They arrested seven staff from the hospital staff quarters. They also searched each and every room under the pretext of looking for those staff. It is said that they also broke supplies and equipment there, but this is not yet confirmed. They erased slogans written on the walls.

An hour long pen down strike was launched in this hospital on the 23rd February to protest the shooting of unarmed people by the government. In this connection, the chief of this hospital had left to obtain clarification or to report on this situation, but has not yet returned. According to the information received from the hospital, Dr. Prasai was supposed to go out for only eight hours. Hospital staff are fear-stricken by yesterday's raid and are going to launch a pen down strike against this government hooliganism.

Teaching Hospital staff's response to the police lathi charge was to run its Outpatient Department outside on the spot where the charge had taken place, thus reclaiming the space as hospital territory where police did not belong. On March 24, the NMA issued a press release:

> Dear Colleague, March 24th
> Nepal Medical Association would like to draw your attention to the current human rights situation in Nepal. You might have been aware from the international media that our Government has launched an unprecedented suppressive action against unarmed and peaceful demonstrations demanding the establishment of democratic norms and values in the country.
> The extreme brutality of this action is exemplified by the use of bullets which were banned by the international community. In this context of violation of human rights, our members have shown their concern and stood against this deplorable affair. The Government responded by detaining many physicians, nurses and paramedics. But, we are determined to release our colleagues and stand against this gross violation of human rights. We send our documents to you with the hope that you will get a glimpse of the present situation in Nepal and express your concern too, to the international community as well as to the Government of Nepal.
> Thanking you for your kind cooperation.
>   Yours Sincerely,
>   Dr. B. R. Joshi
>   Hon. Gen. Secretary

Its action plan, beginning with the press release just quoted, was as follows:

> Action Plan:
> 2046/12/15 Wednesday Strike in all the valley group of hospitals
>   (except EMERGENCY SERVICES)
>   including closure of PRIVATE
>   CLINICS with BLACK BANDS
>   around arms. (28th March)
> 2046/12/19 Sunday   Closure of PRIVATE CLINICS,

BLACK BAND around arms and strike
in all hospitals of the whole country
(except EMERGENCY SERVICES).
5:00 P.M. Further action will be decided
in a meeting held at Siddhisadan
(1st April).

It followed this action plan with a statement to the Nepali government:

Nepal Medical Association on March 24, 1990, issued a press
release demanding the unconditional and immediate release of
all detained and jailed health personnel. NMA called for closure
of all hospitals except emergency services in all hospitals in
Kathmandu Valley on March 18, 1990 if the Government failed
to meet our demands. On that day, the Government intentionally
gave a false assurance to doctors regarding the release of these
health personnel in order to create an environment of confusion
and to stop this programme.

NMA strongly condemns and regrets this false assurance and
betrayal by the Government as only a few health personnel
were actually released. Several health personnel are still either
in police custody or in jail. NMA reiterates its call for closure of
all hospital services, except emergency services in all hospitals
and private clinics throughout the country on Sunday April 1,
1990.

NMA strongly condemns today's barbarous police violence
(lathi charge) inside Teaching Hospital, Maharajganj, in which
several students, doctors, nurses, general public and even a child
were seriously injured. Medical students were also arrested by
police.

NMA warns the Government not to give deceitful statements
and false assurances in the future. NMA cautions the
Government not to repeat the use of violence and intrusion into
the hospital premises. If such shameful incidents and deceptive
assurances are repeated, the Government will be fully responsible for its consequences.

On March 29 Dr. Mathura and some of the health professionals were
released from prison but medical staff pursued their hospital strike to
protest the fact that none of the other prisoners had been released, as the
NMA had demanded. When it became clear that the government was not
going to respond favorably to the doctors' demands, the NMA issued a
schedule for hospital shutdowns from April 2.

Today, the 19th of Chitra 2046 [Sunday, April 1, 1990], the Council of the Nepal Medical Association met at the central office of the Medical Association, and having discussed in detail their concerns and responsibility of the Association towards the current situation of the country, the following demands were set forth unanimously, and the following action plan was submitted for the fulfillment of the aforesaid demands [in other statements]. All the members of this Association, health co-workers, and general people are cordially requested to extend all possible cooperation to make this program a success.

Schedule for Protest: 2nd: close down of hospitals and clinics except emergency services in Kathmandu Valley; 3rd: sole use of NMA prescription pads throughout the kingdom; 6th: close down of hospitals and clinics in entire kingdom; 8th: provide outdoor patient services on alternate days only; 9th–13th private clinics of kingdom will remain closed; 2nd, 6th, 9th, 11th, 13th April doctors working outside hospital will be on pen-down strike.

The outpouring of public support for the doctors and other health professionals in the movement was exemplified in an episode described by Dr. Joshi, a physician working at the Institute of Medicine during their outdoor protest:

I was standing just outside of my hospital when one prisoner was brought with handcuffs, and he was brought from Bhairawa, you know. He had a retinal detachment, and he was referred from there. He was beaten so badly in police custody that his eye was damaged, like that. And when he saw the doors were closed and everybody was outside . . . because he was a political prisoner, I don't know which party he was involved with, but he said, "What is the problem here?" And we said, "We are on strike for this and this cause," and he said "Yes, yes. You are doing a good thing. If my eye goes blind, don't worry. But you are doing a good thing." I said, "Why should you go blind? What is your [health] problem?" He said, "I've been referred here, but your strike is more important than my eye, for success of the movement." I told him that he was an emergency case and we could check him because it was an emergency. We took him there and the emergency doctor checked him and he eventually was fine.

The next thing I noticed was that at that time everybody was praising us. People were praising and we had a lot of expenditures [he was secretary for the NMA], and the legal association spent so much money. One day the decision was made very coolly, without calculating how much we would need. We felt that to close the hospital quite often was not in the interests of the people. We did it a couple of times, and then we felt that even though we are doing emergency services, our patients are still suffering. So, what we did was we said that we should find another way of protesting. We said, "We will not write on the government pad." It was a big decision to refuse to write on the government pads. For government servants, this was a big decision. By doing this, we also asked the people [patients] not to pay the tax [registration fees recorded with the pads], because this pad was sold by the hospital for rupees. By doing so, we were asking the people not to pay the revenue to the government hospital. And then it was decided that we would make our own pad... no one calculated how we would pay for them.

Everybody agreed to that decision, so I went and ordered from the press ten thousand pads. Then a big bill came, and the ten thousand pads were finished in two days! I said, "My God, I don't know how we will pay these bills!" But the next day, I got a telephone call from the press saying that "Your bill is already paid!" So who paid? I still don't know who paid. This was the support we got from the people. We had no money, but we organized, and people started coming and saying that they would give us money.

By April 2, more protests had occurred around the city. Students protested at most of the campuses in the Kathmandu Valley and many were arrested. Civilians protested in major towns outside of Kathmandu and some were shot. In Patan, protestors were setting fire to public buildings, blocking roads, and stoning windows. The police were using tear gas, guns, and lathis to break up protests and arresting those whom the government was still calling "extremists." At more and more government offices, civil servants were engaging in pen-down strikes, attending their desks but refusing to work, or conducting actual walk-outs. At Teaching Hospital, bolder and bolder critiques were being launched from graffiti and posters on the walls, critiques which targeted the king and queen, rather than simply the panchayat system.

In one incident, three youths slain by police in violence in Kirtipur were brought to Teaching Hospital. The police attempted to remove the bodies before the families could, and the physicians and nurses refused to let them do so. This confrontation lasted several days. The police refused to give the bodies to the bereaved families, for fear of public demonstrations and the use of them as martyrs, and the doctors and nurses became central players in the conflict, first demanding on behalf of the victims' families that the bodies should be returned to them, and finally, becoming mediators between the police and the families. At one point the police vans came into the courtyard, and before many of the staff had noticed police had managed to obtain the bodies and place them in a van for a quick getaway. When the nurses saw and blocked them, the police ordered them at gunpoint to move away. They refused to move, and one nurse said: "If you must, then shoot us. You will have to kill us if you want to take the bodies." She even lay down in front of the wheels of the van to prevent it from moving forward. The police eventually backed down, but not until after difficult negotiations.

A proposal had been made to cremate the bodies at the hospital with the families present, but physicians rejected this as compromising the hospital by turning it into a cemetery. Finally, they all agreed to a funeral party consisting of some members of the families, some doctors, and some police. They all accompanied the bodies out of town to what they considered a safe place for cremation – Sundarijal, a small village north-east of Kathmandu, where it was assumed the cremation would not arouse public outcry. Even with the government's efforts at secrecy, and revealing their typical underestimation of village networks of information, one woman from Sundarijal who worked at a Kathmandu women's sewing cooperative told me that she had known what was going on with those bodies when they brought them that night to her village. Later, she explained the significance of the doctors' participation this way:

I think it [the movement] would not have been successful if the doctors had not supported it. Nobody would have known that the people were killed if the police had hidden those dead bodies. There would have been no proof if the doctors had not told so. They were just killing anybody . . . people on the streets, people who were looking out of their windows. We came to know later when we had gone in a procession that a seven-year-old child was killed. People looking out of their windows were killed.

First success and setback: multiparty system declared

On April 6, the movement reached its culmination. The king had issued a declaration that seemed to dismiss rather than attend to the government's failure to treat the deaths of citizens as human rights violations. His government had promised to form a constitutional reform committee and a committee for inquiry into civilian deaths, but the king's speech seemed to indicate a lack of concern over these issues. As a result, over 300,000 people gathered at the open-air theater (Tundikhel) in the center of Kathmandu to demonstrate their displeasure, carrying home-made flags and chanting slogans against the regime. Although a *chakka jam* (interdiction against motorized traffic) had been called by a less visible leftist opposition group, the United National People's Movement, the arrival of this many people could scarcely have been due to any one political party's efforts but rather represented mass popular dissent.

All over the city, people were out in the streets on foot (avoiding motorized vehicle traffic) ready to pelt with stones and bricks any official vehicles which might pass them. A group of doctors and nurses from Teaching Hospital tried to make their way to the Tundikhel in an unmarked bus from the hospital. They had made it no closer than the northern outskirts of town (Chabahil) when their bus was surrounded by protestors. Hands filled with stones and bricks, the people began coming towards them. Those inside were fearful that the bus would be overturned by the crowd.

Then one doctor stood up to call to the crowd at the exit door, and a protestor outside recognized the doctors and nurses by their white coats – clearly on their way to the Tundikhel where they would join the crowd in support of the movement. He yelled, "It is the doctors!" The people dropped their stones and bricks and slowly they moved towards the bus, and to the astonishment of the passengers within they began to kiss it.

What began at the open-air theater as a peaceful verbal assault on the panchayat system turned into the chanting of vituperous slogans again aimed at the king and queen. On the stage at the Tundikhel, there were only two small microphones. The person who rose to chair the occasion, impromptu, was Dr. Mathura, and he was joined by other doctors, lawyers, writers, teachers, and others. One speaker after another voiced support for the movement, articulating the justifications for their cause, restating their need for multiparty democracy. After the speakers had finished, the crowd began to march through the city, undaunted by police lines. They marched towards the palace, but no one was really sure what their destination was. At Durbar Marg they met with paratrooper army units called in by the home minister. By the time they reached the statue of King Mahendra, only a block from the palace gates, the armed servicemen had positioned themselves in combat lines, lying down in the street and taking aim to mow the protestors down with gunfire. From the roof of Bir Hospital, Ganesh Man Singh, Mangala Devi Singh, K. P. Bhattarai, Man Mohan Adikhari, and a handful of the major organizers from health and other professions had taken refuge and watched as the crowds continued forward and, finally, police opened fire into the crowd. As Dr. S. K. described it:

Then, you see, the army began shooting. We were on top of Bir Hospital. A lot of doctors were there, and right in front of us we saw . . . I think somehow I did not comprehend what it was. I then did a very stupid thing which I would not have done otherwise. [He went down to help.] Coming back, we were six or seven doctors, the young boys were there, in the streets – six or seven of us, and the military was going in there with trucks. Paratroopers were going toward Bir Hospital, and I stood right in the center of the road, jam-packed. I didn't feel a bit afraid. It's all emotion or something, but I never felt any fear, and I think everybody felt that way.

From their rooftop perch, others watched the opposition at work. Ordinary citizens posed as medical workers, carrying stretchers and claiming that they were paramedicals – first to help the injured but also to ward off the police and army, who they thought would try to direct their bullets away from obvious first-aid efforts. Patients were brought by the dozens into Bir Hospital. Its floors were overflowing with the injured and dying.

Plate 5 Makeshift ambulances used by civilians during the protest (reproduced with the permission of Dr. Bharat Pradhan).

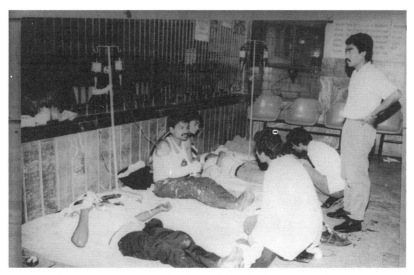

Plate 6 Entryway of Bir Hospital lined with patients (reproduced with the permission of Dr. Bharat Pradhan).

Doctors and paramedicals made temporary beds in the hallways and ran from one makeshift surgical procedure to the next with inadequate supplies, inadequate sterilization, and inadequate manpower. Dr. Mahesh Maskey, in a poem written on April 6, 1990, described the events as follows:

April 6
Waving red flags high in the sky
Like a fort that won't crumble
Stand, proud and majestic
Bir Hospital

Outside march the people, the flag, the slogan
    the chorus of anger, shriek in the air
Outside charge the police, the military, the gun
    desperate are their efforts to spread the terror
Under remote control
Robots take aim, slowly, on people unarmed
Blood Splash!
And turns red the white walls of the premises
But, fearless, like a revolutionary warrior
stand proud and majestic
Bir Hospital.

Inside are wounded, the bodies of the dead
    their dear ones engulfed in sorrow and revenge
Inside are health workers, hands that care
    and a resolve to halt the march of death
        yes, they dare
A wounded is not yet through dressing
And another enters
The sound of bullets time and again
Makes windows tremble
But unshaken and unperturbed
Like the Himalayas
Stand, proud and majestic
Bir Hospital.

Have I
The witness to the undying courage and sacrifice
Of heroes and martyrs unknown and unclaimed
    become a part of History itself?
Lying dead before me is a teenager
And a catapult peeps through his pocket
In this fateful night
When stones and clayballs forced
    guns to retreat
The verdict of Time
As if, quietly followed

The actor and the audience of this drama untold
And holding them close to the heart
Keeping dreams of martyrs alive in the eyes
Like a sleepless Hill
Waiting for a new age to dawn
Stand proud and majestic
Bir Hospital.

Several physicians contacted the International Red Cross by phone and requested relief (which was not forthcoming). They then began to send faxes to Reuters, API, and UP notifying the international press of a massacre. Finally, they contacted friends in foreign embassies in order to request, again, that foreign governments issue statements of denial of all foreign aid until the king capitulated.

From that day the king issued a general curfew. On the evening of April 8 he read a statement agreeing to remove the word "partyless" from the constitution. He installed a new prime minister, L. B. Chand, to form a new cabinet, and the National Panchayat was to be summoned into session to work out agreements for a reform in government. This was cause for a general celebration, but although the opposition leaders called off the movement the curfew had not been lifted. Army and police units were still dispatched to maintain order in the city, and when some young protestors came out into the streets to celebrate their victory they were shot by officers still under orders to shoot curfew violators.

The tragedy increased that night, when six persons were killed after the movement had provisionally ended. Some of the doctors were locked in at Bir Hospital because of the curfew. When the in-charge senior surgical physician there, Dr. Pradhan, was notified about an injured person lying in the street near Indrachowk, only eight or nine blocks from the hospital, he took an ambulance and tried to go there but was repulsed five times by police and army uninformed of what they should do in such a case. He finally had to return to the hospital, from where he tried to call the home minister in order to have these officers ordered to let him pass. Unable to get the minister's support, he left on his own again in the ambulance. This time he made it as far as the second or third roadblock and then was threatened at gunpoint by a soldier. He was forced to leave his vehicle and move towards a group of people who were under armed guard, tied up, lying on the ground. One, he learned, was another doctor who had been accosted in his ambulance while trying to rescue his own injured brother. Finally, although he was unable to rescue the wounded person he had been trying to reach, he was able to persuade his captors to allow him to take the prisoners back to the hospital for treatment. His anguish increased when he learned that the victim at Indrachowk whom he had been unable to retrieve was a boy of twelve who had been shot in the underarm. He had only a flesh wound and died that night from loss of blood before anyone could get to him.

Second-wind efforts

The time after the multiparty system was declared was a very tense one in the city. Although much of the public was celebrating having achieved the right to have political parties, the doctors' groups and other intellectuals on the left recognized the potential transparency of the king's decree. Aside from having made parties legal, it had really changed nothing. The same corrupt politicians were in power even if the king had appointed a new prime minister. The panchayat structure was still in place, and the king still held absolute control. On the basis of the treatment of the doctors the night of the declaration, the NMA stepped up its demands for bolder reform. They insisted on the resignation of the home minister for his abusive treatment of the doctors on that night of the 8th and denounced the government, aiming at unseating those still in power.

> Press release from NMA:
> Everyone knows the fact that we, all the medical professionals, had to come out in the movement in Nepal for the protection of our professional responsibility and dignity, and against the violation of human rights.
> We apologize for the inconvenience caused to the people in general during the movement in spite of our efforts to harmonize the situations wherein on the one hand there lies the importance of providing necessary medical services to patients and on the other hand the need to protect human rights and to maintain the responsibility of professional concerns.
> We, all medical professionals, are grateful to the people in general for their support, cooperation and good wishes in spite of such inconveniences. People holding responsible positions in this country are mad at our movement, and are engrossed with the feeling of vengeance and retaliation against all medical workers. Therefore, the government has not even hesitated to violate doctors when they tried to fulfill their basic responsibilities such as providing medical care to save the lives of people who were shot during the movement and assisting in undertaking the funeral rites of those who were dead. We present a few examples of the government's violations:
> –doctors were threatened and forced by the administration to do

postmortems ignoring even the minimum preconditions required for this work;
– ambulance services are generally allowed even at the time of war; but they did not allow the ambulance to carry gunshot victims and other patients to the hospital;
– doctors and gunshot patients taken in ambulance with due pass were stopped and held at gun point on the road and then turned out of their vehicle, made to lie flat in the road while they were kicked, beaten with lathis and trampled cruelly and inhumanely;
– doctors going from their quarters to the hospital were lathi charged even after presenting their identity cards;
– knowing that people celebrating after the announcement of the formation of a multi-party system were being shot, we requested them to stop, but the response of the person holding such a responsible position as Home Minister was "I will surely shoot. Why shouldn't I? I'll shoot all of you doctors. I'll also destroy your hospital and ambulances." He used slanderous language that an educated person should never use against the chief surgical doctor who was on emergency duty and also threatened him.

Therefore, under the present condition wherein the responsibility of the national security lies in the hands of such a shameless, cruel, and irresponsible Home Minister, we feel that we, the doctors, are not secure, causing a great difficulty in fulfilling our responsibility to serve the people.

The Nepal Medical Association denounces all such despicable activities, and in connection with such condemnable activities, the present Home Minister must tender his resignation within three days on moral grounds. Otherwise, we declare through this statement that the Nepal Medical Association will be bound to make a strong move.

By the middle of the following week public protests were mounting again, and the pro-democracy leaders had refused to join the government of the new prime minister. It was still not clear whether the king would respond nor whether he would actually disband the panchayat system. He only declared that a multiparty system would henceforth be legal, but this left the panchayat structure intact, along with his monarchical rule. But the desire for a completely new government and new society was finally clearly articulated for the king by the Professional Solidarity Group soon after the party leader of the Nepali Congress party sat down with the president of the United Left Front before the king and appeared to accept his plans for a new multiparty version of the existing panchayat monarchical system. Many physicians and intellectuals saw the main opposition leaders as having caved in to palace interests, and this, for them, amounted to a betrayal of all they had fought for. After more public arousal by radical leftist groups, even these party leaders started to doubt whether the king was serious in his offers of a new government as opposed to the same old government with a few new players and possibilities. Soon, they were denouncing their own compromise with the king and as a result the United National People's Movement called for a *chakka jam* and open-air meeting at the Tundikhel to protest the agreement. In keeping with the NMA's role in articulating the movement's agenda for a wider audience, it helped formulate a statement demanding a truly democratic government that would greatly reduce the king's power, among other things:

> The movement launched by the Nepali Congress and the United Left Front on February 18, 1990, with the objective of installing multi-party democracy within the framework of a constitutional monarchy culminated into a truly people's movement with the active participation of all sections of the Nepali community, including various professional groups. First of all, therefore, we must pay homage, with great respect, to the Nepali people for their great sacrifice and fortitude. All Nepalis are united by the conviction that it is this sacrifice and determination that carried the movement to this juncture.
>
> Seen in this perspective, the communiqué issued by the Royal Palace on April 8, 1990, and the comments of the leaders of the Nepali Congress and the United Left Front showed disregard of the glorious sacrifices made by the Nepali people in the course of the movement. In addition, the nation has been engulfed by confusion and contradictions as to the present outcome of the movement vis-à-vis its objective.
>
> We, therefore, strongly appeal that the representatives of the Nepali Congress and the United Left Front take a firm stand in their talks with the Monarch on the following points and save the movement from being derailed by a possible conspiracy. Otherwise, the leaders of these political parties too will have to face the verdict of history together with the insensitive rulers they have faced:
>
> 1. An interim government with representatives of various political parties be formed immediately.
> 2. All political prisoners including those fraudulently charged with criminal offences be released.

3. The citizens who lost their lives be appropriately honoured and their families compensated; the injured be given full and free medical attention.

4. All units of the Panchayat be dissolved and a new constitution framed for ensuring the dominant position of the people.

5. The killings and repression perpetrated during the movement be investigated and the guilty punished.

6. The wealth amassed and kept within and outside the country through abuse of authority during the 30 years of Panchayat rule be investigated and nationalised.

7. The names of all citizens who sacrificed their lives for democracy during the last 30 years be compiled so that these citizens are declared as "martyrs" and their families be compensated.

Finally, we make a special request that the spirit of solidarity and mutual cooperation between the Nepali Congress and the United Left Front and all political forces that have supported the peaceful movement, thus reflecting the historic unity of the Nepali people, will be maintained even more firmly in the coming days so that the people's will runs supreme, as always.

Signed, On Behalf of Nepal's Intellectual Community Chaitra 29, 2046 [April 11, 1990]

This statement, formulated by the Professional Solidarity Group and signed by Dr. Devindra Raj Pandey and Dr. Mathura, was exemplary of the sort of statement which boldly claimed the priority of the people of Nepal above the king's. They paid no homage to the king whatsoever, itself a great contrast to past norms which would have felt obligated to mention the desire for "his will" to be carried out and to offer the best wishes for his health and well-being. Rather, they referred to "the monarch" (his institutional not personal title) as an obstacle to their goals who would prevent democracy by conscripting even the leaders of the opposition into an alliance with him. Their statement was accompanied by another to the effect that the doctors would go on a hunger strike from April 15 until the home minister resigned and a new government or council of ministers was formed under new leadership as an interim government and a constitution for a true democracy could be drafted.

After the Royal Proclamation declaring a multiparty system in Nepal on the night of April 8, 1990, the army and police mercilessly riddled innocent people with bullets who came out in joy to celebrate this momentous occasion. When doctors and other people brought these incidents to the notice of the Home

Minister, these doctors and innocent people were abused in the foulest language possible and threatened to be killed by the Home Minister. The army and police then went on to brutally beat up doctors and stopped the ambulance while doctors in the ambulance went out to rescue innocent victims of gunshot injuries in different parts of the city. Doctors on duty, within hospital premises, and even the driver of the ambulance were physically assaulted.

As the Home Minister was directly responsible for these ugly incidents, Nepal Medical Association condemned the arrogant and oppressive attitude of the Home Minister and released a press statement on April 10, 1990, describing these incidents in detail and demanding the resignation of the Home Minister within 3 days as these incidents were against international norms.

As the Home Minister has yet to resign and continues to behave irresponsibly, NMA has decided to go on an indefinite relay hunger strike starting at 7:00 a.m. on April 15, 1990 in Bir Hospital premises until the Home Minister resigns on moral grounds.

NEPAL MEDICAL ASSOCIATION

The doctors' hunger strike elicited an amazing flood of public support. They were recognized as spokespeople for the public cause. Doctors kept a log of comments offered by visitors to the hospital, and citizens expressed themselves passionately in voices long repressed. One log collected over 4,000 signatures from people pledging their support. The other log collected 413 statements attesting to the support of the public for the doctors' actions and describing their feelings about the revolution, among them the following:[9]

31. Respectable Health Workers: The Face of human beings is raised upward proudly because of your steps. Hearty wishes for your success. – A citizen of Nepal

38. The steps taken by health workers against the present treacherous oppression is praiseworthy. It is understood that this government is trying to divide intellectuals like you. You should not be victims of this conspiracy, and we hope you will demonstrate your determination and sole unity. We intellectuals wish you success in each step you have taken and express our strong agreement with this. We will all be one among you in whatever type of more difficult steps might have to be taken than at present. – Thank you, Intellectual Persons at Tribhuvan University.

41. On behalf of the conscious persons, we heartily congratulate you, responsible citizens in the medical field, for carrying out the most historic occupational challenge in the history of Nepal. – On behalf of People from the Terai Region.

42. However many sectors there are in society, they are angry, and restless because of this fascist Panchayat system. This sort of divisive character of the Panchayat is hardly to be witnessed in any country today. It is intolerable the way that health workers, carrying out humanitarian services, were treated. So, the whole Nepali community should be ready for creating a healthy democratic atmosphere in the country by cremating, immediately, the dead corpse of the Panchayat soon. – A person from Nuwakot

143. I express my respect to lovers of medicine for showing their unity in the course of the Jan Andolan for restoring human rights. It is my thinking, the unworthy Home Minister must ask forgiveness by immediately resigning for misbehaving against the doctors' group. Jindabad [long life] to Unity of the Doctors. Murdabad [death] to the unworthy Home Minister. – Dhanusa District

163. The Medical Association has not got involved in politics; it has enhanced politics and medicine. – A student from Kathmandu

382. The effort of the medical persons for the purposes of arousing sense in a senseless administration which plays on human values is praiseworthy and deserving utmost respect. All human beings are equal. All must get equal opportunities. There should not be any discrimination on caste, creed, sex, occupation, and religion. This Jan Andolan is the example of this fact and participation of the people toward this Jan Andolan is a sacrifice for that. All have understood the important role played by the doctors. This way, the medical persons should be always motivated to speak up in favor of humanity. – A citizen of Nepal, from Kathmandu

Despite continued negotiations between party leaders and the king and his new cabinet, it became clear to the opposition that the palace was not going to go far enough towards real changes in the structure of government. On April 15 a meeting was held between the old government and the party leaders in the Royal Nepal Academy. Catching the government entirely off guard, protestors surrounded the building and prevented the Chand government heads from leaving. The leaders were held hostage inside the Academy for a day and on April 16, with the leaders still in captivity, the king, perhaps finally more fearful of the crisis that would ensue if he did not agree than the one already at his doorstep, agreed to a new government. He asked Ganesh Man Singh to be the prime minister of an interim government that would provisionally rule until a new constitution was drafted and accepted. Singh declined for health reasons and suggested that K. P. Bhattarai take office instead. On April 17 the hunger strike was called off, and the NMA issued a final statement:

It is known to all that, according to the press release of Nepal Medical Association dated 31/12/2046 [April 13, 1990] doctors, nurses and paramedical workers have been on relay hunger strike for an indefinite period of time from 7 a.m. 2/1/2047 [April 15,

1990] demanding the resignation of the Home Minister Nayan
Bahadur Swahr. In this context, as the Council of Ministers is
dissolved according to the announcement of His Majesty date
3/1/2047 [April 16, 1990] and as there is going to be a new
Council of Ministers under the chairmanship of Mr. Krishna
Prasad Bhattarai [Nepali Congress]; cordially agreeing to the
verbal request of supreme leader Mr. Ganesh Man Singh [Nepali
Congress], the relay hunger strike is discontinued.

The Nepal Medical Association, on behalf of all medical
workers, cordially congratulates the new government, and trusts
that it will respect the people's will and dignity, and dedicate itself
to the establishment of complete human rights in Nepal. Nepal
Medical Association is eager to extend its full cooperation to the
new government in order to carry on the development of health
services in the country. Also, we express our gratitude to various
workers of political parties, professors, lawyers, engineers,
artists, students, civil servants, and people in general who supported and sympathized with our move.

Although the government had capitulated, for health professionals the
fighting was not over. More clashes occurred as people putatively paid by
the police called *mandales* roamed the city engaging in various acts of
vandalism. Some suspected that their goal was to destabilize the country
enough to undermine the authority of the interim government and justify
a monarchical coup. The outraged public began attacking anyone suspected of being a *mandale,* anyone discovered with a walkie-talkie or a
gun. The victims were taken to Bir Hospital, and there police (in what
must have been an enormous confusion over loyalty) became violent,
releasing anger at the medical professionals that had been pent up during
the movement. They demanded the release of the police victims for fear
that the doctors – now seen as part of the opposition – would not treat
them fairly. The doctors demanded that the police stay out of the hospital
and assured them that all patients would be treated fairly. The police
began to throw stones through windows and to fire into the emergency
ward. Several outsiders were injured, and finally the army was sent in to
control the police. Eventually, however, the patients were given to the
police and taken to the army hospital.

The army's intervention on behalf of the doctors and the new government became important. Later, when the human rights activists who had
demanded inquiries into the disappearances of prisoners came to power,
such inquiries were called off for fear that betraying the army would lead
to a military coup against the interim government.

The aftermath

One of the major successes of the doctors' involvement in the movement was their ability to both articulate and arouse public support for the sort of social order they envisioned. Although many of their activities were no different from those of other protestors, many were possible only because of the symbolic authority vested in them as *modern* professionals and in some cases as medical professionals in particular. The doctors worked with a type of authority that derived from their role as moderns and experts and as persons who were capable of making life-and-death decisions wholly different from those made by the police and the military. At numerous points the battle was drawn between the guns of the police and the authority of the doctors, unarmed, to declare the police unwelcome. To some extent, the protests and the manner in which they were carried out by health-care workers were a microcosm of what was occurring in Nepali society as a whole, a contest over what criteria would be used to establish social order. If wearing white coats offered more protection than carrying a gun, and if professional organizations could exert more pressure than a personal favor or whim of the king or the weapons of terror used to protect him and the interests of those around him, if a vision of democracy was articulated around a society in which health equality, like social equality, was fundamentally a political act justified by a rhetoric of universal and objective truth, then it would be safe to say that modernity was already at work in Nepal (at least urban Nepal) despite the country's overall lack of visible development.

As for the doctors, it was a demand for democracy which kept them going – a democracy which was for them articulated around notions of objective, universal human rights and principles of fairness, efficiency, and objective truth. The monarchy ended up looking as if it were fighting a losing battle not for peace and national security but for patrimonialism, the personal interests of the palace elite, and the security of its privilege. The doctors to some extent redefined the debate not simply by turning it into a fight for human rights but by turning it into a debate over the kind of power that would prevail in Nepal. The medical professionals' strategies were clever by any standards of revolutionary action, but they were often also indicative of the type of productive efficacy one finds in modern societies, where citizens cannot be forced to conform to social norms but must decide to live by them of their own "free will." The "prescription for health," the hospitalization of the leaders, and the use of high-tech communication to create pressure from professional groups were the kinds of things modern citizens do to participate in power. It was discourse about a vision of a type of society – a civil society – that came to motivate the professionals and the people, and this vision is rearticulated in modern societies in clinical encounters, in classrooms, in media resources, and in actual political processes.

The people of Nepal supported the doctors because doctors were able to claim that they were appropriate spokespeople for their countrymen – that they voiced the will of the people. In this, they conflated the ideas of development, efficiency, fairness, opportunity, modernity, truth, and human rights with scientific practices of medicine which, by definition, were instruments for obtaining access to universal truths that were believed to be, by nature, "apolitical," despite their overt politicization in the revolution.

It is not surprising that the doctors were able to polarize the public and the police, for the police ended up having no popular vision of a society which could be organized around anything but repression and the will of the monarch. It was only the monarch who could sustain a vision of a beneficial and protective society organized around the principles of family and patronage, and the monarch failed to replicate this vision in the everyday lives of his subjects. The health professionals helped articulate and make visible an image of a police force whose main job was to protect the palace and not the people – to control subjects rather than to protect citizens. Nepalis who saw themselves as citizens, however, needed authoritative visions of a society where force and coercion were minimized and people believed they could live by following truth – where life would be better because such truths enabled this. This, many Nepalis imagined, would be possible under multiparty democracy. During the revolution, authoritative or expert knowledge – taken as more potent than guns – and human rights were operationalized through discourses of culturally and politically transcendent truth.

In the days after the movement, Nepalis witnessed serious threats to their newly gained political system, for so long as the public adopted the methods of the police to implement social demands (lynch mobs and vigilantism), there would be no democracy of the sort the intellectuals had desired. This would have made visible that which was effectively concealed until then: that the battle was over whose versions of truth were taken as "objective." The health professionals managed to turn the battle into one between truth and corruption, rather than one between whose versions of truth would reign. The interim government was eventually able to quell the disruptions, and, as a gesture which signaled its desire to regain its position as defender of truth and to restate its vision of a democracy based on truth, in all its modern glory, asked Dr. Mathura to become its first minister of health. This government quickly articulated its priorities for primary education, primary health care, potable water supply, rural transportation, and environmental concerns (Shaha 1993: 257–58).[10] When he was sworn in by the new prime minister, K. P. Bhattarai, Dr. Mathura (and another appointed member, Nilambar Acharaya) swore not by God in the traditional manner of cabinet members but by "truth and conscience" (Shaha 1993: 216).

5 Dividing lines: motivations of the medical professionals

The revolution for Immanuel Kant, Foucault (1988: 89, 91) has argued, is not an event which makes a difference as in the overthrow of empires but a sign of the disposition of those who put their lives on the line for it:

> "Do not expect this event," [Kant] writes at the beginning of paragraph VI, "to consist of noble gestures or great crimes committed by men, as a result of which that which was great among men is made small, or that which was small, made great, nor of gleaming ancient buildings that disappear as if by magic while others rise, in a sense from the bowels of the earth to take their place. No, it is nothing like that." In this text, Kant is obviously alluding to the traditional reflections that seek the proofs of the progress or non-progress of humankind in the overthrow of empires, in the great catastrophes by which the best established states disappear, in the reversals of fortune that bring low established powers and allow new ones to appear. Be careful, Kant is telling his readers, it is in much less grandiose, much less perceptible events. . . . The Revolution as spectacle, and not as gesture, as a focus for enthusiasm on the part of those who observe it and not as a principle of overthrow for those who take part in it, is a "signum rememorativum," for it reveals that disposition, which has been present from the beginning; it is a "signum demonstrativum" because it demonstrates the present efficacity of this disposition; and it is also a "signum prognosticum," for, although the Revolution may have certain questionable results, one cannot forget the disposition that is revealed through it.

If it is true that revolutions leave their mark not so much in the visible transformation of society as in the refinement of the event as a sign of a new and modern disposition, then the Nepali revolution is no exception. The Nepali People's Movement is a sign reflecting, demonstrating, and predicting a type of modern and scientific disposition upon which Nepalis believed a democracy could be built. But I wish to explore both dimensions of this meaning of the revolution; first by probing the sign of it in the new disposition found in motivations of health professionals, and second by probing its failure to radically transform society (in the upcoming chapters) revealed in the revolution's demand that medicine be politicized under conditions of modernity which are ultimately troubled by this stance. Whereas for Kant, and even Foucault, the mere presence of modern dispositions signal a form of success of the revolution, I would explore the traces of the old, the non-successes, within the dispositions of the new in the post-revolutionary period. First, the motivations, then the problems of merging medical science with politics and the remaining traces of the old in the new.

Weariness of corruption and the repression it provoked was a principal motivation for revolution among Nepalis in general and fighting against these was, for most urban medical professionals, articulated through several positive social agendas: the desire for an end to social inequality as a basis for an end to health inequality, and the belief that ending social inequality began with creating a true political democracy. But the motivations of health professionals were not entirely uniform. All could be said to reflect a modern disposition, but in different ways. The majority of physicians, nurses and paramedics who participated in the movement had two specific interests already described: long-standing commitments to political reform, which were, for them, the key to health for all (entailing a commitment to politics as a form of medicine) and the desire to protect fundamental human rights in the face of government terrorism. There were some, however, who, lacking political allegiance to the cause, simply wanted to avoid being left behind on a sinking political ship. Finally, there were some health professionals who declined to participate because they believed that in principle medical professionals had no business getting involved in politics.

This last category of professionals were often dismissed by others as panchayat loyalists, devoted to a politics the majority did not support. I found, however, that a number of these professionals were not aligned politically with the king's government. Rather, their concern was with the fine line between *medical science practiced for political purposes* and *compromising medical science and practice by politicizing its truths*. For them, the idea that scientific truths could be put to political purposes seemed dangerously close to the idea that scientific truths were themselves constructed (brought into existence, even in extreme cases, invented) to meet the requirements of specific political, cultural, and social agendas. They, more than others, were sensitive to the ways in which the very complaints their colleagues made regarding government corruption could easily be turned against them. But their views were contested by others. In all their modern dispositions, we can see the way in which the revolution operates as a sign of modernity – offering the possibility of an objective and apolitical practice of truth.

Political commitment

Some of the principal organizers of health professionals during the movement were doctors and nurses who had been involved in politics for most of their lives. For Dr. Mathura and Meena Poudel, for example, were not unusual in that for them medical practice was shot through with political considerations. Ill health was for them directly related to social and political inequalities and conditions, and therefore health was possible only in the right political climate.

Dr. B., in private practice as a gastroenterologist in Kathmandu, put it this way:

I was born into a political family. My elder brother was a political activist. When B. P. Koirala was arrested in 1960, he was a member of the Youth Congress [Tarun Dal]. The Youth Congress existed during the time of the elected government as a sister organization of the Nepali Congress to educate the young people and make them politically aware. So my brother, he remained in exile for a number of years [after the elected government was disbanded by King Mahendra], and then he came back in this country to launch a student movement. This brother of mine was arrested and spent a lot of time in jail. So, basically, the family was aware of the need for political freedom in the country. That was certainly a motivating factor in my case.

But I think there is an even stronger motivation for me. It is a fact that when you are a doctor in Nepal, you see about a hundred patients a day, and they are in various capacities. You see, if you are a primary care provider, some patients are young and some are older, but the doctor has to see and dispense with more and more, larger numbers of patients over time. Now, over the years, what has happened to me is that I have seen one patient in tatters and the next moment somebody in a gabardine suit walks in with fancy gold ornaments and diamonds and things like that. So a doctor is always exposed to much but insistently exposed to these gaps – these inequalities – in society. . . .

So that gets hold of you – always seeing the perpetual gaps in the social structure. We are a limited number of doctors. The haves as well as the have-nots come to us. So we are perpetually exposed to that stress – the stress of having to live with tremendous differences in social standards. So that, I think, was probably the most influential factor in motivating me, in preparing a doctor to go out and speak. This motivation – it translates to a recognition of inequality. Different standards of living make the difference. It is the reason for inequalities in health. It was this way in seventeenth- and eighteenth-century England, and it still is this way in Nepal.

This inequality was caused by a political system that deprived people of their say in how the society functioned. For example, if I don't listen to you and I have enough power to get the things I want, then, given time, you are going to be in a worse situation and I am going to be in a better situation. And the gap is going to get wider and wider. So I think my involvement was basically to see the society change into a freer one. Freedom in terms of politics, political freedom to bring about some sort of social justice. I was terribly excited before the people were actually gunned down. I was still attending my clinics, doing my regular practice and all that. And then when people were gunned down and initially some of them were denied treatment in Bhaktapur, then I thought: "This is enough. I think we have to speak up. I, as a doctor, cannot sit back and condone denial of treatment." That is how I felt.

Another physician, Dr. K., discussed the problems in much the same way:

You see, doctors are probably one of the leaders of society. They have a social impact and aspect that is tremendous, for we meet people from all walks of life. For example, a doctor taking the position of opposition to the government sees everybody – from poor to rich. Everybody goes to the doctor, so he has a very important social aspect. The doctor is exposed to inequalities and is probably more sensitive than others to these. So in that way we become more vocal, because it is our responsibility to do something to change the situation of inequality. We are also more educated, and we know that change is possible.

Another activist, Dr. M. had insights on the links between health and politics. He had been assigned to conduct a three-month research project funded by IDRC in the Tanahu area, and the results had proved disappointing:

I totally failed. You see, the data I got was totally erratic, and I wrote my resignation because I believed that I had been unable to complete my job as promised. But if I had not failed, I would probably not have been attracted to community medicine. So I resigned, but my dean refused to accept my resignation. Rather, he called an expert from Johns Hopkins University to find out why I failed.

First, we found problems with the research questionnaires. It was too long, and people got tired by the time we were halfway through. We also asked the wrong questions. For example, people thought that diarrhea among children was very common, and they said that none of their children were suffering from diarrhea because they thought that if children did not pass a loose bowel motion, it was abnormal rather than normal. That we didn't know, you see? Or, for them, if a middle-aged woman did not have a backache, she would be abnormal. If the old man would not have a cough, he would be abnormal. So when we investigated together with Johns Hopkins researcher, we found that the social aspects of medicine were important. Then I became attracted to community medicine, you see, because without knowing these things – the culture, social aspects, their belief systems, interpretations, their knowledge, and their social conditions – we cannot really know the problems. . . .

I found a different dimension of medicine. I will tell you a very interesting story. Before, I took American medical students, via a program run partially by Carl Taylor [founder of the Johns Hopkins School of International Public Health], in the Kali Gandaki area. In that area, you see, we saw one big problem of scabies. In that area, the hillside was mostly where the rich people stayed, and most of the rich people owned the good lands on that side of the hill. But we found that scabies was very common among the rich people there. There was the river, and in the dry upland area across the river from the rich people, very low-class people lived, but among them scabies was virtually absent. We didn't know what the reason was. I thought it was a mistake on the part of the student [who collected the data], but I checked it myself and it was correct. But we didn't know why. So we gathered together the people in the village and we presented our data, and the students said, "This is what we found, and we cannot explain it, but if anybody in the village can answer this question, we will be much obliged." So, you know, unexpectedly, one illiterate woman of about forty years of age and who was a bit drunk volunteered the answer, and, she provided a very scientific answer. You know what the answer was? She explained that the dry area was without water, and so the poor families' children had to take their animals across the river each day to the forest area on the other side of the mountain, and so each day the children had to go swim along with the cattle in the Kali Gandaki River. And they had to swim back, to go to the school or other work, and then go back in the evening to take the cattle back from that place. And we asked about the Brahmins and these upper-class rich people on the forested side. They only had a few wells for water, but they didn't have sufficient water to take baths. So that was very interesting to show how health is related to ecological and to economic conditions.

I always believed, but in actuality it is very hard to bring politics in health. It is the most important thing, but politics is unfortunately called slander. The word "politics" is itself, these days, slander. Many people understand politics as party politics or politics for power or intrigue. But politics is actually only people's participation in their health. The level of people's participation in politics in Nepal is very high. That is why people are critical of doctors. They are skeptical, because they are so involved in politics. They should be critical and have critical awareness, because, you know, there are some doctors who are just false. They are like *zamindars* [landlords]. They make their practice just like their landholding, and they make money out of their certificate and out of false assurances, false attention, instead of giving the right information, the right kind of information or right kind of treatment. They always muddle the information for their own benefit. . . .

But, here people do believe in doctors, that is why they are suspicious of people who are not good. They still believe doctors, and they have no other way. You see, if they don't take the doctor's word and the doctors advise blindly sometimes, someday the doctors will be forced to behave properly, sharing proper information to the people about their own ability and about their own findings. If they are not able to diagnose a condition, they should be frank and say that. Normally, they do not say that they are not able to diagnose someone; they go on creating what is called the "next opportunity" and deceiving the people. In this way, people will also learn the limitations of medicine, and it will help to bring medicine onto real scientific footing. Real scientific footing in my concept includes people's participation in the practice of medicine. People's participation in terms of understanding, in terms of sharing and getting interest to get information and be skeptical about their doctors. And also in terms of behaving in order to prevent as well as to get relief of any suffering or problems.

Many of the health professionals who became involved as organizers in the People's Movement blamed health problems on corrupt politics. Paramedicals who worked in rural areas, in particular, were highly motivated and politically conscientious. I was told by the president of the Nepal Paramedicals' Association that this was true because not only were they continually confronted with the conditions of living which caused ill health among the Nepali people but being placed in rural clinics which were chronically understaffed and undersupplied only exacerbated their consciousness of the corruption and political impediments to health. They argued that even if they had medicines, the health problems they confronted were not going to be solved by medicines alone. Mr. S., an officer of the Nepal Paramedicals' Association, explained the paramedicals' involvement in politics as follows:

In fact, many people in the health sector, and in the health service – say medical, paramedical, nurses – they are very politically conscious. It is very interesting. You see, it is because they interact with the people. They know the living standards of all the people. They follow their patients and have new conversations with fifty to one hundred people, and all the time they see how these people are living. Then, we also see what happens in the villages when a *pradhan pancha* [mayor] comes to the people and he tells the people he wants them in his pocket, and they pay the people or make big promises for hospitals and better services, like that. But they never bring these things – better services – only people end up in a worse condition. So, you see, we see the conditions and the way the politicians work, and we feel that we must be political – to help people become politically conscious.

The Department of Community Medicine at the Institute of Medicine (begun by Dr. Mathura) taught that primary care included teaching villagers about political empowerment and community organizing.

Community-health-oriented doctors in general in Nepal were influenced by radical Western intellectuals such as Marx, Sartre, and Lenin. Additionally, those who went on to study public health abroad were often exposed to the writings of Western critics of biomedicine such as Ivan Illich, who wrote *Medical Nemesis* (on biomedical iatrogenesis), Thomas McKeown, who wrote *Medicine: Dream, Mirage, or Nemesis?* (questioning the validity of claims that improvements in morbidity, mortality, and longevity rates are due to medical advancements as opposed to basic infrastructural changes), and Vicente Navarro, who wrote *Medicine Under Capitalism* (a critique of the commercialization, profits, and class inequalities of medicine in the United States). Upon their return to Nepal, these doctors were implored to promote the WHO and UNICEF's Alma Ata primary health care programs. Although overtly offering a commitment to politics, this agenda's politics were not, as aforementioned, so straightforward.

The strategy designed at Alma Ata was to correct the failures of international health development programs to date, notably the failure of vertical (disease-based) eradication programs to improve the overall health of recipients (Foster 1987). Indirectly, Alma Ata represented a response to the increasing presence of political leftists in the Third World. Recognizing the widespread acclaim in the 1970s for both China's and Cuba's successful communist health programs for the masses, ironically, the conservative interests of the bilateral and multinational agencies funded largely by the Western nations of the so-called free world saw medical intervention as a way to ensure that poor countries would *not* become communist. Aid agencies offered interventions that co-opted the political rhetoric of basic health care but usually advocated an approach that worked to depoliticize it. Even though their goals made recipients more aware than ever of the need for revolutionary political action when they used a rhetoric of "political will," multilateral development programs often deployed explicitly apolitical techniques. Few bilateral or multilateral health development agencies ever actually advocated "revolutionary" activities against existing regimes for doctors or allied health professionals. At the most, it was assumed either that a democratic infrastructure already existed and so "political will" could be aroused without destabilizing the government, or else it was assumed that setting impartial medical goals and then helping nations to achieve them through technical interventions would propel the target populations towards democracy.

It was often assumed that by calling for "political will" for health, development programs could be undertaken without running the risk of being accused of meddling with a country's internal political affairs. (Again, see Morgan 1993 for a case study.) "Political will" came to be translated as "community participation" at the village level but was accounted for only in terms of politically sanitized statistics on morbidity, mortality, fertility control acceptance, parity, immunization acceptance, growth rates, and clinic visits. In Nepal, the same was true. The lack of infrastructure in Nepal was treated by development programs as a problem of material resources (income, roads, products, transport systems, etc.) but seldom as problems of politics, power, or corruption. Rural health development meant clean water, sanitation, nutrition, family planning, and first aid but not taking up arms to overthrow an oppressive regime which denied these opportunities by siphoning off most of the country's money for its ruling elite.

What was designed in communist-bloc countries as a health agenda devoted specifically to promoting the political interests of the nation became in non-communist regions a health agenda that would serve scientific and objective truth rather than political agendas, or at least not overtly so. Even when, among health development donors, the indirect goal was to promote democratic forms of government (and to keep communism at bay), this was seldom explicitly stated. Most of their programs were identified as serving the interests of medical truth rather than the political interests of donor nations. Many believed that democracy was a neutral government system which merely gave expression to competing and contested political views rather than a politically and socially hegemonic system already invested with specific economic, social and even cultural preferences (e.g., free markets, nuclear families, individualism, wage labor, etc.).

In Nepal, however, local "experts" in health development were instrumental in setting up programs which would operate under the perceived neutral rubric of medicine and medical aid (partly to promote this idea of a neutral government), but they would go farther than most program donors would possibly have wanted them to in repoliticizing medical agendas in order to make them speak for a revolution. For example, courses in community medicine under the guidance of these politically committed health activists were required of all doctors and nurses receiving their education in Nepal, and these actually focused on the role of politics in health care. The framings of health problems delivered to classrooms usually reflected the technical orientations of multilateral agencies, but the teaching by Nepali doctors often focused on the political issues underlying those problems.

One series of Department of Community Medicine lectures I attended involved guest speakers from development agencies, one of them a US public health physician from the WHO and another an Egyptian physician from UNICEF. These visitors consistently referred not to social or political involvement but to disease pathways, vectors of transmission, infectious conditions, monitoring strategies, impact reports, and statistical evaluation techniques. The WHO representative focused on cold-chain storage strategies for live attenuated viral immunizations and education about the virological sources of polio, entirely avoiding such important questions as how villages would be selected for immunization services in the first place or what mechanisms might be in place for ensuring parents would be able to afford to bring their children for immunizations when workers arrived in their villages. The UNICEF lecturer discussed the problem of "implementation" in primary health care and the important role of supervisorial management. Clean water, hygiene, and nutrition were treated as if their acquisition and practice were simply a matter of knowledge and desire rather than a complicated process of negotiating social relationships among caste, class, and ethnically divided populations. Summing up, he said: "All the ingredients of primary health care are there. You need to make the health worker better trained, better motivated, better supervised. You have to see that your worker is there, your logistics are there, your supervision is there, and then make assessments accordingly." He never once mentioned that social inequality, differences in gender or ethnicity, or political hierarchy might complicate the implementation of even his general technical prescriptions (again see Justice 1983 for a case study).

In contrast, the Nepali professor, Dr. Mathura, referred to social motivations and activism among villagers, noting that the physician or nurse or paramedical posted in a rural area would have to take a more socially involved and politically active role in the health of villagers and try to make villagers themselves more aware of the politics of their own health care. He stressed the fact that a young physician working in a rural community would need to pay attention to community-defined needs, including perceived needs to eliminate social inequality.

In Nepal, then, "Health for All" was taken by many health professionals as a call *for* very specific sorts of political action. Politically committed Nepali medical professionals took advantage of the fact that, unlike foreign advisors who only behind the scenes spoke and taught Nepalis to see their nation as bedeviled by corruption but had to remain publicly politically neutral, they came to see that they would have to speak out politically, even if it was risky. They demonstrated that the outcomes of health development imported from the metropole were in some ways inevitable. Nepalis' internalized a vision of corruption as an obstacle to health. Its eradication would be through apolitical techniques of intervention which were nonetheless able to show "political will." But Nepalis also showed the unpredictable in the sense that this politicization of health agendas reached its apogee in the 1990 People's Movement which led to a destabilization of the existing government and a revolution which, for at least the time being and several years after, was not clearly committed to Western-style as opposed to communist/socialist versions of "democracy." Although foreign donors wanted to see an end to corruption as much as many Nepalis, they first responded with hesitation, fearing political instability more than poverty and ill health. Eventually, they supported the movement when it became clear that the government would be placed under control of the Congress and not communist factions. Nepalis learned to critique themselves and in this sense learned perhaps better than their foreign advisors how to carry out the Alma Ata promise.

What is interesting in this process is that Nepali medical professionals also internalized one of modernity's enigmas: they advocated political reform without compromising their professional claims to objective and impartial truth. The idea of politics as medicine on a grand scale was for them not the politicization of medical science but the practice of good medicine *as* good science. Politics became a necessary component of science for these doctors because it compelled them to work in the interests of those patients they served. But what if it compelled them to work in the interests of the politics they served rather than the patients? What if the interests of the patients were not served by the same actions as were the interests of politicians? In their approach medical truth was juxtaposed to corruption rather than being seen as something that could itself be corrupted. Corruption had become the enemy, truth would be the victor. Politically committed doctors, in particular, quickly pointed out that although there were corruption problems within their own professional ranks, the problems of the overall health infrastructure and poor health-care delivery systems were principally problems of government corruption, the elimination of which would eliminate perceived corruption within their own ranks. Doctors had been known to have been beaten by villagers when they were unable to save patients' lives or supply them with needed medicines. This sort of corruption was attached to government, not medicine; it was because the government consistently refused to incorporate doctors in the planning processes at the Ministry of Health and instead regularly placed non-physicians in positions of authority at the district-level health posts. Instead of seeing problems of corruption as inevitable within the framework of a politicized scientific practice, they blamed the problems on corruption belonging to government. If the government were to rely more on their expertise than on traditional systems of patronage and favoritism, then their problems would be solved. The health system of the country, some contended, should simply be run by medical experts rather than government agents who had little technical or scientific training but who happened to land important posts because they were well-connected. They believed it possible to run the system as medical experts not as politicians despite that fact that it would be political action that would bring them into that role.

Thus while the politically committed health professionals went far beyond the expectations of most Western health development agendas by turning medical practice into political practice, those who shared this motivation believed that they were being absolutely consistent with such metropole interests. A critical evaluation of the metropole agendas would see this outcome as inevitable. What the medical professionals could not foresee was what risks they would run by becoming so political under a modern regime that demanded a clear boundary between politics and scientific truth.

Human rights

Another of the most potent rallying motivations for doctors was the concern for human rights. Dr. S. K., who worked at Teaching Hospital, explained this motivation in these terms:

During the Panchayati time we wanted a health system that would have a separate health act which would give us more autonomy. It would give us more freedom to make decisions as professionals about what happens in the health sector. This is a positive aspect of our profession, and it is also true of persons in the government. If you have a separate health act . . . well, we had even proposed that going on strike would for doctors be illegal, you cannot jeopardize the health of people who are ill. You cannot say, "I am on strike. I won't see [the patients]." It is against the Hippocratic oath. So you have to see patients when they come to you. We wanted that, and the medical association was active in debating that. We felt that medicine is an essential service, you know? Like the postal system. So we could not strike.

But during the movement, it was not something we planned – we never planned that we would go on strike, because it was spontaneous; it all happened within a short time. When the government began to kill so many innocent people, we felt we had to do something. Personally, when I saw the victims, they were just young boys, and I was very angry. And I thought, "I cannot stand by idly while they are shooting innocents." So when we agreed to go on strike, we still ran our Out-Patient Department services through emergency, but only those people who came to the hospital knew that. From the outside, it looked like a complete strike. We were even planning to run it outside the hospital. That way we could give some service to the people, and especially those people who come from such faraway places . . . we could not just turn them back.

So, in that regard, doctors on strike – that strategy – was the most effective as compared to others because the doctors are considered quite high status in the society. We are providers of health care.

Dr. S. K. saw protesting government killings as a form of medical service. Professional responsibility for him meant following a code of conduct which transcended particular political currents of the day. It meant living by medical truth, not politics. Ultimately, the decision to go on strike was made by many physicians because of their recognition that what was at stake was not party politics but fundamental human rights, over which, they argued, physicians must be concerned. The killing of innocent protestors by the government was the catalyst for them; it made no sense to continue to work for the government to bring about health if the government insisted on producing ill health, even death. Their participation in protest under the rubric of universal human rights was, however, complicated by physicians' social status.

Many of the doctors were members of the Nepali elite. Indeed, few urban professionals had the financial and social wherewithal to go to medical school and many of the physicians in Kathmandu had become physicians because their families were wealthy and had "source-force" which paid off in such things as scholarships for study abroad. Even when merit was a consideration, persons without "source-force" were seldom in a position to make use of such rewards. Not all doctors were born to well-to-do families, but becoming doctors usually guaranteed them financial security that few Nepalis had. Thus, one might have expected the majority of physicians to resist involvement in a movement to change the status quo for fear of losing their social positions of privilege, especially if communist agendas replaced current ones and regulated their industry and its profits. The majority of physicians who had worried about going on strike indicated, however, that their concern was not with losing personal privilege. In fact they argued the opposite – that eliminating the corruption of the status quo would bring them greater professional privileges based on standards which were more efficient and more fair. Instead, they worried that going on strike would alienate the public – that people might feel that they, as doctors, were not living up to their professional responsibilities if they shut down services that these very clients depended upon for survival. The human rights rubric was therefore important to them as a rationale for activism and professional solidarity without compromising their commitment to alleviate human suffering. Violations of human rights redefined the nature of their professional responsibility and demanded political action. After Dr. Mathura accused the government of using damaged bullets, in clear violation of human rights, the majority of physicians and nurses joined the protest. Although the public might well have viewed physicians as epitomizing an elite and blamed them for the ordinary Nepalis' suffering, they instead came to see physicians as spokespersons for the "people." They had the moral upperhand because they stood by the truth. One example of this sort of support came from a young man whose sister had died a year after the movement, when hospital staff failed to tend to her while staging another political strike. Although he felt the strike which led to his sister's death had not been justified, being for better wages, the strikes during the revolution were justifiable:

Whatever doctors did during the Jan Andolan, it was okay. It was supposed to be done and they did it in order to bring about a change in the system. The change in the system took place; their demands were fulfilled, and the people are happy. During the revolution, the doctor's role was very important. They took part in the revolution and democracy came in only fifty days time. If they had not taken part, it would have taken longer. Because the doctors took part, everybody supported. They played an important role because, when the panchas killed by shooting, the doctors said, "You are continuing to kill, and on our side, we are continuing to save lives! We will quit saving, if you are going to continue killing, we will not continue saving lives!" This is how they challenged the Panchayat government at that time. So, their protest was justified.

In contrast, he was angry about the death of his sister because the actions of the hospital staff at that time revealed their elitism; they were on strike over improved wages and working benefits which he felt "was not a matter of right or wrong. It was an agitation for themselves. . . for their own interest and it caused the death of general people like this. It cannot be said to be fair."

Despite the possibility that the public would oppose the health professionals for denying them care at this critical moment in their struggle for precisely the same reasons as seen after the revolution they instead embraced them, largely because these professionals were able to articulate a moral position that effaced their elite status by putting that status to work for the popular cause. More than anything else, human rights discourse gave the health professionals this ability to align their interests with the public in a manner that would not compromise their professional claims on truth.

Abandoning the sinking ship

Predictably, there were some health professionals who joined the movement only reluctantly. These people, I was told, often invoked professional responsibility in arguing that they should not go on strike, while others suggested that what was really at stake for them was their commitment to an old system from which they personally profited. It was apparently not until these professionals recognized the writing on the wall, literally and figuratively, that they came over to the side of the protestors. Some of these physicians were of the older generation who had experienced Rana rule and may have considered the system already dramatically liberalized. Their reluctance to participate in the movement was articulated not around either a desire for stability (although clearly some did support the system because of this), or a commitment to an apolitical science, but around what they would personally lose by joining the opposition. Should the revolution fail, these professionals reasoned, their participation would guarantee their removal from the ranks of power, prestige, wealth, and professionalism. Ironically, I was told that they argued that they were not political, although being in the good graces of those in power meant engaging in a personal politics every day. These professionals did not want to be seen as revolutionaries, but as good doctors. They did not want to jeopardize their ability to practice by falling out of favor with those who guaranteed them jobs. Ultimately, however, they apparently realized that if they did not change allegiance in time they might sink with the old system.

Dr. B. G. felt that most of these professionals were less clinical, more administratively oriented than the "full-force" participants:

Most of the doctors who did not immediately participate were people from the ministry . . . they were not clinicians. They were basically attached to medical administration, office workers, etc. A doctor has to be somebody who is in constant touch with his people. Perhaps it is not fair to call them "people," but I am in constant touch with my "clients," so I can relate to their problems, to their day-to-day chores, things like that. But these people had us between them and the real people, so maybe because they were in very gleaming [desirable and powerful] government chairs, they were afraid to lose their positions.

My interviews with lower-level civil servants in the Ministry of Health revealed that many of them were participating covertly in the movement from its inception, so one should probably read Dr. B. G.'s comments as applying to mostly high-level administrators who were sometimes but not uniformly the most reluctant participants – the most at risk of losing their jobs. In some cases it was these professionals who had the least faith in their professional expertise to provide social and financial rewards. Their privilege had come from social affiliations, therefore risking it was not an option.

For many who reluctantly joined the revolution, the idea that they were motivated by self-preservation was never forthcoming in interviews as hindsight. Rather, they claimed either that they had secretly wanted to participate all along and only felt it was safe to do so once it was clear that it would be successful or that they had felt responsible to their professional duties regardless of political upheavals of the day. None of these people allowed me to tape my interviews with them. One hospital administrator said that she felt it was her duty to maintain the efficient operation of the hospital whether or not the superior to whom she was beholden for her job was being thrown out of power. For her, the idea of allegiance to her superior was not an issue, but to others commenting on her actions it was the primary reason, as evidenced in her acquisition of the job in the first place.

Eventually, these professionals joined their colleagues in protest because they were convinced by the activists that they would be excluded from the new political order because of their identification with the old system. Dr. P. told me that he had appealed to his reluctant colleagues' sense of duty to profession but also to their sense of logic and reasonableness in view of the outcome if they appeared to be siding with the panchayat system. His comments offer telling commentary on a certain ambivalence about the potential for the revolution to really change things: he reveals the perception that political favoritism would persist beyond the revolution despite the efforts to overthrow this sort of thing by revolutionary means. He said to them:

This is Bir Hospital, and don't you know what that means? This is a difficult place. We have been fighting for many years, and the medical profession has contributed many things professional. And yet the situation of Bir Hospital, the people's hospital is never given any value. They always neglect the issues. But this is a government hospital, and whatever decision is made, whatever happens in this government . . . if there is a new government and we have won, then whatever decision will be made, it will be with a new policy and new rule. Power will be transferred and all this sort of thing. We have to see reality. We have to see that it will be a few who will be victimized for being part of the pancha system. If you are going to go against the majority, you will suffer under the new system unless you support them [the revolutionaries] now. You must also think of your profession. If this is the professional decision, you should consider what is the loyal thing to do, what is the right thing to do.

Medical professionals who jumped on board eventually but only reluctantly did so not necessarily because they were politically motivated as citizens but because they found that participating gave them a safe place in which to wait until they could see where the power landed in the aftermath of the movement. Some of them were successful in giving the impression that they were supporters of the movement and loyal to a higher power in their profession, and they have curried favor anew with the contemporary holders of power in the new democracy. This is true partially at least because pre-revolutionary relations of power have been sustained in post-revolutionary Nepal.

Principled non-involvement

A few medical professionals were opposed to participation altogether. Some of them, like those discussed above, were motivated by the fact that they held positions of authority and power and were opposed to the multiparty democratic movement, completely convinced that panchayat democracy was a good thing. Others were not necessarily committed to the current regime but felt that under no circumstances should medical professionals use their medical expertise and authority for political purposes. These resisters offered an interesting critique of the politically committed health professionals because both explained their stances in terms of professional responsibility. But each came to different conclusions regarding the method of adhering to it. Whereas many activists felt politicizing medicine was necessary, their opponents' logic was that health professionals had no business in politics, for politics compromised one's professional reputation and, more important, one's "scientific objectivity." Dr. D. O., a former Bir Hospital administrator, explained this sentiment:

My main interest during the Jan Andolan was in keeping the hospital functioning. I was always ready to respond when I was called upon by the institution. Other doctors might say that their hunger strike was important, but I would say that more important was our responsibility for the care of the injured, and that means keeping the hospital functioning as usual, in its most efficient and effective capacity. If nobody were to look after the injured, then life has no importance. For me, life is important, as is care of the injured. I will say that doctors should not go on hunger strikes. All of our interests were the same. We all wanted success with the movement. But, I think the bottom line is that you cannot compromise patient care for political purposes. If you do, then you are telling them that politics is more important than their lives. The responsibility of the profession is to care for the people, not to care for the politics.

O. I., a nurse at Teaching Hospital who steered clear of any political involvement during the movement explained her motivations similarly:

Because you are professionals you have some responsibility to get involved politically insofar as it makes a difference in terms of being able to do your job correctly, but there is a fragile boundary beyond which you should not go because when politics is too influential, you compromise your ability to do a good job. You compromise your political, your professional power, your professional duties, and also you are compromising your professional welfare.

Of course, everyone will have some kind of political thought. Assuming you are a professional person, you will have a civic conscience. You can and you always should have. But let that not influence your work. Don't let it interfere with catering to your professional needs, protecting your professional rights and interests. Otherwise, what happens is that politics is always seen as the reason for your actions. Let's say that someone at the top has one political thought and a few others have other political thoughts. When it comes time for promotions, who do you promote? How can you do it without seeming to make a political judgment? If the person who is chosen is recognized as being of one political thought, then he is identified for that. Now, the other people who are his juniors or other people who are working with him who might harbor other thoughts are just no longer confident that that person will do justice to them or that they will be given a fair chance.

You see, when politics get involved, it is impossible to see things otherwise. People then become afraid of losing their job or losing something because they may not support their bosses politically. What can they do? Now, is that any way to run a hospital or to teach? We have to worry about that sort of compromising within the profession. Who will suffer in the end? It will be the patients, the people. Professionals should take their own power rather than boosting some political agenda – some political person's ego.

You see, because that is the nature of a democracy. People must learn to be self-responsible. That is what being a professional is all about. People want a democracy, but they really don't know what democracy is. They want all the freedoms of a democracy without any duties. What a real democracy is, I feel, is following duties. So, if they don't have a sense of responsibility for a society – they all talked about wanting change and wanting freedom, total freedom, but they think that democracy means total freedom without any rules at all. This is wrong. The main thing is that a democracy entails self-responsibility, self-responsibility, and people don't yet have a sense of self-responsibility. That is the main problem. Even the health professionals have this problem, you see? They do not even have a sense of self-responsibility to their profession.

The concern of those who opposed participation was not simply that the public would lose faith in these practitioners but that practitioners themselves would lose faith in their practices if they were politicized. In fact, the reputation of physicians among the public was positively affected by their political involvement in the movement, but the idea that a politicized medicine would somehow compromise the profession overall, and especially from within its own ranks, is not so easily dismissed. O. I. identified what might be considered a critical feature of some version of democracy when she said a strict boundary (or at least the belief in one) between politics and medical science was necessary. This boundary maintenance was for her something which emerged with the discipline and responsibility of being a modern citizen.

However, the problem she identified as inevitably placing medicine at risk was for other politically committed professionals precisely what would make their professional practice strong and effective. One could not avoid politics in health care in Nepal; therefore, they felt, it was important to embrace a politics which worked scientifically – that would be a democracy. This meant, for some professionals, trying to ferret out the difference between party politics, subject to corruption, and real politics, tied to scientific truths about health and disease. Dr. R. S. articulated the nuances of this argument for himself by noting that there was a difference between party politics and politics:

The majority of the people have the sense that they were suffering during the time of the panchayat regime. What is the suffering of the people at this time, though, and has there been any decrease or any change in the general level of suffering of the people? Is this the kind of democracy they wanted or is this the kind of democracy they had visualized and dreamt about? Is this the situation for which people have devoted themselves, fought, and got killed? There should be some signs and symptoms of improvement. You cannot cure a disease that has been there for so long, but there should be signs and symptoms at least that the patient is getting better or the severity of the disease is decreasing. You can find out some indicators of the development thus far. Has there been any change in that? That is my question, because there is a problem with political participation. I am political in the sense that there should be some improvement every year. Like, after every five years, we should at least see some improvement in the developmental indicators, or at least in the general sense of the people. There should be some improvement.

You see, there are problems that cannot be solved by individuals, and that is why we come in groups. That is why the majority of doctors are concerned with their own profession only. They do not belong to any major political parties. So if politics means acting as a professional for the good of society, as a group, then we must be political. But this is not necessarily party politics. We have no concern for one political agenda or another.

This physician's view that party politics was not the same thing as general political consciousness was one which many who politicized medicine shared. Those who declined to participate did so on the principle that any involvement in politics at all had the potential to become party politics, thus precisely the sort of thing that could corrupt the scientific and objective practices of medicine. After all, they noted, it was resistance to political corruption that had motivated their colleagues to incite a revolution in the first place. The danger of politicizing medical practices was precisely the sort of danger that corruption posed to democracy. Their concern was with the ease with which a situation of health as politics could become transformed into a situation of health as party politics wherein health professionals were pawns for particularistic party goals. The position of these health professionals revealed how easily claims to universalist, scientific truth *once politicized* could be rendered vulnerable to charges of corruption. In fact, in 1993 I found that doctors and nurses who had worked hard to make medicine speak a new political language had become frustrated by the suggestion on the part of their critics that their work was necessarily partisan politics, however neutral and objective in orientation they thought it was. Physicians believed that their medicine would make patients politically aware, in Freire's sense, "conscientized." The idea that their interventions would be read as partisan truths was for them anathema, but for others inevitable.

In the end, the merging of medicine and politics in the People's Movement came to be seen by these non-involved health professionals as an obstacle to creating a society organized around impartial institutions. For these critics, the revolutionary tactics invoked placed politics at the center of the scientific stage and incontrovertibly turned medical truths into politically convenient ones. In their view, if medicine was corrupted by a politics of affiliation before the democracy movement, then the strategies of the Nepali health professionals to politicize medicine in the name of science and democracy only further infused everyday practices, including medical practices, with politics. They turned impartial institutions into sites for the deployment of specific political agendas.

The motivations of the Nepali doctors, nurses, and paramedicals resonate with the concerns of other scientists, physicians, and scholars, revolutionary and conservative, over a long international history. Comparison with instances of politicized medicine from different regions of the globe makes it clear that the link that Nepali medical professionals saw between a scientific medicine and a democratic political system was not inevitable.

6 Medicine and politics: a triage of truth in the practice of medicine

> For a long time I have been conscious of the fact that I stand free and open-eyed in my times, and assimilate their trends early and quickly. I have often misjudged people, the times never. This has given me the advantage of being now not half a man, but a whole one whose medical beliefs fuse with his political and social ones. As a natural scientist I can be but a republican. The republic is the only form in which the claims derived from the laws of nature and the nature of man can be realized.
>
> Rudolf Virchow 1985 [1879]

It seems ironic today that a person considered one of the nineteenth-century's leading scientists, a forerunner in the use of the scientific method for pathological anatomy, Rudolf Virchow, could have been so committed to the idea that science, and particularly medical science, was also deeply political. So deep were politics in science, for him, that it was only under certain political circumstances that scientific truth could be made apparent. So political were his truths, however, that he was considered a radical by some of his contemporaries – a person more interested in politics than medicine and one who would prove them correct by eventually taking up a political office. Virchow identified the dilemmas faced by many Nepalis in the wake of their revolution. His story and those of others who have tried to merge politics with medicine are instructive for understanding the Nepali case.

A boundary between science and politics

Despite the absence of laboratory science in either academic or public-sector enterprise in Nepal, the assumptions found in cultures where laboratory and experimental science exist are also found among Nepal's educated. Among the assumptions Nepali biomedical professionals share with their colleagues in the wider world is the inviolability of medical facts. People who believe in science generally hold that a scientific fact is a "fact" because (1) it is independent of the social and political conditions of its production and (2) it is not arbitrary; it pertains to existing and confirmed understandings of the real world. The medical facts around which practitioners organize their diagnoses and interventions are, in this sense, objective.

Returning to Steven Shapin and Simon Schaffer's (1985) analysis, one of the origins of this notion of objectivity is the experiment. Experimental objectivity entered popular discourse in the European world as partly a product of the mid-seventeenth-century debate between Thomas Hobbes and Robert Boyle. Their debate was over what counted as knowledge: the facts which emerged from the experimental apparatuses (such as the air pump) of Boyle that were collectively observable and confirmed by one's educated peers or the facts made clear by the laws Hobbes established through reason. For Hobbes, laws of nature were objective; they transcended the political and social contingencies of the moment. At the same time, he knew that, because they emerged as philosophical concerns, they pertained specifically to social and political domains. This, he presumed, would also be true of experimental facts.

At stake in the debate between Hobbes and Boyle was the boundary between science and the larger social and political entity within which its facts were pondered. For Hobbes, philosophy was itself a science that could attend to the task of keeping social order and peace by reasoned argument and principles outlining uniform relationships of cause and effect that constituted laws of nature. Hobbes' perspective led him to argue for the necessity of a strong sovereign and a rule of law, even one which might authorize coercion in the event of sectarian conflict. For Boyle, in contrast, it was possible to "achieve peace and to terminate social scandal in natural philosophy" only by "securing a space within which a specified kind of dissent was manageable and safe" (Shapin and Schaffer 1985: 107). This, for Boyle, was the experimental space defined by the laboratory. For Hobbes, such a space would ensure just the sort of dissent he believed needed to be curtailed, the sort of dissent which could lead to social conflict and perhaps even civil war. The idea of a separate experimental domain was, for Hobbes, untenable; laws of nature would pertain inside as well as outside it and therefore dissent within would be cause for dissent outside.

Was it reasonable to assume that an ideological boundary could be drawn around science in such a way that gave the space of the experiment priority in ascertaining truth? Hobbes would not concede that facts produced in such a space could constitute truth because they did not fulfill the requirements of a philosophy; no such separation between experiment and the social condition was possible to imagine. The laws of nature did not shift depending upon which social domain one was in. Facts from experimentalists were, for Hobbes, suspect because they were no more than subjective observations, no more valid than assumptions of faith, since they failed to conform to more general philosophical tenets that could explain the whole of nature, the whole of social life. But for Boyle, facts produced in such a space constituted truthful knowledge in part at least because they were subjected to verification and scrutiny through dissent by educated peers. More important, among the desirable qualities of laboratory truths, for Boyle, was that they could be discovered *without disrupting the socio-political order.* They were neutral and objective, above and beyond politics, more eternal than what could be found through philosophy or politics.

Whereas Hobbes started from the assumption that his laws of nature were in part born of the historical moment of their production (in his case the civil war and the eventual restoration of the monarchy in Britain), Boyle created an ideological space within which it became reasonable to assume that independent of political and social currents scientific discussion and discovery could be undertaken and be productive of facts. In the end, Boyle won the day; it was this idea that certain truths, certain facts, exist apart from any social or political, even cultural, conditions which has continued to operate even into the late twentieth century in much of the world where modern European science has penetrated. Nepali doctors inherited this view when they became trained in biomedical techniques of inquiry and care giving. They voiced this belief during the revolution, when they held that their knowledge and expertise were more authoritative than those of the king, because they were based on science.

But Shapin and Schaffer show that it was Hobbes who was right. In retrospect, one of the main reasons Boyle's approach was considered more desirable than that of Hobbes was that it suited the socio-political circumstances of his time – a post-civil war Restoration England witnessing the rise of educated professional organizations. Notably, unlike Hobbes's contentious position *vis-à-vis* the church's claim to authoritative knowledge and his belief that only an all-powerful sovereign could provide the stability needed to prevent war between sectarian religious or professional factions, Boyle's laboratories offered a model for a society that could rule itself peacefully. "The experimental philosopher could be made to provide a model of the moral citizen, and the experimental community could be constituted as a model of the ideal polity. . . . In the debates on the effects of toleration and the achievement of assent, the experimenters in the 1660s showed how their community acted as just such an ideal and stable society" (Shapin and Schaffer 1985: 341, 303). The achievement was both tremendous and subtle: Boyle's contribution was in being able to legitimate the social interests of his day precisely by creating a domain of science devoted to the exploration of objective knowledge – knowledge that was not conditional upon the social interests of the day! Shapin and Schaffer (1985: 343) ask:

What sort of society is able to sustain legitimate and authentic science? And what contribution does scientific knowledge make to the maintenance of liberal society? The answer then given was unambiguous: an open and liberal society was the natural habitat of science, taken as the quest for objective knowledge. Such knowledge, in turn, constituted one of the sureties for the continuance of open and liberal society. Interfere with one, and you will erode the other.

The birth of experimental science marked a turning point in the sciences of nature. Henceforth it would be commonplace to treat scientific facts as if they were objective, as if they transcended the particular historical, cultural, political, and social conditions of their production. No matter how scientific "facts" might be used for political purposes, that they might themselves be political constructs was seldom considered because they emerged from an experimental space that was ideologically insulated from the socio-political world around it. But if Hobbes was right, no such domain could exist outside of the social or political context of its production. This would raise the question of how Nepalis managed to maintain the fiction that such a domain not only existed but also could map itself onto a political system it was supposed to transcend. The position adopted by the Nepali medical professionals in order to use medical science to fight for democracy was the position adopted by a long list of others before them who had engaged in similar projects.

Politicizing medicine as good science

Virchow lived from 1821 to 1902 and began writing as a professor of pathological anatomy in Berlin. At the time the dominant *Naturphilosophie* was vitalism – the theory that organic bodies were acted upon by and able to produce transcendental forces or unifying powers (vital forces). Like other vitalists, Virchow first maintained that living matter was separate from the rest of nature in its vitality (its life force). Later, he became an important figure in the reconsideration of vitalism, abandoning the belief in transcendental, invisible forces, and eventually a proponent of a mechanistic, empiricist, materialist theory of physiological anatomy, focusing upon the unit to which, he believed, all life could be reduced: the cell (Mendelsohn 1974).

Virchow was also a product of his political times. He witnessed the "unnatural" rise to power of the Prussian monarchs by military force and dynastic ambition in his homeland and watched these sovereigns promote German hegemony via the same military power. He witnessed and opposed the monarchs' efforts to legitimate and humanize their actions in terms of the dogma of the church. Instead, he defended "science" and "free research" as antidotes to political repression and the church's attacks on the "materialism in medicine, i.e., the natural scientific method" encapsulated in his studies of the cell (Virchow 1898: 9–15). In a manner reminiscent of the Nepali democracy struggle, he wrote (p.15):

> The great struggle of critical thinking against authoritarian rule, of natural history against dogma, of eternal human rights against arbitrariness, a struggle which has already twice raged through the European world, broke out for the third time and victory, provisionally, was ours. On the 18th we were promised a constitutional monarchy but only after the iron mouths of the cannons had spoken in vain; and only on the 29th, were the broadest foundations added, i.e., the democratic principle, the supreme will of the people. This movement will not come to an ultimate halt until we have attained a cosmopolitan point of view, that of scientific politics, that of anthropology or physiology (in the widest sense).[1] And in the face of such a movement we are told that medicine has nothing to do with politics! In the sweep of such a movement is it possible that we, who on account of our materialistic standpoint are so well aware of our smallness and finitude, are accused of personal passions when we attempt to draw the consequences of the grand idea of the progress of mankind to the various institutions of the state?

From a historicist perspective, for Virchow the relationship between cell and society was not metaphoric but logically scientific. Oswei Temkin (1949: 172) describes Virchow's writing of the "democratic cell-state" in which the individual cell was not simply *like* the fundamental unit of society, the individual citizen, it *was* the individual unit of society, being the fundamental unit of the individual. The individual was made up of cells and amounted to a social institution, just as many of these together formed the larger social state:

> The cell, Virchow maintained, was the fundamental unit of life. All plants and animals were sums of these vital units. It was the relationship between the cells that determined the structure and function of the multicellular organism. "Hence it becomes evident that the composition of a larger body, the so-called individual, always amounts to some kind of social institution" [from Virchow 1879]. This cell state, moreover, was patterned after a republic. There was no special organ, no single cell representing the individual. Individuality as something simple and integral was altogether a subjective phenomenon of our minds without corresponding biological parallel.

His vision of the sort of state that would be modeled on the natural body, as it came to be understood through the scientific method – that is, the natural state of society in its utmost efficiency and optimum state of organization – was that of a democratic republic. He wrote about democracy (p.15) as a state that:

> desires the welfare of all citizens, since it acknowledges the equal rights of all. Inasmuch as equal rights lead to self-government, the state also has a right to hope that everyone will know how to find and attain a state of prosperity by his own efforts within the limits of the law established by the nation itself. The premises for well-being, however, are health and education, and it is hence the duty of the state to provide the means for the maintenance and improvement of health and education to the greatest possible extent by public health and public education facilities.

Virchow became most vocal about an application of his theories of the cell to society and politics after he was commissioned by the Prussian minister of culture to report on the typhus epidemic in Upper Silesia in 1848. As a pathologist and medical examiner, he collected information about the epidemic which would help him to understand the cellular processes and causes of the epidemic and found that these cellular processes were conditioned first and foremost by the deplorable living conditions of the people. Poverty, lack of sanitation, lack of food and clean water, lack of both industry and political voice, heavy taxation, neglect by the government, compulsory labor for landlords, and overcrowding in houses were the main reasons for the epidemic. He reported that because of these iniquitous conditions, the people's spirit was broken. They lacked any desire to help themselves not because of their culture but because of their social conditions of deprivation (Virchow 1898: 217):

> Would it be an impressive sight indeed if this abject population which has carried the heaviest of shackles for centuries, rose up for the first time like a young giant lifting up its head and stretching its powerful limbs! Surely it would be worth the while of a benevolent and clear-sighted politician to attempt the solution of such a problem. Medicine, as a social science, as the science of human beings, has the obligation to raise such problems and to attempt their theoretical solution; the politician, the practical anthropologist, must find the means for their actual solution.

But Virchow pursued his politics principally as a scientist. He provided an exhaustive review of the known types of typhus (including a broad spectrum of fevers thought to affect the nervous system that are now considered separate diseases) and a deductive analysis of similar outbreaks and available data on typhus from elsewhere. He considered the effect of weather changes on crop production and living arrangements which might have produced a condition known as hunger typhus (starvation) and distinguished between types of exanthematic (or spotted fever) and abdominal typhus. He wrote as an advocate of the scientific method. He amassed volumes of information which made possible detailed comparative, inductive work, all of which promoted the idea that cellular processes, materially and empirically verifiable, also produced disease. His particular brand of positivism saw linkages between the material conditions associating cellular with larger social processes and states. In contrast to theories of invisible, transcendental vital forces, his notion of the cell was materialist, functioning in the body and in society. Social conditions which were empirically verifiable clearly played a role in disease. For his work in deciphering different types of typhus, he is recognized to this day in the United States as a champion of the scientific method in medicine.

Virchow became an original advocate of public health and produced a journal devoted to the advancement of science in the service of social causes. Before Prussia had become the German Empire of Bismarck, Virchow had also become an active politician, elected to the Berlin town council in 1861 and to the parliament in 1862. He founded the Progressive party and served as a member of the German Reichstag from 1880 to 1893. Even as a politician, he remained a medical man and advocated a political role for medicine. "Medical organization," he wrote, "is to be reformed not so much for the benefit of physicians as for that of the patients; the physicians are actively involved, but their position as regards the question of public health care differs from that of elementary teachers. . . . The physicians surely are the natural advocates of the poor and the social problem largely falls within their scope" (Virchow 1898: 4). The republic was for Virchow a democratic solution to scientifically perceived problems. It was a democratically organized political system which would promote the sort of freedom necessary to implement scientific solutions to social problems.

Virchow's particular style of linking politics and medicine has reappeared in diverse locales and eras, but the politics emerging from a "scientific" worldview has not always been what is today called democratic. Soon after Mao's communist army had finally established itself throughout the Chinese countryside and founded the People's Republic of China in 1948, the communists set about the task of creating a public health system which would bring basic health interventions to the masses in a manner costing the least and benefiting the most. They designed a program of "barefoot doctors" as a "Maoist model of medicine that emphasized a wide distribution of preventive medical activities, supplied by minimally trained health workers and traditional practitioners, and financed mainly by the local community out of collective resources"(De Geyndt, Zhao, and Liu 1992). Adapting some of the techniques of biomedicine to a communist social regime, the barefoot-doctor program replicated Virchow's sentiments regarding the call for political solutions to basic health problems. The barefoot doctors were sent out not simply as medical experts but as party cadres who could provide political and ideological training for the advancement of the communist party and its perceived health benefits among the masses.

The training manual for the barefoot doctors attended to both scientific and political goals. It began by stressing two cardinal public health principles: a hygienic environment and safe water. It also directed doctors to spread and implement the principles and policies for health work formulated by the state; to put prevention first, promoting patriotic public health campaigns aimed at eliminating the four pests (flies, mosquitos, rats, and bedbugs) and bringing diseases under control, providing technical guidance over the disposal of sewage water and night soil and the maintenance of wells, toilets, livestock pens, cooking stoves, and the environment; to perform preventive inoculations; to report on the epidemic situation and control infectious disease; to offer preliminary medical treatment and first aid, and refer difficult cases to hospitals; to provide professional guidance and sponsor training courses for health workers and midwives and to spread health information; to offer advice on maternity, child care and family planning; and to gather statistics and make reports on local health conditions (Chen and Zhu 1984: 113).

The PRC's medical strategies intended to combine the best of the political processes envisioned for a communist society with the best techniques of biomedicine. During some campaigns of the Cultural Revolution (beginning in 1966), however, high-technology orientations became an object of scorn, and so the basic essentials of scientific medical intervention were recast in a framework that made national medical traditions appropriate for health care in the Chinese countryside. The barefoot doctors were political by design; that was a prerequisite for their recruitment and their mandate. The barefoot doctors were intended to serve as a political instrument for consolidating communist power at a time of great medical flux, particularly during the Cultural Revolution when the quality of medical expertise fell into decline as a result of campaigns to support "Red" versus "Expert" knowledge in the countryside. Their health agendas were aimed at convincing people of the political underpinnings of health and the benefits of following a Maoist agenda to achieve it. One writer describes the orientation this way: "In China health behavior is more accurately described as health conduct. The older connotation . . . of 'conduct,' meaning moral behavior, is appropriate here because health acts are 'political.' For China and the 'New Man'[2] no act is devoid of political factors, which define the purposes and direction of the society. Thus health conduct is moral conduct laced together by the cognition, ideologies, actions, and spirit of the socialist state and of the socialist citizen"(Chen, cited in New and New 1977: 510). We also learn that China shared this approach with other communist countries: "China and Cuba . . . made conscious efforts to radically alter the health structure by infusing political ideologies into health care" (New and New 1977: 504).

The admixture of politics and medicine in the barefoot-doctor model was not considered problematic by many international agencies in the postwar period. In fact, the impact of the reported success of the Chinese system was to be felt throughout multilateral agencies such as WHO and UNICEF for decades to come. James P. Grant, executive director of UNICEF, in his opening address to a WHO interregional seminar on primary health care in 1983 in Geneva, explained this impact as follows (WHO 1983: 10):

> Above all, the Chinese barefoot doctor system, which began using the approach adopted by WHO and UNICEF in 1978 of health for all by the year 2000, was begun in China in the 1950s. . . . The first factor was a change in the direction and dynamics of the government and the people, a change which manifested itself in the confidence that age-old problems of poverty, starvation, illiteracy, and ill-health could be resolved; and that the responsibility of organized society was to bring the good life to all its people, with particular attention to the vast and neglected rural population. In the vocabulary that has grown up around the primary health care movement, this change of spirit has come to be called "national political will," a serious commitment at the highest level in government to the social goal of health for all. This will has been evident in China since the early 1950s.

However desirable the marriage between politics and medicine among barefoot doctors seemed to international aid and multilateral agency leaders, these public health medical orientations, as we have seen, were divested of their specific political orientations in WHO and UNICEF practice because of the latters' need to dissociate themselves from communist ideology. By turning political orientations into a neutral "technical" category based on scientific knowledge, they could be shed of their associations with contested power and ideology. Rather than seeing a medical commitment to politics as advancing totalitarianism, these metropole agencies were able to promote political involvement as an instrument that was like their vision of democracy – neutral because it served a higher, natural, and objective truth. This approach reiterates Virchow's view of the "good" medical scientist who is able to advance medicine for the sake of democracy and democracy (for him the republic) for the sake of medical health. But this view fails to acknowledge the possibility that a politicized medicine might serve *any* political regime, not only democratic ones, simply by the fact that it is a political instrument. Moreover, in becoming politicized, medical truths themselves run the risk of being perceived as politically motivated.

When Sir Douglas Black, Professor J. N. Morris, Dr. Cyril Smith, and Professor Peter Townsend wrote *The Black Report* in 1980 under the Department of Health in Britain, they noted that political bias was built into medical truths. The report was submitted to the Secretary of State but thereafter suppressed, and as a result it received a great deal of public attention. The burden of the report was that there were enormous regional, class, and sex inequalities in health care and the overall health of the British population that had not been recognized by the National Health Service and that the government should have been investing far more money in health care. At a time when welfare was being cut, affecting vital systems of health care and shifting much of the health burden to the private sector, *The Black Report* revealed that inequalities would only be exacerbated under a non-nationalized system. They argued that money should be reallocated to attend to more basic preventive social medicine to affect the living and working conditions of the poor. The authors of *The Black Report* invoked Henry Sigerist, who (following Virchow) argued that promoting health was a social act and medicine basically a social science (Townsend et al. 1982: 45). They also pointed to the WHO's concept of health as more than merely the absence of disease or infirmity, a more comprehensive state of being than the concept being employed in the medical professions.

The report politicized medicine in a manner consistent with the practice of many of the world's mainstream public health agencies. What was perhaps slightly bolder about it, however, was the way in which it transposed not simply medical priorities but medical concepts of disease and health on to a political field. If economic class is brought under the rubric of the medical profession, then prescribing drug therapies for ill health that is produced by socio-economic conditions becomes "band-aid medicine," treating the symptoms rather than the causes. The implication of this stance is that practitioners would have to be either ignorant of the realities affecting their clientele or willingly engaging in a politics of obscurantism. *The Black Report* falls into the same tradition as the critical materialist medical writing of the 1970s such as that of Vicente Navarro and Ivan Illich.[3]

A politicized medicine like that in *The Black Report* advocates politics as a medical intervention. But a politicized medicine that achieves its goal also requires the inverse postulate and its concealment: a medical science that is a product of politics or political interests cannot risk the appearance that its medical facts are no more than political inventions. For example, if ill health is caused by social inequality and political reforms are required to end social inequality, then effective political reforms will at some point claim poverty as a *disease* not as a *social* problem. *The Black Report* called for political processes that would restructure health care in order eventually to restructure the distribution of health and disease in society. A political system which is sensitive to the medical needs of its citizenry will, by definition, attend to the structure and allocation of medical resources and the practices of medical science overall. But this arrangement reveals the thorny side of the relationship between politics and medical science: When does the idea of medical truth itself become compromised by the visibility of its political underpinnings? If *The Black Report* contended that medical facts could be produced by political conditions, then how did they defend themselves against claims that their own medical facts were not also produced in this way? I return to Virchow to pursue this issue.

Virchow was, by the standards of his day, an advocate of a materialist and mechanistic reading of anatomy and the causes of its disorders. He was reductionistic in his approach to the cell, especially his idea that the cell was the fundamental unit of society. All disease, he believed, arose from cellular pathologies, even when those pathologies might be caused by social or economic deprivation. Again, his understanding of the relationship between science and socio-political structure was not metaphoric: for him "history proceeded according to laws as precise as those governing the natural sciences; he saw it moving in the direction of greater personal freedom" (Boyd 1991: 30). The task of the scientist was therefore to ascertain the laws of nature, visible in history itself, by which this progress was made. The scientist who could grasp these laws would then be able to apply them to the improvement of the human condition through politics. Thus, for Virchow, medical attempts to restore the health of individual patients were analogous to the politician's ability to heal a diseased society. The physician scientist could do both.

Politics, for Virchow, was not simply about governing; it was about finding a scientific method of organizing society so that it followed laws of nature rather than violating them. By the same token, medicine was not simply about scientific healing; it was about finding a politics that suited the natural optimal functioning of the individual. The relationship of cause and effect went both ways: good medical science made good politics and good politics made good medical science: "Anyone committed to the goal of sweeping away prejudice and superstition in order to establish medicine on a basis of scientific laws must, through application of the same cast of mind, desire to remove political power from the hands of the

privileged hereditary ruling classes and place it in the hands of the people.
. . . It was the duty of the state to guarantee to all its citizens the right to a
healthy existence; a state that failed in this respect had sacrificed its claim
to their allegiance" (Boyd 1991: 36).

Everett Mendelsohn has noted that Virchow's orientations towards
politics and science were shared by other scientific intellectuals of his
time. Virchow wrote nearly one hundred years after Boyle at a time when
the idea of an experimental science had matured into that of a "pure
science." His position did not challenge Boyle's notion of objectivity; it
presupposed it and then went on to demand that such objectivity be put
to good political uses. Science was at its best, Virchow felt, when it was
invested in social causes and derived from social interests. He "challenged the philosophical confusions which he saw in his day, a confusion
[which could be listed in a single phrase:] 'Science for its own sake.' 'It
certainly does not detract from the dignity of science,' he wrote, 'to come
down off its pedestal and mingle with the people, and from the people
science gains new strength'"(Mendelsohn 1974: 413).

Virchow maintained that the best science would be democratic – grown
from the people and their needs. At the same time, he argued, resting his
case indirectly on a hundred years of tacit cultural assumptions framing
his own research, that scientific methods could produce objective truths
about the optimal political "organism." Such truths would not be arbitrary, nor would they be fashioned according to the political whims of the
day. On the contrary, they would be fashioned after the sort of polity that
observed the scientific laws of nature. Nature, by the logic of the experimental conditions under which it was uncovered, could be the model for
this polity. In order to be useful, then, it would have to apply itself to
society and derive its data from that society according to the rules of
science.

Pure science was for Virchow juxtaposed to applied science. But the
knowledge derived from science was never, in his mind, corrupted by
applied concerns. It was made more "pure" by being applied to social and
political concerns. This, I venture, would strike some observers as problematic. For many people who are raised in cultures of science, the distinction between pure and applied science is an important, if not sacred,
distinction. Applied science is distinguished from pure science by the
applied interests which support it. Often such interests are seen as
influencing the scientific work by limiting or otherwise arbitrating the
parameters of inquiry and even, in some cases, the results by the same
pathway. Pure science, in contrast, is believed capable of offering more
accurate truths because it does not run the risk of being influenced by
applied concerns and interests. It is driven in its questions and results

only by its own concerns. Again, this idea of pure science takes us in some sense back to the experimental space of Robert Boyle in the mid-seventeenth century, to the idea that laboratory science could produce truths unrelated to the social or political conditions of their production. Today these conditions include concerns over funding, not simply social and political interests for the validation of one "fact" over another.

But should the distinction between pure science and a socially engaged science even be taken seriously when the science under discussion is medicine?[4] Medicine is often juxtaposed to pure science because of its very definition as a humanistic science. In fact, for most of those who practice medicine, although political concerns and cultural ideologies may become involved in the application of medical truths, they do not constitute its truths. Medical practitioners and researchers the world over tend to hold that whereas politics and social processes may be usefully attended to with the help of medical facts, those facts are themselves objective. A pure science of medicine thus always has applied intentions and sometimes they demand political action. In fact, Virchow's politicization of medicine, like that of politically active medical professionals in Nepal, merges two insights: (1) that medicine must become political to eradicate the causes of ill health and (2) that medically scientific truths are usually formulated in contested political contexts. Those who have worked under conditions of repression know very well how truths can be repressed until more favorable political circumstances make them visible. Beyond this, there are those who recognize that the very truths which are sought out and made visible are themselves politically constituted. The fact that one truth prevails over another has as much to do with politics as with objective criteria. Virchow and Nepali medical professionals argued that recognition of these insights about medical truths makes them more valid and objective, not less. Once grasped in this way, however, medical truths immediately become vulnerable to accusations of being political and false as opposed to objective, rather than being objective *because* political. How can politics be both the application which corrupts truth's validity and that which establishes truth's utility?

The idea that social and political circumstances play a significant role in constructing the "factualness" of medical truths is not new, and related, I would say, to questions about the political construction of medical facts. Certainly the claim that medicine is by definition an applied science is a starting point for this idea, but even before the distinction was made between pure and applied science, philosophers of a "scientific" mind thought about medicine, the body, and health in terms of cultural models of the social. Exploring debates about the social construction of medical facts may shed light on debates about the political constitution of medical truths. Virchow's metaphorical notions of the democratic cell-state, for example, were consistent with a long line of nineteenth-century (and earlier) thinkers who "imaged" biology through metaphors of society – that is, whose medical "facts" were constructed in terms of preexisting cultural idioms.

Biological truths reflect cultural predispositions, but they are naturalized into forms taken to be objective and "pre-culturally" real. According to Oswei Temkin (1949: 170–72), this trend is quite old:

> When we speak of an organism we think of a natural object where all parts function so as to maintain the existence of the whole. Now this biological order also seems applicable to human society, as is expressed in the old parable by which Menenius Agrippa is said to have brought back the revolting plebeians from the Mons Sacer, where they had seceded in 494 B.C. Jealous of the stomach that received all the good things for which they had to work, some other organs of the body decided to go on strike. But, as a result, they too starved until they finally recognized that the stomach was as important to them as they to the stomach, and that in order to exist the body needed the proper service of each part. The moral of this story was obvious. The stomach is the patrician caste, the other parts are the plebeians, the body as a whole is the Roman state.
>
> The political theory of the Greeks [that of the pre-Socratic philosopher Alcmaeon] described disease as a "monarchy" of any one of the qualities. Some six hundred years later, the Greek city-state had lost its freedom. The Roman Empire ruled the world not only by its armies but also by its laws expressed in the maxim: To each his own. This did not imply everyone's having equal claims; rather, it meant that everybody ought to share according to his rank. In the second century Galen, the last of the ancient anatomists and experimental physiologists, used this concept of justice again and again to make the anatomy of the human body understandable. The various parts of the body differ in size: this is only just, because nature has apportioned their size to the usefulness of their functions. Some parts have few nerves: this too is just, for they do not need much sensitiveness. As we shall see later, the comparison with a social organism was not Galen's main biological metaphor. Nevertheless he found the concept of social justice valuable just as he used the simile of the food supply of a city for explaining the function and name of the veins of the portal system, which carried chyle to the liver just as many routes carried food to the city's bakeries.

Virchow's theory of the cell-state also reveals the cultural underpinnings of medical facts, this time in a model that unites cell with society through the concept of the organism. The metaphors we live by enter into and configure our understanding of the natural world around us; Mary Douglas (1970) noted that we think nature through culture. But what if we take seriously the claim that the organism for Virchow, according to

Temkin, was to be taken not simply as a metaphor, but as a biological "fact"? The living organism, he argued, "is a free state of individuals with equal rights though not with equal endowments, which keeps together because the individuals are dependent upon one another and because there are certain centers of organization without whose integrity the single parts cannot receive their necessary supply of healthful nourishing material" (Temkin 1949: 175). We would be hard-pressed not to see this reading of biology as in some sense metaphorical today. The cultural scripts of his time found their way into his conceptualization of the natural world, so that we could say he viewed the relationship metaphorically.

Virchow sheds light on the problem of the relationship between politics and medical science, for by claiming that pure science is problematic he is able to incorporate into an objectivist stance the idea that even truths produced from explicit social agendas can stand for objective, scientific truths. He suggests that what come to stand for "matters of fact" in any science are in fact matters of social negotiation and politics, but acknowledging this makes them all the more "factual" (*pace* Harding 1994). Put otherwise, revealing the sociopolitical contingencies of matters of fact in medical science does not undermine their objective validity.

Ludwig Fleck approached this problem of a transcendent objectivity in science in a manner different from Virchow. In his 1935 book *The Genesis and Development of a Scientific Fact*, he foreshadowed the work of some contemporary scholars of science and technology.[5] He argued that scientific facts emerge as products of "thought collectives." Facts are "distinguished from transient theories as something definite, permanent and independent of any subjective interpretation by the scientist" (Fleck 1935: xxvii), and yet they are also always derived from pre-scientific notions via theories formulated from shared knowledge that is historically and culturally contingent. This inquiry did not lend greater credibility to an objectivist position, but it did raise questions about the possibilities of an entirely transcendent scientific stance.

Thought collectives are, I believe, best considered as constellations of cultural, political, and social conditions and ideas that both allow for creativity and constrain innovation. The workings of the thought collective are, from a Durkheimian perspective, like those of social facts: "The explanation given to any relation survives and develops within a given society only if this explanation is stylized in conformity with the prevailing thought style" (Fleck 1935: 2). As did Durkheim, Fleck used the analogy of the mob which compels the individuals who make it up to act in ways they would never consider alone. He argued that once a structurally complete and closed system of opinions has been formed, it offers constant resistance to anything that contradicts it: (1) a contradiction to the system appears to be unthinkable; (2) what does not fit the system remains unseen; (3) alternatively, if it is noticed, either it is kept secret; or (4) laborious efforts are made to explain an exception in terms that do not contradict the system; (5) and despite the legitimate claims of contradictory views, one tends to see, describe, or even illustrate those circumstances which corroborate current views and thereby give them substance. Thomas Kuhn (1962) would later explain how, even with this conservatism, paradigm change is the norm in science.

The cultural character of the thought collective is, according to Fleck, one in which every age will have its own conceptions, including remnants of past ones and rudiments of those of the future. Fleck argued that this inscription of cultural forms on scientific facts is not simply ideological, for the thought collective is embedded in social structure, including political and social relations out of which are produced scientific facts. Inscription processes include those familiar to the technologies of science, which ensure that certain questions will be pursued while others will not in the construction of and techniques for uncovering truth. These are like the "technophenomena" that Gaston Bachelard (1934) identifies to describe the material formations within which scientific ideas and truths are both formulated and brought into permanent material and social existence.

One of the routes by which conventional knowledge finds its way into scientific thought is via what Fleck calls vademecum or "handbook" science. Expert science is made up of the combined workings of journal science and vademecum science. Whereas journal science is filled with highly technical descriptions, indefinites, and inconclusive and sometimes contradictory results, vademecum science is used in teaching manuals, and public fora and as a means of achieving consensus among scientists. It is in vademecum science that one finds remnants of pre-scientific cultural thought (Fleck 1935: 119, 121):

> It governs the decision on what counts as a basic concept, what methods should be accepted, which research directions appear most promising, which scientists should be selected for prominent positions and which should simply be consigned to oblivion. . . .
>
> Let me give an example. The etiological concept of disease entity is not derived directly from individual contributions to the journals. Emerging originally from exoteric or popular ideas and from ideas formed outside the collective in question, it gradually acquired its present significance in the esoteric communication of thought and now forms one of the basic concepts of vademecum bacteriology. . . . But once part of the vademecum, it is taught and generally used. It forms the keystone of the system and thus exerts a constraint on thinking.

Unlike popular science writing, vademecum science is a crucial part of expert science itself. Fleck's primary example of the way in which society and culture are embedded in scientific facts is the evolution of syphilis and the creation of modern theories of bacterial infection via the Wassermann test. Syphilis was initially called a carnal scourge, and along with most diseases in the Middle Ages, it was believed to be caused by demons that infected the blood. The notion of "bad blood" or "change in the blood" was associated with theories of humoral pathology; it was held, for example, that melancholic blood, "because it is infected with a noxious property, is not properly transformed into a nourishing substance" (Fleck 1935:11). The assumption that blood was the site of pathology convinced researchers that they should be working on a blood test for syphilis. Such a test would satisfy the presence of a moralistic concern that syphilitics had "impure" or "befouled blood."

The Wassermann test was initially an attempt to find a reaction with mercury mixed with blood of the syphilitic because mercury treatments were used on other skin lesion patients (although it did not improve syphilitic rashes). Eventually, Wasserman and others developed a method for producing a reaction based on antigen presence, but even here, initially, the reaction occurred only 15–20 percent of the time in cases of confirmed syphilis. In fact, researchers found that blood tests produced the same reactions in healthy individuals. Nevertheless, the viability of a blood screening method was already accepted by the thought collective. From its initially poor results to the final test, which showed 70–90 percent accuracy, the scientists engaged in a detailed and painstaking refinement of the test procedures. "The optimum intermediate position between minimum nonspecificity and maximum sensitivity had to be gradually established. This, however, is entirely the work of a collective consisting of mostly anonymous research workers, adding now 'a little more,' now 'a little less' of a reagent, allowing now 'a little longer,' now 'a little shorter' reaction time, or reading the result 'a little more' or 'a little less' accurately"(Fleck 1935: 73).

Eventually, the refinement process produced the appropriate equation. The point, though, is that the circumstances for the production of that particular equation had to be produced first. The equation, in some sense, had to already exist as an idea in order for it to be "discovered." The issue has not to do with the validity of the test for ascertaining the presence of the disease (nor with the truth of the disease), but with the inevitably culturally constructed character of them. Fleck notes that Wassermann's assumptions about the diagnostic factor were largely wrong, according to later scientific theories of how the test worked. It was largely an accident that, beginning with his assumptions, he was able to come up with a "viable and reliable" test. But, Fleck notes, Wassermann found his reaction not by chance but because he looked for it, proceeding quite systematically, naturally on the basis of the then current knowledge (Fleck 1935: 75). He was looking for a syphilis substance (not an antibody) and indirectly produced a test that would work to distinguish syphilitic "blood" (Fleck 1935: 73, 77):

> Collective experience thus operated in all fields related to the Wassermann reaction until, with disregard for theoretical questions and the ideas of individuals, the reaction became useful. But this rewarding and tedious work of the collective was carried out only as a consequence of the special social importance of the syphilis question and of the problem regarding change in the syphilitic blood. . . . Had it not been for the insistent clamor of public opinion for a blood test, the experiments of Wassermann would never have enjoyed the social response that was absolutely essential to the development of the reaction, to its "technical perfection," and to the gathering of collective experience.

The idea that the blood is the site of syphilis has long prevailed in medical inquiry, precluding investigation into numerous other locales of the body or society which might have been considered (constructed as) the causes of syphilis or identified as likely sites for its manifestation in the body. Blood tests which reveal a syphilitic agent may be correlated with the disease, as are potentially many other factors. What makes the blood the site of its pathogenesis is largely the theories current in the thought collective of this nineteenth-century European community. Thus, Fleck's work makes a case for the idea that medical "facts" about diseases and their diagnosis, treatments, and cures are not simply examples of human apprehension and management of a raw and objective nature but rather instances of the apprehension and management of a nature already constituted through culture. In the case of syphilis the collective encompassed socio-political relations between nations and between groups of people. It reiterated political relations among those who took it upon themselves to distinguish between the "pure" and the "impure," notably anticipating a twentieth-century focus on blood as "breed," a rising nationalism in Europe, and eventually a Nazi politics of fascism.[6]

If medical facts are constituted within a field of contested social relations and these relations find their way into any construction of the facts, how could biomedical professionals claim, as the Nepalis did during the revolution, that the truth was "on their side" without realizing the dangers of such a claim? Panchayati truths were arbitrary, in that they were often invented to serve the interests of corrupt palace and panchayat elites. Surely one could say in this instance that the truth was on their side too. But the truths of the medical professionals were thought to be different

from those of the regime because they were objective. Politicizing medicine did not necessarily expose medical truths as culturally or politically
constructed; on the contrary, politicizing medicine involved taking objective medical truths and putting them to work through politics.

Politicizing medicine can, however, lead to a fundamental skepticism
about the validity of medical facts because such actions bring the visibility
of cultural and political "constructedness" (bias) to the surface. Again, in
the case of Costa Rica described by Morgan (1993), community
participation strategies designed to improve health care by involving
recipients in the planning, promotion, and care-giving activities of
primary care ended up also arousing political participation. Planners
failed to acknowledge that local and national governments were themselves sites of contestation for power among differing interest and political groups. Once the politicization of primary care had occurred under
the call for "political will," the ability for this strategy to work as health
intervention was compromised by the pre-existing conflict between political parties. If community health was on the platform for one party, its
programs were abandoned by the opposing parties once they came to
power. In one sense, what can be seen in this case is that politicizing medicine had the effect of making the utility of community participation seem
like an arbitrated and negotiated "truth." The case reveals two levels of
skepticism: doubt of the objective characterization of health problems
and doubt of the strategies promoted to solve them. What was promoted
as a medical "fact" by the international aid community – that community
participation is required for better health – became seen as a politically
constructed truth once it was absorbed into a political platform. At a
more critical level, the risk in politicizing medicine is not simply that
policy and strategy may become contested but that ideas about pathologies – the causes of suffering, the nature of diseases – themselves may be
placed in contested terrain.

It is hard to imagine any public health strategy not being a topic for political debate. Consider the parallels between the 1832 cholera epidemic in
England (Morris 1976) and the case of AIDS in the United States in the
1990s. When cholera first emerged as a disease that was largely affecting
the poor, public bans were posted alerting people to the dangers of the
drinking water. Legislation to improve the welfare of the poor was being
debated in Parliament at the time, and the poor first interpreted the bans to
mean that the wealthy who opposed the proposed poor laws wanted to be
rid of them and were therefore poisoning their drinking water. Some
believed that cholera had been invented as a diversionary tactic by opponents of the poor laws but did not actually exist. When public health
officials forbade public funerals as a means of containing the spread of the

disease by limiting access to the corpses, again the poor interpreted this as a tactic against them. They believed that by preventing funeral marches and watches over the deceased at the cemeteries, the elite could confiscate the bodies of their deceased loved ones for use in medical autopsies and research. The case has more recent parallels. Initially, popular and mostly apocryphal theories about AIDS deaths in the United States in the early 1980s included the idea that it was a disease invented by the CIA and that the lackadaisical response by the Reagan administration reflected his genocidal attitudes towards those who had it. Even after it was widely acknowledged that HIV was a cause, public health measures to stem its spread were hotly contested. Attempts on the part of public health officials to distribute sterile needles to the illegal-drug-using community of New York City, for example, were loudly criticized by members of Latino communities, who claimed that clean-needle programs would hasten the death of large numbers of Latino drug addicts, again, a form of genocide.

The point here is not that medical truths are arbitrary but that medical truths are never formed outside of a socio-political field of relations wherein people vie for power in the form of authoritative truth. When certain truths do take hold and are accepted as objective the act of politicizing their delivery can have the unintended effect of making truth itself appear to be arbitrarily manufactured for the benefit of the political interests behind them. Politicizing truths makes them seem more visibly socially constructed. While it is easy to argue with critics in the above cases (the poor, these activist Latinos) and to make the case that they are simply wrong about the medical truth of cholera or HIV/AIDS and its modes of transmission, it is less easy to see where truth lies when debates over, for example, funding of research are made visible. If virologists vie with immunologists over control of AIDS research funding and virologists win the day, what sorts of research questions are effaced by this fact (e.g. are magic bullet searches for "vaccines" for HIV pursued while research on multicausal models of cofactors triggering full blown AIDS is sidelined?) (Patton 1990). One interpretation of making such sorts of debates visible is that the possibility of being able to see the politically and culturally constructed nature of medical facts is not a result of a corruption of good science, when politicized, but an inevitable artefact of it.

A final example of the politicization of medicine comes from the Vietnam War. Marine Corps physicians were recruited to deliver care not only to wounded US soldiers in Vietnam but also to the Vietnamese (3D Marine Division 1968, Stolfi 1968). Medical personnel joined this mission not simply because they believed in "the cause" but because they believed that as physicians, nurses, and aides they would be able to help suffering persons. Their medical services were used as political instruments, however, precisely because officials and health profession-als alike maintained a belief in the apolitical character of their services. The Marines opened a Children's Hospital (later an orphanage) at Dong Ha, some twelve miles from the demilitarized zone. This location, it was assumed, would have the effect of using the medical infrastructure as a shield against incursions from Viet Cong because it was assumed that medical personnel would be seen not as political personnel but as tech-nical, professional personnel on a humanitarian mission. (The boiler-plate case of this is the Swiss Red Cross, which has been able to accomplish its goals by promoting this view of humanitarian neutrality for decades.)

Medical teams were also sent by the Navy to villages in Project HAND-CLASP (begun in 1963). This was designed as "part of the Navy's people-to-people effort and overseas community relations program" (Stolfi 1968: 73). They brought clothing, food, pens, soap, vitamins, worm pills, sewing needles, thread, salt, books, and other medical sup-plies to villagers in an effort to win over the villagers to support the Government of Vietnam. By March 1966, however, the tenor of the program had changed (Stolfi 1968:75) making the political goals more obvious:

> County Fair was a joint Marine Corps/ARVN operation designed to destroy Viet Cong influence in chosen hamlets and to re-establish the authority of the GVN (Government of Vietnam). Marine Corps units provided security during the County Fair operations by cordoning off chosen hamlets with riflemen alert for a possible break-out by Viet Cong guerilla fighters. . . . ARVN forces and GVN political workers then entered the cordoned area and moved all of the villagers to a central area where they were interrogated, processed for identification, fed, and exposed to propaganda lectures, drama presentations and movies. While this combined military and civic action was being carried out, ARVN forces conducted a detailed search of the hamlet for hidden tunnels, food, munitions, and hiding Viet Cong.

Medical interventions were routinely carried out as part of the County Fair program. One Marine physician communicated that he remembered cases of physicians arriving with soldiers to perform surgery for villagers while the soldiers interrogated village headmen for information about Viet Cong activity. Among participants, it was felt that these activities "impressed the villagers with the power, efficiency, and benevolence of the GVN. The operations in their refined form were a traumatic surprise to the Viet Cong, who emphasized in captured documents the necessity to take immediate countermeasures against the new technique" (Stolfi 1968: 75).

The ability to use medical interventions as an instrument for health and as a political weapon is obvious in this case. The irony of this use of medicine, however, is that it both presupposes the necessity of thinking of medical practices as scientific and therefore "objective" (i.e. the belief that villagers would see that antibiotics and surgery work not because of the political rubric under which they were introduced but because of their scientific bases; why else would the villagers be impressed?) and at the same time as a useful political tool. A politicized medicine does not necessarily compromise its claims to truth among those who deliver its services, but recipients may view interventions not simply as scientific techniques but as politically contingent truths, the validity and utility of which are dependent upon political consensus. Hence the reported response of Vietcong countermeasures against the "new techniques." As a hermeneutical instrument, I remind readers of the account depicted in the phantasmagorical film *Apocalypse Now* (Copolla) in which Colonel Kurtz describes his conceptual turning point that enabled him to "win" his battles against the Vietcong by internalizing their techniques of terror. It was the discovery that Vietcong village leaders had lopped off the arms of all the children whom his US squadrons had vaccinated the day before. Although of quasi-fictional provenance, we might consider the message the story suggests: when life and death are the outcomes in the political uses of medicine, who is to say where truth lies? At what point can we suggest that villagers' belief in the utility of vaccinations is seriously compromised by the fact that its consequence is an amputated limb? At what point are we forced to acknowledge that the politicizing of medicine renders medical truths vulnerable to opposing political versions of truth?

The Nepali doctors managed to place themselves, because of their particular historical, cultural, and social circumstances, in the scientific positions of Virchow and Fleck and, perhaps – although clearly with different outcomes – the US Marine physicians. Medical practices were deliberately politicized for the sake of promoting a form of health care that was more neutral, fair, objective, and scientific – in a word, "democratic." At the same time, I return now to a description of how their use of medicine as a political weapon left them vulnerable to some critiques that they had politicized truth. The political processes in which medicine came to participate made medicine seem to some observers antithetical to good science, as promoting truths based not on neutral and technical universalist principles but on the *partisan* interests of those who promoted them. When social, personal, or collective interests become visible in medical practices, are these a sign of a politically invested objective medical science, Nepali-style, or are they a sign of corrupted medical science?

7 Post-revolutionary political medicine: corruption or validation of truth?

Doctors involved in the Community Medicine program at Teaching Hospital responded to the call for a politically active medicine. This medicine would combine the best of a socially conscientized political activism with the highest possible standards of scientific medicine. Writing on the role of the Institute of Medicine in health system development in Nepal, Dr. M. Maskey et al. (1994) described this in a discussion of "excellence" in primary health care:

> The experiences of some medical colleges which have assumed the responsibility for health care of the population of defined geographical area, and thus exposing their students to an extensive range of health and socio-economic problems, were emphasized and highlighted in the report [from the Edinburgh Declaration of the World Federation for Medical Education in 1988], despite resistance from some corners with the slogan "for standards of excellence." The sixth theme of the declaration emphatically stated: . . . "such exposure to the actual health needs of the community is likely to influence fundamentally the curriculum of a medical school and is sometimes resisted for fear that it will detract from the standard of excellence of scientific medicine. But in the words of the Alma Ata Declaration the highest standard of medical education for any country is that which is most responsive to local needs."

If the mandate in primary health care was that rural community development, with its emphasis on social action, take precedence over hospital-based curative care, with its emphasis on scientific research and technology, Maskey was not entirely in agreement (1991: 99–100):

> In the evolution of health services, hospital-based and community-based services came into being out of necessity and served the society they intended to reach. But later development of hospitals was often associated with increased glamorization and sophisticated care and a mystification of medicine. Hospitals came to represent the main concentration of health resources, professional skills and medical equipment, but at the same time the hospital also became more divorced from community health services. These came to be looked upon as separate entities and as rivals. This . . . is a false antithesis. . . .

Primary health care doesn't simply mean community health services or primary medical care in the conventional sense. It can be looked at in several different ways:

–as a range of programmes adapted to patterns of health and disease of people living in a particular setting;

–as a level of care (exact definition depending upon the country concerned) backed up by a well organized referral system;

–as a strategy for reorienting the health system in order to provide the whole population with effective essential care and to promote individual and community involvement and intersectoral collaboration;

–as a philosophy based on the principle of social equity, self-reliance and community development.

Maskey suggests that the allocation of health resources in a poor country like Nepal should be equally attentive to the rural community and the creation of extensive resources for curative hospital care. For him hospitals offer the best of scientific practice, but the standards of care there should also be applied to rural community care. In both places attention to local patterns of health and disease as well as social conditions producing them should be foci. Primary health care does not compromise the "excellence" of curative scientific standards: on the contrary, it demands it. He is particularly keen to translate international agendas into plans that make sense for Nepal. In the same way, he identifies both sites for care as places where political conscientiousness should play an important role. His training under Dr. Mathura Shrestha is evident here. Dr. Mathura argued that the best medicine would be found in a society wherein people were politically aware and educated in order to empower themselves politically, even to be skeptical of medical practitioners. Arguably, the tactic of both doctors is thoroughly modern in that they want to both hold truth as above social contingency and yet reinsert political consciousness into the process of using that truth. Truth not only could but *must* stand above social contingency because it provides a basis for impartial decision-making. But truth which could not be used for political purposes would not ultimately serve "the people." Their approach raises the question: if pre-revolutionary Nepal was characterized by partiality, repression, and persistent use of social connections and if the "modern" invoked to counteract this situation was associated with abstract principles, standardized rules, equality, development, meritocratic procedures, and impartial institutions associated with individuals, then what happened when political interests were visibly rejoined to medical sciences under a multiparty democratic modernity?

Three years into their democracy, Nepali health professionals were rejoicing in the fruits of their hard-earned political efforts. With fewer government regulations great numbers of medical non-governmental organizations (NGOs) were begun with the intention of providing better health care to a wider audience than had hitherto been effectively served. Political parties were highly visible and seemed to, at least rhetorically, attend to the needs of local populations over the needs and demands of the palace. More students than ever were enrolling in medical education programs. Innovative health programs between Nepalis and foreign donors were starting to emerge. At the same time, some were having difficulty negotiating a politicization of medicine without compromising their claims to impartiality as held by their profession. As we have seen, medical professionals invoked scientific truth to establish the legitimacy of their political struggle. They argued that violations of human rights, social inequality, and lack of political freedom could be sources of ill health and that these violations arose from government corruption. Corruption had led to a situation in which only a privileged few benefited while the masses suffered. So opposing corruption had thus meant practicing a medicine that was politically and socially aware of its outcomes and uses, ensuring that it did not benefit only the elite. But ultimately, a politically conscientious medicine was hard to distinguish from a medicine corrupted by favoritist politics. Initially, corruption served the privileged few by using favoritism, familism, and partiality, while scientific medicine served the masses. But both entailed awareness of the political and social interests behind and benefiting one's medical resources and one's truths. In post-revolutionary Nepal, political parties had become legal and so they were increasingly seen as a new locus for corruption. Social affiliations through parties were now used to obtain privileges serving specific individual, social, *or political* goals.

A politics of affiliation persisted in post-revolutionary Nepal, ensuring that partiality was still an operative mode for social life, even if organized around parties. Instead of being based only on family, caste, or *aphno manche* groups, affiliations were now also based on profession, party, class, and even a reified notion of ethnic group. At the same time, such affiliations became seen as new bases for obtaining *aphno manche* advantage. That Nepalis called a politics of affiliation corrupt may seem ironic since in most democratic nations the idea of party favoritism is commonly held as an inevitable outcome of a well-functioning democracy, not a corruption of it. But many Nepalis viewed party favoritism as the same kind of corruption that existed in pre-revolutionary Nepal. Because social affiliations became labeled as corruption and were rejected by revolutionary action, even politics that worked through networks of social affiliation became seen as corrupt and therefore to be avoided in post-revolutionary

Nepal. The question confronting many Nepali biomedical professionals in 1993 was therefore whether politicizing medicine only tied it to new forms of corruption expressed as the privileging of one interest group over another.

Fears that a politicized medicine would corrupt not only professional authority but also the very basis for democracy were expressed to me by Dr. M. D. As a physician he was concerned that medical professionals were allowing their political party interests to affect their professional judgment; political interests were for him the same as personal interests:

Two years ago [1991], I wrote up a little flyer. You see, I was so disturbed with our so-called intellectuals behaving just like prostitutes, prepared to go with any idea for their own gain. After the revolution was over, I found our professionals were behaving just as before. If just in the heat of the moment everybody behaved well, but after the heat was over the government came in and they began to go after ministers to get this post or that post through the same way as before, using aphno manche and all this corruption. Then, the revolution was for nothing. So, I wrote this, and I distributed it to different parts of Nepal. I distributed it to members of parliament, standing in parliament. I sent my mandate to distribute to all of the members. One or two items I just want to tell you are these:

"7. When the progress and development of our country are shaken, let us all intellectuals keep aside our personal interests and political impressions for the time being and fulfill our responsibility to direct the country toward the right path, by giving out opinions and suggestions without any fear, and by marking out to the people that what is right is right and what is wrong is wrong.

8. Let us all Nepali people fulfill the responsibility of our respective professional areas of expertise for the development of our country, through the implementation of individual skill and capacity with full enthusiasm. Nothing will be impossible to accomplish for the Nepali people provided that we cooperate with each other, remain under discipline in every area and respect the dignity of one another, ignoring minor disputes but holding onto what is right. Therefore, we – all Nepalis – today have to dedicate our lives to the struggle for the progress of the nation so that our posterity may be happy and prosperous."

This is against the leftists and any politicians who are speaking certain things under their professional title for personal gains.

At the time of the revolution, the intellectuals were put on high pedestals. "Oh! The intellectuals have done it." But what I saw was that the intellectuals did do this at the heat of the moment, but thereafter they went back to their old ways. You understand, it was "Speak for the cause of the nation" during the revolution, but now it is "Anything for the cause of development." But intellectuals must forgo their political leanings. They must separate their political leanings from their personal gain. They must leave their politics for a certain moment. They must stay away from that. They must look at the issues in the proper, professional perspective and give their opinions based on their knowledge of their field and mould public opinion on that basis, but not to look at everything from your political party perspective. If you don't do this, then people will be led on the wrong path because of your self interest or your political leanings. Today, the doctors are not on a pedestal any more. They have fallen down. They are seen as being very mercenary. They have become mercenaries.

The fact that many Nepalis understand their medical practices in terms of party politics is partially a natural outgrowth of a political movement which all the more closely allied medicine to politics. But it is also a predictable outcome of the continuation of an encultured practice of everyday life that has always placed high priority on the socio-political consciousness of one's privilege (or lack thereof) in terms of social affiliations. Now that parties are legal, parties themselves are constituted in terms of the social affiliations that have always dominated as a mode of power in Nepal, and as medical practices continue to be tied to party politics, so too do they continue to be seen as opportunities for corruption. The risk of having politicized medicine was that practitioners and patients alike would come to see medicine as only serving political above medical purposes.

Charges like Dr. M. D.'s that doctors were prostituting themselves for specific political goals (whether for health or not) were based on the idea that some doctors had let their political interests guide their expertise or even become more important than their professional duties. This accusation was aimed at those physicians in government who had the ability to "shape" and design medical infrastructures in Nepal along specific partisan lines but also at the many clinical practitioners who advocated political positions which would give them more freedom, but also more ability to personally profit from clinical or other medical practices. But from the point of view of those whom he criticized, there was no corruption in their practices. Physicians in government who were setting health policy believed they were using medical truth to establish viable socially oriented medical policies. Also, clinicians who wanted private practices wanted this in order to work "freely," under no constraints but their professional standards of excellence. Particular debates over medical truth were now being debated in a multiparty political field, making party politics the influence that could corrupt truth for specific personal and political goals.

In fact many Nepalis perceived an ongoing politics of affiliation in the post-revolutionary period, as if the revolution had not changed much at all. This was made obvious to me in a conversation I had with two Kathmandu women at a sewing cooperative. R. U. was a student activist who had been involved in helping to organize protests for the revolutionary movement and D. V. was a housewife and mother of three. These women believed that good doctors were the ones who delivered care "democratically," equally to all, they said, but that in fact social connections still played an important role in health-care delivery. As D. V. put it:

The doctors did a lot of things for the Jan Andolan. They fought for democracy. But, compared to before the Jan Andolan, things have not changed much with the doctors. Before, they were afraid [of recrimination by the king], and that is why they were treating patients well, but only some patients got good care – only those who know the doctor – friends, relatives, same caste. Now, they are not afraid, and all in all they are still treating people well, but only if you know someone. If the doctor is related to you, or if you have somebody you know in the hospital, then they take good care. Otherwise, they are not taking good care . . . . I have taken my child during emergencies to Kanti Hospital, over the last two or three years. We were always taken by surprise. He would be playing and suddenly get a fever of 103 or so and faint. It would happen all of a sudden, and saliva would drip from his mouth. We took him to Kanti Hospital, because that is the children's hospital. And sometimes they would make us wait. I would shout at them, "Look at my child." But they didn't check him right away. Even when we told them we are scared and that our baby is very serious, they just tell us not to worry. They said everything would be all right. The doctors have good medicine, but sometimes they don't treat well. We have to push them, or we have to have a friend help us.

Many revolutionary doctors would agree with D. V.'s indictment. This sort of favoritism would seem to them a form of corruption that was fought against during the revolution. If continued, it would undermine their medical and professional credibility. But favoritism of an only slightly different sort was used by many of these same health professionals when they engaged in medical practices that were politicized, arguing for certain kinds of political processes and privileges which would benefit some persons over others. This elision of favoritism of individuals with favoritism of political party was partly a result of the problems of the new democracy which were the same as the problems of panchayat Nepal. A politics of affiliation was recast and was now indexed in perceptions of political freedom. If one did not have social connections to meet one's needs, then it was often perceived to be because the system was unfair and needed to be more "democratic" and "egalitarian." The same was true in the aftermath. Political freedom was thought to provide this sort of egalitarianism, because it was believed to ensure equal access to resources. But political freedom did not provide equal access to resources; it merely provided new and different avenues by which to gain access to them, especially using party affiliations. Nor did political freedom eliminate the need to rely on the people both within and outside of one's caste, family, ethnicity, or religious group who could help one to achieve one's goals. Because the revolution provided new official avenues for gaining access – namely, parties – one's achievement of access was used as a gauge for the success or failure of democracy. If one had access to and gained resources and privileges, one thought one had democracy. If one did not, it was thought that one was being denied democracy. Moreover, the inverse also applied: those who were denied access to the privileges others received felt that those others must have used corruption to obtain them (at one's own expense). I have also heard Nepalis who obtain access to resources and privilege attribute others' disgruntlement over being denied access to the others' unwillingness to play by the rules of democracy. In all cases, both access and exclusion were seen as a result of social affiliation of one sort or another, but one was seen as democratic while the other was seen as corruption depending on whether one gained or lost in the ongoing struggle for resources and privilege.

Conversations in Kathmandu and surrounding villages indicated to me that people were not entirely convinced of the benefits of the new democracy. For example, G. K., a Chettri (high-caste) working class laborer from a village outside of Kathmandu described the situation as follows:

The panchayat system was not good for us. We were oppressed. The poor people could not make any advancement. They were pressured, always. The panchayat ran the country for 25–26 years [actually 31 years] and now people wanted the multiparty system. The Jan Andolan was started by the people, but first it was the leaders [of the parties] who gave the push and kept it going. The people did not have facilities; there wasn't even enough water in the capital. This is when the doctors got involved. You see, they went on strike. They said "Why should we watch this hardship of the poor people?" and they went on strike. The government employees also went on strike. The doctors said, "Why should we keep quiet when ordinary, simple people are being killed?" After the killings, the doctors decided to go on strike. They went on strike. They closed the hospital. They said, "We are not willing to go there. We will not treat people. We are not able to give adequate treatment for these killings." The employees also helped them. Everyone – doctors, employees, students – became united. At that time, our movement became very strong. . . .

At that time, the doctors had a big role in our Jan Andolan. They wanted to bring our democracy, because in a democracy all people should get equal rights. Everyone should get medicine when they need it, and education. Even in villages, the children should be well-educated, and then people should be given jobs that suit their qualifications. But really, I haven't seen much difference since our Jan Andolan. The only difference is that prices have skyrocketed. It was the same, politically, as during the Panchayat regime. I wonder, is this democracy or not? After the constitution was written, everyone was talking about democracy, but there is no difference. How can this be called democracy? What I see is that we can go someplace and talk. During panchayat, action would have been taken against us. If we were in government service, we would be fired. But now we can go and speak against the government, they don't care much, but during the panchayat, we could have been sacked or even put in prison for two to four months.

So democracy has come, everybody says so. But democracy has not been able to work properly. Whichever system comes, there won't be changes. Whether it is Emale [Ekikrt Marks-Leninvadi, or UML, United Marxist Leninist, also Emale, short for Communist Party Nepal-UML] or the panchayat system, what I see is that the leaders hide and motivate the public to carry out agitations. The result is that it's the public who get beaten up and killed. After the leaders succeed, they don't recognize the people. It's good that democracy has arrived, in one way it is good, but the thing is that there are too many parties here. There are quarrels and fights as to where development is to be taken. This is property of Congress [Party], that is property of Panchayat [Party]. Even among doctors, there is fighting between parties. At the time of the Andolan, people were happy with the doctors. What the doctors are doing now [though] is what they did during the panchayat system. They are concentrating in their [private] clinics, rather than in [public] hospitals. They are spending more time at their clinics, and they don't serve the poor people. Many incidents have taken place in Bir Hospital and in village health posts. The government sends medicines, and the doctors hide the medicines and only give it to their patients if they support them. The politics is even in the health posts. To become a good doctor, he should distribute the medicines properly that have been given by the government . . . for the treatment of the patients. There are a lot of poor patients without money. These people should be helped by providing money from government grants, etc. This is what I feel will be good. But only the parties decide who will get benefits and who won't. If one area is in the pocket of one party, then they give money and grants for development. If they don't support them, then they don't get money. It's the same as the panchayat time.

Democratic medicine was for G. K. a medicine that did not favor one group over another, but all around him he saw doctors following the rules of politics, not what he associated with democracy for democracy was supposed to be like science, impartial. Parties were deciding who got the benefits and who did not. A variety of instances of post-revolutionary medical practice add substance to his concerns.

New medical non-governmental organizations

Throughout the late 1980s and early 1990s, with International Monetary Fund structural adjustment policies putting pressure on local governments to curtail their spending on health, coupled with increasing emphasis on "user-financed," self-help and people-centered orientations in development, non-governmental organizations (NGOs) devoted to health proliferated throughout the developing world. In Nepal, physicians with an interest in rural health care were particularly enthusiastic about founding NGOs for rural health care. Typically, an NGO took a specific rural area – a village or series of villages – as its target community. Along with village representatives, in keeping with people-centered development agendas, these doctors organized and deployed health programs which were predominantly aimed at primary care. NGOs offered specific interventions, including clinics in the community, health education training programs for villagers who would become village health staff, and "health camps" (short-term specialty interventions for target communities, such as sterilization programs, health education, eye surgeries). One

NGO ran a hospital in Kathmandu which gave priority to patients needing hospitalization from the community served by its health program. Another had targeted a community in the terai, where it conducted frequent health camps. Another focused on eye care in health camps throughout rural Nepal. Still another focused on women's health needs and primary care in a series of villages an hour's drive south of Kathmandu. Having received funding from the American Foundation for AIDS Research (AMFAR) via Save the Children, USA, it also conducted research on sexually transmitted diseases and blood testing for HIV seropositivity, along with an education program on HIV/AIDS. Finally, one NGO was developing a total health-care system for a community about five hours by bus west of Kathmandu, in the middle hills. It was designing and raising funds for a community hospital which would eventually be operated, supplied, and staffed by the community itself. Its goal was a medical system entirely run by the community.

All of the organizers of NGOs with whom I spoke indicated a desire to meet the highest medical standards. They used epidemiological methods and remained up to date about theories of disease and treatments. At the same time, they almost all also promoted grass-roots approaches to rural health care as advocated by international funders. In the process of delivering their health messages, however, NGO medical professionals were often accused by urbanites and villagers alike of using their programs for political purposes. In fact, in order to advocate messages about self-help and the importance of education and political participation, the NGOs often used local politicians or regional parliamentary representatives who visited their health camps to augment their visibility and political clout. In the new democracy, the idea of political empowerment was combined with messages about self-empowerment in the area of health, and so, to the villagers involved, the medical acts these doctors and nurses performed could not help but be interpreted as political acts. M. B. T., a young farmer who had spent some time in school in Kathmandu, offered this account of the relationship between medicine and democracy, after a long introduction to his understanding of democracy:

Briefly, as I understand, I suppose "praja" means people, "tantra" means rule. Isn't it so? Hence prajatantra (democracy) means "rule by the people." The difference between the panchayat and democracy, I think, is that the panchayat government was one-sided (absolute) rule. For example, our words made no difference to them. They did whatever they liked. A plough-man used the oxen to plough. If the government said that that is how it must be done, then that is how it was done. Otherwise, such and such a punishment would be given. Serious action would be taken. A death sentence would be given. . . .

In a way, whatever is happening as a result of democracy is okay. It is being allowed to work according to our own desires. It is being allowed to speak whatever occurs to our mind. That right is given. But, it comes to my mind, when one is allowed to do anything one likes, and speak anything one feels, it might create trouble someday. When one is allowed to do or speak anything, then people think of development in the country, construction, and this and that – everyone exchanges ideas and suggestions. It is good in this sense. . . .

In fact, whatever is happening now is very good. Trainings are taking place. I also got the opportunity to get training. It is because of the democratic development. Great people like you, doctors, and others, who are far superior to people like us, have come all the way to our villages. I feel very happy at this. And doctors are part of democracy. Doctors have to get good training and do good diagnosis and good treatment. But the doctors also do politics. So I cannot tell the difference between doctors and politicians. Of course they both do different jobs. The doctors come here to do trainings, and this is political work. The [NGO] here today also has politicians to get people involved. They both do social work, that is the same. In the democracy everything is politics. Even the doctors do politics for the party they support. People think the democracy is just freedom – indiscipline – but it is really about awareness, about wanting to develop for ourselves. This is about politics.

This young man sees the deliberate attempt to politicize villagers in regard to health and health care as an intrinsic part of democracy, but the ambiguities in his sentiments are many: he supports the idea of a politicized awareness of health and development, but also shares in his fellow villagers' skepticism, afraid that democratic politics will promote a free-for-all of political expression – a permission to do whatever one likes. He is also skeptical about village knowledge. It is outsiders who have medical expertise, yet outsiders arrive to promote politics. In his mind, it is clear that politics and medicine are intertwined but he suggests that this should not be at the risk of creating indiscipline, when political party interests promote no more than old-style favoritism. As it is, the system seems to be at risk of indiscipline – a sort of chaotic situation in which everything is politicized by doctors and in which one cannot tell the difference between doctors and politicians.

As a result of this blurring, some medical professionals opted to promote the view that medicine is not political, and that medical interventions should steer clear of politics if at all possible. Dr. M. D., above, adopted this view. Dr. K., son of Nepal's first elected prime minister, also did. He described the problem of villagers reading his health efforts as political campaigning as follows:

We have an organization which is in my father's name. It gives people incentive to do that work because of that name. It is called the B. P. Koirala Memorial Health Foundation. We have been conducting camps at various places, in so many places, you know. But all the time, whenever we visit, I say even to the leftists there, "This is not a political camp. We are here to help you. I only use this name so that people will come. I need this name so that doctors will come." You see, party politics is not part of this organization, but it is a big problem. How do you prevent politics from becoming part of it? It is very difficult.

We are now conducting a very big camp in Jhapa [the terai]. We have done six from November through March. All of them are multipurpose. We are thirty doctors or so, all professionals. We have been channeling patients [making referrals] and doing surgery. We combine an AIDS program that the program has received funds for from AMFAR. We have also been offered medicines from Direct Relief International. But what happens is that everywhere we go, we are thought of as political. Now we are going to Jhapa. We chose Jhapa because of the prevalence of AIDS cases. But in Jhapa we are going to have by-elections soon, and now they will put two and two together and say that we are organizing a camp there for political reasons [supporting Nepali Congress]. So what I plan to do is to take several of the leftist doctors from here, and I will tell them to come along and see for themselves and to show the people in the village we are not political. You see, we are interested in humanitarian projects, not in politics.

The idea of reading beneficial health programs as politically motivated is closely related for villagers to the idea that the medical truths promoted in these programs might themselves be constituted for the benefit of one political interest over another. Take a case in point for this – the alternative interpretations of tuberculosis as a disease caused by a bacillus or one caused by poverty, can result in the promotion of one truth and the exclusion of another. One truth does not necessarily have to preclude the other, but when one gets aligned with a political party and the other aligned with a different party, they inevitably do appear to have to preclude one another. Among village Nepalis, truths about health are often offered as "new" knowledge to them every time they receive visits from urban health professionals. The labeling of a disease or a condition of suffering at any given time cannot help but be read by villagers as in part a product of the social relations which produce that label. N. D., a nurse who ran the health camps in a region outside of Kathmandu, explained that this was sometimes a problem. She, like other health professionals, seemed to be caught off guard by public skepticism over putting apolitical truth to work for a politically activist medicine:

We want the villagers to know we are not coming for one political party or another. We are interested in their medical problems only. If they have one disease or another, it doesn't make a difference if we are communist or Congress. The incidence and prevalence of HIV, for example, is the same regardless of political party. But, you know, the villagers always think we are only there for politics. When we tell them about HIV, they think this is a political issue, not a disease. But we want them to know that our party politics doesn't matter. Whether communist or Congress, what matters is if they understand that their health is in their hands, and this is political in a different way. Of course, we need to educate them about the disease, but they have to be involved, and they should be involved politically. We want to solve the problem of HIV in a sustainable way – by building a sustainable health infrastructure that they support. And this means they have to become political.

This professional, like many others, walked along the delicate boundary using politics to improve health while trying to avoid accusations of political bias. In one coherent thought, politics are both rejected and celebrated as a part of health care. The fact that this NGO recruited two of the communist members of parliament to speak at the opening of its health camp in the village only exacerbated the problem this nurse identified. When I spoke with several villagers about the health camp, they confirmed that politics was an intrinsic part of the NGO that had set it up, but, they noted, this was not unusual. In fact, they said, it was no different from the situation before the revolution. These NGO personnel, they said, were new resources for them as villagers, but they were also resources for politicians. Some villagers thought the NGO personnel would become patrons through whom they could obtain scholarships for their children to study in Kathmandu schools. They even hoped that external aid from foreign development agencies would be funneled to them via new social connections arriving with the NGO. They also knew that politicians saw NGOs as resources through which to obtain votes in the next elections. In my conversation with Mr. B. T., who came from this village, I learned that he hoped that the NGO I had arrived with would someday repay his diligence as an agricultural worker for their project by sending him for further education on a scholarship. It seemed to him that the NGO would provide him with the *aphno manche*, the "source-force," the affiliations he needed to obtain "democratic" privileges.

Health NGOs often struggled with the tensions emerging from their desire to promote health as at least partially political – in the sense that they believed people needed to be political to be able to help themselves – and health as political *in a party sense* (biased in favor of one political party or one politician over another). That health camps set up by NGOs in the local communities often employed political rhetoric as part of their health goals only convinced villagers that their loyalty to these NGO personnel and their political perspectives would provide them, in classic *aphno manche* style, with great opportunities not only for health but for overall social improvement. Meanwhile, the politicians whom NGOs typically recruited for gaining the confidence of the local people made speeches in which they announced that the NGOs' goals were decisively non-political. Thus, although these organizations were set up with apolitical health goals in mind, the party politics of their founders necessarily emerged in their practices. In one village, the NGO director gave an opening speech for a three-day health camp, introducing the fact that health was a product not simply of medicine but of social opportunity, gender equality, and self-help. The director was particularly interested in raising women's awareness of the need for regular gynecological check-ups along with their need for increased literacy, both of which she announced were basic human rights. At the same time, she continually stressed that the NGOs' goals were not political in the sense that they were supported by one party over another. They were only political in the sense that to be truly healthy meant to have social equality and opportuni-ties for nutrition, education, and health services. Of course, the presence of three politicians from leftist parties at the opening events discredited her claims of political neutrality in some eyes, but even without them villagers had already perceived a political message in the issues she raised.

Villagers at this health camp expressed the opinion that if they towed this NGO's political line they would gain access to its privileges in the same way they used to obtain privileges from their local politicians. They had always known that loyalty brought rewards, and in the post-revolutionary context the system had simply been recast in terms of party politics and the work of NGOs. Villagers were very politically astute. One man, for example, from a family of wealthy landowners in the village, had been involved in village leadership since soon after the Rana era; he had been in power during the panchayat regime and was still mayor in the new democracy. He offered a revealing illustration of the ambiguities that arose with the merging of democratic politics with politicized medicine:

Democracy is a good thing, but it is in its infant stage. It takes time to grow up. I feel democracy has to be made more sturdy and strong. Is democracy right or wrong? It is absolutely right. Democracy is freedom of speech; people can talk openly about what they feel. It is freedom of the press. As a social worker, there are different things it means to me. But now I feel democracy is being misused by politicians. It can be found in many developed countries. It is not only here or in Kathmandu's politics, but misuse of democracy can be found all over the world. These types of actions [political partisanship] do not support democracy but hamper it. There should be total freedom of speech, the press, to gather and com-municate about politics. This is why I favor the Nepali Congress. I respect [its leader] for his outstanding character. The leaders say that Nepal is a mountainous country and so to develop it we must start from the villages, i.e., from the founda-tion. And this is very much the truth – democracy's truth. Let us say feed those in need, learning for the illiterate, cure for the sick. Democracy means power to the people where the public can apply their personal rights. Development is part of this, applied to the social field. In other words, politics and development are parts of the same boat. But politics and health are different. Politics comes to the people through the constitution. The power is with the people. Whereas social health means, if my stomach is hurting – I go and show it to the doctors.

Let us take the example of a school. School is not for personal benefit. It is for everyone. It is for Congress, for CPN (Communist Party Nepal), UML (United Marxist Leninist), for Jana Morcha. It is for everyone's children. Here the parents also get involved. So school is a very pure organization. Medicine should be the same. If politics is played here, it is going to spoil the school. This is why development and politics differ. This is why health and politics differ. It is like a river with two rivulets joining it. Democracy runs a country and for this a very powerful team is needed, so that it cannot divert and go the wrong way. Due to lack of knowledge and poverty, it is easy for people to be bought, and they sell out. They sell their votes. A person is bought and sold for his vote. If the Communist sold the Congress bought. In politics, some are gained and some are lost. Even the NGOs they are buying votes with the health camps. They don't pay money, but they bring votes by bringing medicines.

As mayor and Congress party supporter, he was particularly uncomfortable with the fact that the NGO had recruited two communist members of parliament to speak at the opening of the health camp. For him, democracy represented a merging of politics with development in a manner that brought benefits to the people, he expected health programs to be apolitical. At the same time he recognized that his own ability to stay in power was contingent on the villagers' not perceiving his opposition to the NGO. He needed to be able to obtain some political credit for it.

The harshest critics said that foreign aid had become just another resource within the "source-force" system still operating in Nepali society. The trend towards establishing a health infrastructure ideologically embedded in universal claims to truth was reproduced locally through the logic of party politics, wherein truths were necessarily interpreted as political messages. Historically, social influence was disseminated from the palace through local political entities; now it was disseminated from the government and foreign aid agencies through NGOs working with local political entities. This mayor went out of his way to welcome the doctors to the village, attempting to make it appear to villagers (to the chagrin of NGO organizers) that he had been partially instrumental in bringing so valuable a resource to the village. These villagers were after all his *aphno manche*, his own people. The flip side of this was that to villagers it appeared that nothing, not even medicine, was above politics. For villagers, messages about scientific truth that came packaged in political wrapping were simply part of the same political culture that had always defined development and health programs delivered by elites.

The assistant nurse midwife crisis

The entanglements of a nurse in a dispute between the assistant nurse midwives (ANMs) and the university administration of Teaching Hospital illustrates a similar situation of medical professionals being trapped in a struggle between politics-as-usual and democratic politicization. Typically, ANMs were chosen from among those rural women who had completed a Class Eight (eighth grade)-level education. They were given training and expected to return to the rural area, where they assisted in deliveries and educated mothers about pre- and post-natal care and fertility control. They worked under the supervision of village health workers or, in district hospitals, under physicians. Prior to 1993, ANMs who had served for a period of time were able to sit for examinations which could, with the right marks for the equivalent of a School Leaving Certificate (SLC), qualify them for further training in Kathmandu in the trained nursing program or for a degree in public health. Because it was seen as important to encourage more of these women towards higher degrees as a stimulus to other rural women and because it was assumed that these women were typically more committed to rural medical work than those from the urban areas (see Justice 1987 on the early history of this program), the university allowed a certain number of these women to enter higher-degree programs even if their examination scores were slightly lower than those of other qualifying students (often urban). It was assumed that their wealth of experience in rural health care would compensate for their lack of formal education.

In 1993, however, the university decided to upgrade the requirements for entrance into the nursing program in order to raise its training to international standards. The provisions for entrance on the ANM track would be eliminated, and only those holding high marks and SLCs would be admitted. Moreover, at the time that the decision was made to upgrade, the administration decided not to "grandfather in" the women who had already entered the ANM program expecting that they would have the chance to continue their education. In response, the ANMs preparing to pursue further education began a hunger strike. They set up their protest outside of the dean's office at Teaching Hospital and demanded that at least those who had already been trained be allowed to continue towards a higher degree. They also argued that removing the opportunities for higher education for the ANMs would dissuade the best-prepared rural women from entering the program by eliminating any chance for advancement. They noted that because girls were typically given far fewer chances for education in rural Nepal than boys, the chances of finding women with a Class Eight education who were committed to working in the rural areas were slight. They suggested that Nepalis should not waste their time making their degrees meet international standards if it meant ignoring the country's health problems, which were different from the international community's. Nepal's enormous rural populations would continue to need rural health personnel who were not necessarily qualified for work in urban or rural settings elsewhere but well-enough qualified for the health care that villagers needed.

L. S. K., a public health nurse I came to know, had decided to become an advocate for the ANMs, arguing that the new policy discriminated against women in that the equivalent training system for men (enabling village health workers to enroll in the MBBS program to become doctors) had not been similarly transformed. She also supported the view that Nepal should live by its own, not international standards. Her approach, she said, was scientific and modern: "If a patient is sick because of dehydration, you must give that patient water. You should not withhold that water simply because it does not meet international standards of purity." She blamed some of the conflict on the new government. She recognized the benefits of the new democracy in medical efficacy and promoting new standards and objective measures for organizing the health-care system so that it was fair. At the same time, she complained about the failures of the new system:

We [nurses] used to be able to go directly to Prekshya Rajya Laxmi Devi Shah, the sister to the queen, who took a great interest in supporting the nurses in Nepal. She protected us so much. Even the big big doctors, the big big politicians, the big big secretaries were scared of her. But now, nobody is scared of anything from the nurses' side. The nurses have lost their support person. Now, I myself am in deep trouble over this ANM crisis. You see I have received this letter from the minister of health, and he has told me that I have broken the law by sitting with the girls on their hunger strike. Actually, I did not sit with them, but I support them. I believe they must have the chance to study. That is my profession, I told them [the administration]; I am not against the government. But they are saying that I am a communist because I support them. I am not communist. I am not Congress. I am a service holder. I have taken no part in politics. I am only supporting the ANMs for the rural health care system. So, in this sense, I think real democracy has not come yet. It is exactly like before – the same kind of politics.

The revolution had reconfigured resources of power so that different persons had access to it than previously, but the perception was that the basic "corrupt" system was still very much alive. In this nurse's mind, her action had been a political act in the service of medical truth, but the perspective of the minister was that her action was based principally on politics. Her protest invoked a professional medical practice aimed at rooting out political corruption, but in the new milieu her action could only be read as a political act. The new system left the nurses adrift, depriving them of the major source of influence they had had before. The irony for this nurse was that her professional organization was trying to become more professional in terms of international standards while the system within which they would exercise those standards had not changed; new wine, old bottles. The minister of health who issued her warning letter saw her activism as not only violating her role as a civil servant but also threatening democracy. The nurse, in contrast, read his threat and his support of the new policy as a way of ensuring that more urban, high-caste, educated women from his social and political circles would gain entrance to the nursing program. She felt it was a way for the minister to gain political favor and pay back his supporters and to rid himself of activists who insisted on impartial rules and standards in their new democracy. His letter suggested that he felt it was she who was violating rules of impartiality to promote communism, who was impeding the progress of modernization by her resistance to upgrading the nurses' profession to international, scientifically determined, standards. Both claimed ownership of objective standards and impartiality, and each accused the other of using socially convenient truths for corrupt political purposes.

As a result, this nurse pooled her resources to create a network of obligations among people who were in new positions of political power who might help her save her job. She visited the home of the health minister every other day. She also seized a windfall opportunity to recruit support from several members of parliament who came to her home soliciting contributions for development resources in her neighborhood. Wasting no time, she contributed 3,000 rupees (several months' salary) and took the opportunity to explain her plight. Now the problem was no longer simply her own: "You see, now the problem I have with the minister of health is also their problem. As members of parliament, they will have to influence him on my behalf." A politics of social reciprocity (now through political parties) fills in where a logic of science fails. With several important parliamentarians on her side, she was able to engage in an ironic politics of resistance to the new demands of her democracy. Despite her desire for an institutional system which would operate according to the most efficient means, she herself had to rely on politics-as-usual to save her job. The debate about objective standards by which applicants should be accepted and promoted into the nursing education program and about her role as a civil servant was not, then, simply a matter of establishing objective standards. Rather, the standards were themselves a highly negotiated, socially constructed matter of debate.

The Sarlahi flood relief effort

In the summer of 1993, the monsoon rains were heavier than usual, and the new dams which helped to direct the flow and amount of water in the river drainage system from the mountains to the southern part of the country were not equipped to handle so much water. The region to the south of Kathmandu was flooded, killing an estimated 10,000 people and leaving entire villages homeless. Immediately, the government began to collect donations from foreign and local sources for flood relief. Helicopters flew politicians down to the damaged areas to assess the problem. Foreign aid agents flew with them and with supplies began to design interventions. As mentioned before, Dr. Mathura and the Department of Community Medicine doctors and students, watching thousands of dollars being "wasted," as they said, on the transportation of politician after politician to the flood site with little apparent result, organized a rescue operation of their own. They collected funds from Kathmandu Nepalis and foreign agencies and flew down groups of physicians, nurses, and students along with basic medical supplies. In the flood-affected area of Sarlahi, they set up temporary clinics in structures which were still standing and devised a network for communication and supplies. They also undertook outreach to villagers who were stranded at a distance from relief efforts. Dr. Mathura described the effort as follows:

We don't work under the government. They are such rascals. We don't work under them. We offered our services, but they don't make use of us because they say we are doing [communist] party business. People supported us, not the government. The government people are also sending rescue teams, but what happened is that first of all they don't have a "people-oriented" attitude. They just go. Sometimes they don't even open the packages which contain relief supplies. They come back in their helicopters without distributing things. The second thing is that there is a lot of bureaucracy; they make a lot of rules. So in one area where we went there are about seventy houses affected, and these people don't have any place to live. They were living on the roadside under very miserable conditions. And the Red Cross had dropped off about 200 things, but it was all locked up. You see, it was terrible. I don't know why they didn't distribute even 70 out of 200 things. And that is already provided, but the government could not distribute it. The Red Cross also became very angry.

So we have organized and sent our own volunteers, and they saw how terrible it was. The roads were all washed out, no bridges, no homes, everything is under water and gone, people living under makeshift thatch shelters, but they have no walls, and at night they are so worried because the snakes come and when they are sleeping they can be bitten. This means someone needs to stand watch all night, and they are exhausted, without food, with diarrheal diseases. And the other thing is that the helicopters are a great disadvantage, you see. Because whenever a helicopter comes, the local people think they have brought food. So everybody comes asking for food, and they are so happy when they see the helicopter – they think that breakfast is ready – but the helicopters sometimes only bring people. Even when it has supplies, then the real ones who need the help, the people who are mourning dead family members, they are just mourning, sitting for thirteen days. They are depressed, and they don't go to collect food or clothes. The ones who are more active who go to the helicopters may not need the things as badly as those who cannot come. But, the expectations are raised very high by this helicopter, and they seldom make a difference.

Already, we have deployed eleven batches of volunteers to six places. We were the first medical teams to reach the victims. They have epidemics of diarrheal diseases, pneumonia, many respiratory and trauma injuries. They cannot burn the bodies of victims and animals, and the flies and dogs are scavenging on them – the dogs are becoming wild and dangerous. The distribution of food supplies is defective, and what food crops are available are just grabbed by one or two people who get to them first. The poorest and most sick don't get anything. Most serious, however, is the social problem. These people, their lives have been destroyed. They are returning to their homes and their homes, crops – everything is gone.

The health professionals' program for relief during the 1993 floods was turned into a non-governmental organization of health professionals devoted to the creation of an emergency health infrastructure in the country – the Health Professionals for the Prevention and Management of Disasters, Nepal. The month after the disaster, they held a public awareness program at an open-air market in downtown Kathmandu. They set up a series of slide shows and photographic essays which described their relief efforts during the floods, produced educational pamphlets and posters written in English and Nepali about the types of natural and man-made disasters which were likely to affect Nepal, and promoted public awareness about grass-roots interventions and, surprisingly, the need for monitoring of technological interventions:

> AWAKE, ARISE, UNITE and DEFEND OUR ENVIRON-MENT and THE EARTH; PEOPLE, ONLY the PEOPLE can PROTECT.

> It is YOU who has to protect the EARTH and the Nature from SENSELESS and PLANLESS INVASION of TECHNOL-OGY.

> 20% of the Total Population in the World lives in the Developed Countries and uses more than 80% of the World's Fuel (gas, petrol, etc.). The Remaining 80% of the population is Living in the Undeveloped Countries, using less than 20% of the World's Fuel. The Main Reason for increasing Pollution is Unlimited Industries and the way of Living in the Developed Countries which is entirely to Their Benefit only.

Their exhibit showed photos of the suffering masses of villagers homeless after the floods, camping out on small dry patches under makeshift thatched structures with no food, little clothing, and looking tragically desperate. It showed the makeshift medical clinics with captions describing strategies for hygiene and sanitation in disaster circumstances. It described the creation of a network for soliciting contributions and distributing essential drugs and supplies. It explained the basic geology of the Himalayas and discussed how the combination of earthquakes and heavy precipitation increased the likelihood of floods and dam collapse, questioning the need for large dams at all. It criticized inappropriate technology and corruption in the building of dams. It argued not against technology itself but against a *planless* invasion of it that resulted in scientifically predictable disasters and often benefited only the elite. It demonstrated first-aid techniques and asked people to take responsibility for their lives by becoming socially, technically, and politically aware. There were several booths devoted to the topic of AIDS and awareness of sexually transmitted diseases. The combination of messages that were anti-imperialist, resistant to Western hegemony, and pro-environmentalist with those that were unswervingly committed to the idea of technologically advanced scientific knowledge was one that cast the group's efforts in much narrower political terms than had been intended.

The medical students, doctors, nurses, and paramedicals involved answered questions for the citizens who visited the exhibit by the hundreds. Those I spoke with were promoting a perspective which attacked development for serving the interests of elites but their attacks left science intact as a knowledge system which could serve the poor. However, what was for them medicine at its best was seen by others as an abuse of medical science – a medicine used for political campaigning for the Left. Although no mention was ever made of political parties or candidates, many visitors interpreted the exhibit as an act of defiance of the Congress government. Engaging in activities as "renegade" health professionals outside of official government channels was seen by Congress politicians and many of the public as support for the opposition parties. The actions of these health professionals were read as politically partisan in a manner that some felt could undermine the authority of their presentation, thus their verbal insistence that they be regarded as apolitical. What was intended as a set of messages about health and human safety became interpreted as an attack on the legitimacy of the current government. One Nepali who accompanied me to the exhibit informed me afterward that she didn't like much to attend these "political events" because they were always the same. She added, "They did good work for the flood area. It is educational." But then she dismissively added, "I don't like all the politics – just fighting between one party and the other."

Surgery with a social orientation

The politicization of medicine in democratic Nepal is also apparent in the experience of a surgeon, Dr. S. One of the first physicians to receive his

MBBS from Tribhuvan University, he came from a rural village in eastern Nepal and had begun his career as a village recruit to the rural health system:

I was a paramedic before I went to medical school. I was working as a health assistant in a very remote health post. I was there for about 18 months. During my 18 months in that very remote area as a paramedical worker, I learned that if you do not do surgery, you are mostly helpless to help people. For example, in a district hospital in a mountainous area, if you cannot perform surgery, you are no longer considered a doctor. That is what I felt during my paramedic time. I never went out in a district hospital as a medical officer after my graduation, but I knew that, while working as a paramedic, there were many surgical problems, for example gynecological problems that could be helped by surgery, but I was helpless because I did not know surgery. I could help a patient by giving drugs. I could prescribe and I could tell a patient to go to a place where they could buy drugs, and I could even help that patient buy drugs. But if a patient needed surgery or any kind of operation, I was helpless.

Then, the only help I used to get was from God. I used to pray to God not to send me any surgical patients for my care. I knew that to be a better doctor, I had to learn surgery. There was no way out. By staying in the community, you get a sense of what is happening in the community and how to help with preventive medicine, but you never get a sense of what it is like to operate on a patient. But being a surgeon with a background in community medicine puts me in a completely different situation. I haven't switched the kind of medicine I practice. I still have an interest in community medicine. Without the vision of community medicine, I don't think any doctor is a real doctor. You can never be a doctor if you leave all the senses that are needed for being a community physician. If you leave that, you won't be a good physician; you will only be a factory robot.

This is not only me. There are many doctors that have a similar kind of feeling here. We sit around every week on Thursday morning and discuss the epidemiological aspects of our work. This is very nontraditional. Our senior physicians never talked about that. Our seniors would always come – and say how many cases they did and what the outcome was and what tools they used, like that, whereas most of us juniors are concerned about the integration of different specialties in giving holistic care to the patient. In institutions of health care, at least in this particular small hospital, which is more scientific? For example, I cannot say I have seen fifty cases done of something. I can say I have seen one case being done this way, so I think this is going to work. But if an old professor comes in and says out of his experience alone that you should do this operation like this, we do not try to follow him dogmatically. We try to judge it against the present available data – data that is available through MedLine. We have that facility available now, and we have a group of us who discuss those things. Before, statistics were never brought into the practice of clinicians. If you talk about our seniors, they were never taught anything about statistics. We, on the other hand, teach ourselves. We try to teach ourselves the basics of statistics which can be used in the analysis or in the delivery of care.

For example, the breast diseases, not only cancer, but all the breast diseases – those women who come to our surgical Out-Patient Department. Our data gives the information that almost one-third of the female population comes with breast problems. This includes breast cancer or breast abscesses and mammillary duct impactions, fibroidenosis, benign tumors, and sometimes just infections. We try to find out why that is happening, why that is so common. We are trying to find out, given the different diseases of the breast, which is more likely to be found in a particular population or ethnic group, or in a particular socio-economic status, like that. We ask questions of our breast cases and take note of it. We do not have a very good format yet, because we need a lot of material and work, and it is hard to do that work while running the OPD. We do not have research assistants.

It is very productive. We are going to publish our findings in the *Community Medicine Journal* also. We are looking at economic factors. We can find out whether people are rich or middle-class or lower middle-class or poor. And we are able to correlate that certain diseases are more common in the lower-income group. Breast cancer is an important case. We know that women in the upper socio-economic class are more concerned about their health and they come to us for check-ups more often and they have a lower mortality from breast cancer. In another case, we see that almost 95 percent of the patients who are burn victims, who die from burns, are female. Isn't that interesting?

Dr. S.'s view that he was undertaking a scientific type of medical practice with the aid of statistics was ironically countered by physicians who claimed that the type of work he undertook was in fact politically motivated. They suggested that he was under the influence of communist rhetoric promulgated by certain major figures in the Department of Community Medicine. The suggestion was even made that Dr. S's political leanings were motivated by his membership in a minority caste and his having been born and raised in a rural part of the country. His work was seen as overly concerned with political matters rather than medical ones. Dr. S., in contrast, considered his work pro-development, exemplifying a physician's role in a democratic society, and he considered this work scientific, not political. He felt that those members of the surgical profession who opposed his views were still wedded to a non-scientific and non-democratic view of medicine.

Government plans for rural health infrastructure

In Nepal, as in many developing countries, the Ministry of Health is putatively in charge of designing the country's rural health system. Foreign development agencies have played an important role in funding the Ministry's plans, and therefore the rural health infrastructure of Nepal has undergone numerous changes which have been the result of pressure from foreign aid priorities over the years (Justice 1987). Before one system is fully deployed and given a chance to establish itself through the process of trial and error, new proposals and revisions in the system are often put forward. When the new interim democratic government was created in 1990, it too devised a new plan for rural health care. The plan developed under the direction of Dr. Mathura, who was interim health minister, was conceived as one that would expand the role of physicians in rural health services and elaborate upon the orientation of his Department of Community Medicine. Because villagers often complained about the lack of skilled physicians in the rural area, and physicians often felt that they were treated poorly by non-physician district health officers, the goal of the new plan was to increase the presence of physicians in the countryside and to eliminate several layers of health bureaucracy between villages and centralized resources.

Biomedical health care in Nepal is delivered by four types of institutions: multilateral and bilateral aid agencies; NGOs and missionary hospitals and clinics; private-sector medical professionals; and government. The Ministry of Health rural health system in pre-1990 Nepal was designed to have a health post in every *ilaka* (nine *ilakas* make up a district and there are 75 districts). At these health posts, a health assistant (always male, with Class Ten education plus two and a half years of health training) was in charge. They were staffed with community health auxiliary personnel (again male, with a Class Ten education and one year of training in health) and assistant nurse midwives (female, with a Class Eight education and three years of health training). There were to be 814 such health posts in rural areas. The health post was designed to offer minor clinical interventions and door-to-door health education, gathering of statistics, guidance for fertility control, etc. Health assistants also coordinated local visits from mobile Ministry of Health or foreign-aid sponsored immunization teams. The government also supported 145 Ayurvedic dispensaries, but these played no obvious role in the health planning for biomedical interventions (which is not to say that they were not well-utilized by patients). Health-post personnel were charged with referring complicated cases to district hospitals.

In the late 1980s plans were made to set up health sub-posts staffed by paramedics in every village. These would refer difficult cases to the health post, which in turn referred its difficult cases to health centers or district-level hospitals (one of which was supposed to exist in each of the 75 districts of Nepal but in 1990 had only 61 operating). Zonal hospitals received referrals from the district hospitals and in turn referred patients to the central hospitals of Kathmandu (Bir and Teaching Hospitals). District and zonal health centers and hospitals were run by Ministry of Health administrators, few of whom were doctors. The district health officer was typically in charge of supplies and staff for the entire district. From the district-level hospitals all the way down to village health posts, Nepal's rural health infrastructure seldom operated with its officially mandated supply of personnel (Justice 1983, 1987). Moreover, the plan to establish sub-posts was never completely carried out.

After the People's Movement, the interim government sought to broaden and fully implement the sub-post plan. Three factors were to be taken into account in determining the locations for health sub-posts: geography, population, and socioeconomic conditions. I was told that these were used because they were the most objective measures and would ensure as much fairness for rural Nepalis as possible. Geographic regions would be designated for posts on the basis of population size and income levels, assuming that the poorer regions would need more than wealthy ones because poorer villagers could less afford to travel far for health care. Health sub-posts would replace existing village health posts, eliminating an unnecessary tier that might stifle access to hospitals instead of increasing it. Hospitals at the district level would be run by doctors instead of district officers who it was suggested were primarily interested in sinecure and contact with their Kathmandu superiors who could promote them than in health matters. Because of this orientation, they were seen to have different priorities from doctors. The idea was that if physicians were given positions in which their decisions would not be overridden by bureaucrats and were able to make decisions about the operation of the health infrastructure, they would be more willing to practice in the rural districts and more effective in providing care based on medical rather than political considerations.

The program which was finally being promoted by the new democratic government in 1993 was, however, a severely compromised version of the initial plan. I was told by the former minister that the criteria of geography and socio-economic status as bases for establishing health sub-posts had been entirely abandoned in favor of political ones; sub-posts were being located primarily on the basis of political constituencies or "voting capital" in government ministers' own districts. Also, most village health posts were being left in place, retaining that extra tier of care in a manner that I was told would impede effective referral to hospitals reportedly because of politicians' fears of losing resources already in their districts regardless of their perceived efficacy. Finally, the issue of establishing physicians as the in-charge in the district was still being debated and it was clear to those with whom I spoke that in the long run there would probably be some sharing of the role between physicians and ministry officials. Despite the fact that this sort of politics is characteristic of democracies in many countries in the developed world, the Nepali doctors I spoke with considered it undemocratic because it co-opted scientific knowledge for politics – they argued that the decisions were not based on the "objective" measures that maximized health efficiency.

Medical science was being derailed by politics rather than politics being used for medical goals, but this politicization of medicine was not in fact that different from what politically active medical professionals had done to create a revolution on behalf of the common man and the voting public. The only difference was that one was done for votes while the other was done for the system which would allow votes to matter. Now that they did matter, politicizing medicine for political goals meant, for many, politicizing medicine for votes. Here again, the case reveals that it was not simply a question of letting politics derail medical truth, but that what got to count as medical truth was revealed as the outcome of a political process.

Doctors and the government

By 1993 many physicians had private practices in Kathmandu. Although government jobs paid next to nothing compared with the private sector, and the government bureaucracy was perceived as interfering with the practice of medicine, nearly all doctors had or wanted to have some government job along with their private practice. I was told that this was partly because the pensions provided a certain amount of security but that the money was not the most important thing. Rather, government positions were important for the privileges which being affiliated with the government still guaranteed. For some physicians this idea of privilege was tied to maintaining an active voice in politics, because for them, again, politics was an important form of medicine. For some, privilege was associated with feeling a need to give service to their country, since, in their minds, many poor Nepalis received biomedical care only when it was "free" at hospitals and clinics run by the government.

By far the most common reason doctors felt it was important to hold government positions was that without connections to government officials it was nearly impossible to set up and maintain a private practice that was safe from demands for *baksheesh* (commission) from government bureaucrats. It was impossible to be considered for postgraduate work and education without connections to persons in the government. Although there were many physicians who could obtain these privileges through birthright and social affiliations, getting a job in government was thought to enhance one's access to those in positions of power who could help one secure privileges. This perception on the part of doctors that it was important to maintain ties to an old network of affiliative politics crosscut their concern for more autonomy from government when it came to making professional decisions.

More than a holdover of the sort of corruption they had fought against, this form of political connection was something doctors and others were having to cultivate anew as a way of gaining political access to the resources and privileges with which to practice effectively. The new democracy demanded political alliances because politics was the new means of exercising medicine. For example, when one health NGO wanted access to government funds for a hospital in their target village, they approached the elected parliamentarians from their district and, from there, requests were made for support all the way up to the upper house of parliament, all through shared party lines. Although one might consider this the normal political process in a democratic government system, another NGO director describing this first NGO's strategy for obtaining funds called it an abuse of the system by using political *aphno manche*.[1]

The physicians' call for a Health Act

In 1993 physicians were pressing for a separate Health Act which would give them more power outside of the Ministry of Health. This issue was raised in discussions of the problem of getting physicians to work in the rural areas. The Nepal Medical Association president in 1993, Dr. Joshi, addressed this issue in his inaugural speech. He began by calling attention to the fact that health personnel provided an essential service to the country, one that differed entirely from that of other members of the civil service because it required higher qualifications and involved different responsibilities. This alone, he argued, should be reason enough for separating the health service from the general civil service. The problem of deputation of doctors to rural areas was occasioned by the presence of corrupt politics within the profession:

The government has been blaming the doctors for being city- and town-oriented and not willing to work in remote areas. I've no hesitation in accepting the fact that most of the doctors like to work in the cities and towns. Nearly two-thirds of the doctors are residing in Kathmandu Valley alone. Though on paper it seems that there are two or three doctors in [each of] the district hospitals, the fact remains that many are without any of them. The Honorable Minister of State for Health will agree with me that besides other factors the politicians are equally responsible for this situation. Each leader demands for doctors to be posted in his or her constituency and in the same breath requests that the doctors, if they happen to be their own relations, should be posted in cities or towns. If this practice is allowed to continue, the Ministry may have to prepare one list of doctors related to powerful persons so that they can be posted in cities and towns and another list of doctors not related to powerful people to serve in remote areas. I think it will never be possible to prepare the second list, because it is not very difficult for anyone to catch hold of a person in the power axis. Hence, for sending medical personnel to all the desired places, to provide health services at the grass-roots level, and to standardize medical practice in Nepal, I reemphasize the need for a separate health service as mentioned already. Posting should be done for a fixed period of time for a certain area and nobody should be transferred before their term is completed. There also should be time-bound promotion and career ladders. The practice of posting on deputation for an indefinite period should be done away with. Transfer as reward or punishment should be stopped, as there are many other ways to reward or punish.

Bemoaning physicians' persistent use of the power axis through which privileges still seemed to be distributed, he then turned to the need for a professional oversight body devoted to maintaining standards in the pro-fession and keeping out unqualified practitioners. This, he said, should be financed by the government:

For standard medical practice the role of the Nepal Medical Council is of utmost importance. A lot of unauthorized medical practice is being openly undertaken in the country, including in the capitol; still, nothing much is done to control this. It's the duty of the government responsible for the people to protect them. Hence, the Nepal Medical Association strongly demands appropriate financial resources should be provided by the government to strengthen the Nepal Medical Council for the ultimate aim of protecting the people.

The present government is encouraging privatization in all aspects. It is good news that privatization in health sector is coming up. New nursing homes and pharmaceuticals in the private sector are examples. They are helping the government serve the people. Hence proper guidance, protection, and standardization is required for the private sector.

Science has advanced by leaps and bounds and is still doing so, but the misuse or ignorance of scientific discoveries and failure to obey the laws of nature is causing ecological imbalance and creating serious health hazards. . . .Finally, I would like to request that the government ban the advertisement of tobacco in media and smoking in public places, public transportation systems, and offices and see that the ban is enforced strictly.

Science, for the NMA president, was the key to health for all and effective health care for the nation. He seems to suggest that one could somehow surgically remove corruption from the medical system by removing politicians who let themselves be susceptible to special requests from their constituents and whose decisions do not medically benefit those whom he feels should take priority. But in the same breath he reiter-ated the call for a medicine which could use politics to produce better health standards for the nation. In his view, politicians were needed to implement scientific truth but not to ensure that doctors adhered to the practices implied by such truth. Politics could both enhance medical practice and lead to its corruption. Like many physicians (not simply those in Nepal) he argued that politics could be a medical tool but medicine should never be used as a political tool because politics was inherently corrupting. But for many the difference between corruption and legitimate uses of politics for medical goals was only a matter of who benefited. If the outcome could be construed as having served a politician's or physician's personal gain, it was corrupt, but if it was shown to be good for the community it was a legitimate use. In fact, the difference between personal and community benefit was not always clear. In many cases, both claims were invoked by opposing parties. A medical profession which so clearly articulated a political role for itself had thus come full circle to facing the problem of its own demands being interpreted as serving their personal benefit. One can imagine the claims made by the industries under attack in this president's public demand. The irony of this scenario was not that it did not reveal the success of democracy insofar as these sorts of political battles are commonplace in any democratic system, but that for many Nepalis this sort of political activity was seen as anti-democratic and corrupt.

Corruption or validation of truth?

I believe many health professionals in 1993 were still struggling to eliminate the old systems of corruption from their society. Shaha (1993) describes this desire as a craze for modernization and sees it having resulted in the creation of a large number of modern institutions that paved the way for the revolution. He notes, however, that even when these institutions have rules based on what are taken to be objective standards, these rules are not always followed, and when the structure breaks down people turn to the loyalty of family and friends. I would add, however, that it is not simply that institutional breakdown results in the activation of old loyalty systems but rather that the criteria for establishing objective standards and medical institutions are themselves also sometimes based on social affiliations which are inherently political. "Objective measures" are themselves political facts serving some interests over others. This is perhaps true anywhere but it is particularly visible in Nepal because of the circumstances which gave rise to democracy and the particular modes whereby power and truth have come to be linked through ideas about impartial truth.

For many Nepali physicians and other medical professionals, the idea that one can both hold on to objective medical truth and engage in a politicized medical practice is unproblematic. I have tried to show, however, that for many Nepalis the distinction between a politicized medicine and one which is perceived as corrupt is hard to establish. In a world which emphasizes social connections in order to ensure that objective truths can be heard, it becomes difficult to avoid using them. The politics of affiliation formerly used to obtain privileges and effect exclusions has been able to find its way into the functioning of modern institutions, especially political parties, through which health professionals try to promote a scientific medicine in the new democracy. Again, this is true in any democracy but rendered visible as a problem in Nepal because eliminating corruption was the reason for the revolution in the first place. Even when medical professionals knowingly avoid nepotism, favoritism, and bribery, they remain vulnerable to criticism by their own professional colleagues and even their clients that they are susceptible to corruption in the form of partisanship. Health professionals struggle with the desire both to politicize medical practice and to resist the revitalization of pre-revolutionary political practices. Sometimes corruption is easily identified, as when a minister offers a prestigious government job to a family member who may not hold the highest qualifications. Less visible is the promotion of a politicized medicine in a milieu wherein every political act runs the risk of being called partisan corruption, such as in politicizing an epidemic or an environmental disaster.

One might suggest, then, not that Nepal's medical professionals are mystified by the force of culture which compels them to rely on "source-force" rather than on objective and professional strategies which have international visibility today but that their behavior and sentiments illustrate the difficulty of dislodging and treating as separable professional practices, indeed, particularly scientific medical practices, from their social and political contexts. The troubles these professionals confront today reflect a transnational desire of those who call themselves medical scientists and those who aspire to democracy for a society organized around institutions, processes, and procedures founded on objective truths. What is important is less whether such a society exists than that a modernist hegemony demands its possibility.

Returning to the project that many Nepali physicians have undertaken of promoting social reform and political intervention as medicine, we may ask how that perspective contributes to the problem these very same physicians perceive in their system when they say that it is *not impartial*.[2] When medical professionals in Nepal promote politics as a deliberate medical strategy with the idea that this makes for a better medical science, we should probably recognize them as being more objective about science than those who insist upon a natural and necessary separation of medicine from politics. Their claim that biomedicine offers objective truths and universalistic methods is not inconsistent with their opinion that medical interventions are also inherently political. In taking this stand they share intellectual ground with a variety of other intellectuals and medical professionals from other times and places. But in Nepal, we can see how easily medical truths become subject to political techniques of control and accusations of corruption. Should democracy depend upon the maintenance of the cultural fiction that there are such things as objective truths which transcend politics and political contexts, then the Nepali doctors have chosen to believe in this particular fiction, for it is an eminently useful one. Consequently, they have also chosen to contend with its accompanying contradiction when each time they assert such truths for the sake of medicine, they are seen as making "political" claims. This is perhaps one of the enigmas of science and democracy, one legitimating the other and sealing off the possibility of questioning either's "factualness." Difficult as it has sometimes become for Nepali biomedical professionals to sustain a view of medical science as both inherently political, an outcome of social contingencies, and inherently scientific, and therefore impartial and socio-politically neutral, they have so far done so with a modicum of success but also some failures. There is in their minds no way to create a democracy other than to let truth speak for itself, even while they recognize the dangers of presuming that truth is ever formulated outside of a highly contested political milieu.

8   Science fetishism, truth, and privilege

> Take away man from his natural surroundings, from the fullness of his communal life, with all its living associations of beauty and love and social obligations, and you will be able to turn him into so many fragments of a machine for the production of wealth on a gigantic scale. Turn a tree into a log and it will burn for you, but it will never bear living flowers and fruit.   Rabindranath Tagore 1917

> Science is afforded opportunity for development in a democratic order which is integrated with the ethos of science.   Robert Merton 1942

The first third of the twentieth century produced at least two reactions to the rising tides of nationalism and fascism. Rabindranath Tagore wrote as a colonized subject against European nationalism suggesting that European society lacked India's tolerance for diversity and commitment to bonds of family, community, and spirituality. He characterized European modernity as maximizing efficiency but transforming humans into no more than appendages of machines – well-organized and scientifically ordered machines called nations (1917: 61, 62, 67):

> And we cannot but acknowledge this paradox: that while the spirit of the West marches under its banner of freedom, the Nation of the West forces its iron chains of organisation which are the most relentless and unbreakable that have ever been manufactured in the whole history of man. . . .
> The monster organization becomes all eyes, whose ugly stare of inquisitiveness cannot be avoided by a single person amongst the immense multitude of the ruled. . . .
> You may ask in amazement: What has she [the West] done to deserve this? The answer is that the West has been systematically petrifying her moral nature in order to lay a solid foundation for her gigantic abstractions of efficiency. She has all along been starving the life of the personal man into that of the professional.

Tagore's romantic vision was of a pre-colonial society that contained and nurtured a sense of collective obligation wherein the personal was not subordinated to the professional, wherein rational principles of efficient organization gave way to the social bonds of family, morality, friendship, and religion and the sacred values invested in these things. In this particular case, his critique is of modern institutions which are driven by the rationality of science and technology. Although the comparison is limited in all sorts of ways, a few of his concerns reappear in the work of other South Asian intellectuals today, for example, Ashis Nandy and Shiv Visvanathan. For these authors science is an instrument of postcolonial modernity that configured oppression under colonialism and continues to configure it under neocolonialist regimes of development. Technologies and techniques of modern science are for them not only inherently violent but their depersonalized and so called objectivist knowledge is capable of contributing to a fascism of science itself. Science is capable of eventually placing the state in the service of its own regimes of domination. The position advocates a return to and recuperation of indigenous idioms of knowledge, experience, and truth.

Less than a few decades after Tagore won the Nobel Prize, as the world moved towards a second world war, this time over fascism, another intellectual offered a different view of modern science. The American, Robert Merton, like Tagore and those who followed him, vigorously opposed the rising fascism in Europe in the 1930s, but he did so not by criticizing science but by embracing it as the means by which to avoid war. Merton argued that science was a critical instrument for undermining fascism because it was built upon the same foundations as democracy. Science and democracy "were expressions of each other and . . . both were threatened by Nazism" (Hollinger 1995: 440). Merton's link between democracy and science emerging from a particular moment in the history of the West, was one of shared values: "Intellectual honesty, integrity, organized skepticism, disinterestedness, impersonality," "freedom of thought," and "respect for the dignity of the human race" (Hollinger 1995: 2). These values were nurtured by a democratic system that placed a priority on the scientific method, and it was precisely these qualities that were lost under fascist regimes, wherein political prerogatives forced intellectual dishonesty, a compromising of skepticism, a denial of freedom of thought, and a preferential respect for some humans over others.[1]

These two responses, so seemingly opposite, have an ironic similarity. Merton came close to Tagore's insights about modernity when he concluded that science was "a cultural system, a pattern of attitudes actually embodied in a community" (Merton, quoted in Hollinger 1983: 4–5) rather than a domain of truth and knowledge external to culture. But for Merton the scientific community was exemplary in its social values and therefore an ideal cultural model for a society that functioned not only fairly (therefore morally) but also effectively. A morality of egalitarianism was fostered by strict adherence to impartial mechanisms for the distribution of society's privileges and rewards. For Tagore, modernity and its demands for impartial efficiency undermined the social fabric of humanity, partly by undermining its notions of sacred and moral duty that were so much a part of South Asian culture.[2] Science held the potential to rip society apart by denying the spiritual, familial, and social side of humanity while promoting a belief in objectivity.

Tagore's writings were readily available in bookstores in Kathmandu and India, where many Nepalis receive their education. The ideas of Nandy and Visvanathan were also discussed among Nepal's intellectuals in 1993. Moreover, Nepali intellectuals' concerns for preserving a distinctive Nepali way of life have been bolstered by their critiques. But, while I never found Merton's writings in Nepal, it was views like his as opposed to those of Tagore and other Indians that were taken up by Nepalis over the course of the revolution. This cannot be attributed solely to Nepali resistance to Indian hegemony, although it should not be overlooked. That Nepalis maintained like Merton that scientific methods were a key to democracy, and that the medical science they practiced functioned ideally like the democracy they wished to see writ large in their society is not a surprise, but why?

Surely lack of a colonial experience may account in part at least for the fact that Nepali intellectuals did not adopt the criticisms of science and modernity emerging from those who had experienced the oppression associated with their uses under colonialism. But this cannot explain it entirely, for surely these critics' calls for a recuperation of a socially embedded way of life resonate with Nepali medical professionals' calls for retaining a distinctive Nepali way of life invested with a sense of community, reciprocity, and moral obligation, as well as retaining their reputation for being a people who have reverence for the sacred (in gods, goddesses, and moral responsibility). In this concluding chapter I interrogate the Nepali approach to science by juxtaposing it in more detail with the views of the South Asian critics just mentioned, particularly the view that sees science as destructive to a morally based society, including a moral duty not simply to the gods, but to others.

The criticisms from India make Nepali medical professionals' desire for a democracy through science appear naive at best, perhaps self-hating at worst. Thus this chapter offers a choice between two different conclusions. One invokes the South Asian post-colonial criticisms of science in order to suggest that Nepali medical professionals are themselves advancing Western hegemony and that their commitment to scientific objectivism obscures their positions as elites within a still highly stratified post-revolutionary Nepal – elites who still benefit from notions of sacred duty held by the public and who continue to feel that doctors are "like gods." The other turns the actions of the Nepali medical professionals into instruments for a critique of the post-colonial critics, pointing out that Nepali doctors overcame their elitism and aligned themselves with the interests of the masses by using science to this end. The struggles for a Nepali democracy used science as a tool not for oppression but for liberation, not for objectification but for collective social action. Thus, some of the critics may be wrong in considering science inherently violent and objectifying, Nepalis say, for clearly it can be used to put an end to domination and the seemingly inevitable alienation its empiricism is thought to demand. In this, Nepalis' actions also speak back to critics who suggest that the sacred is undermined by the secular as an inevitable outcome of modernity. Nepali medical professionals have tried to reinsert morality into medical secularism by politicizing it, and they suggest that domains of the sacred are not undermined by science but allowed to survive by being removed from them and from the domain of the political.

The critics' suggestion that scientific truths are instruments of domination might be revealed by some Nepali professionals as, in its own way, aligned with privilege. Just as universalist definitions of human rights are of more use to those who feel they have been violated than to those who have not, so too are the notions of universalism put forth by science of more use to those whose struggle for democracy than to those who already live in democracies wherein such assumptions are already "matters of fact." Democracy is not a given or a fixed social formation, nor is it tied in any inevitable way to scientific truth, but a process which, according to Nepali medical professionals, must be built upon shared beliefs in such objective truths. Just as science is revealed as not inherently violent, the Nepali case also reveals that science is neither inherently democratic in its conception or implementation or even in its objectivity, nor is it inherently impartial. Rather, science is always formed and exercised in negotiated political fields where either democratic or undemocratic purposes can be served. The Nepali case suggests that if the former is desired, it must be fought for, vigilantly and persistently.

Surely the ability to speak about the culturally or politically constituted nature of either scientific truths, democracy, or human rights in the Nepali context demands attentiveness to the privileged position of the speaker. For Nepalis involved in the struggle against both Indian and Western domination – for those who have employed science as a weapon in their struggle – there is much at stake in claiming science is an instrument of domination. This conclusion thus highlights the relationship not between truth and power but between truth and privilege. With this latter point then, I come full circle back to the views of Ashis Nandy and a third possible conclusion. Nandy pointed to the inevitability of the internalization of Western knowledge systems by the formerly colonized (and "development"-ized), but he also noted the possibility of the shaping of these Western discourses into hybrid local forms. Whatever dilemmas this presents to its practitioners, this is perhaps what the Nepali medical professionals have revealed to us.

Criticism of science in the post-colonial world

Post-colonial Indian intellectuals Ashis Nandy and Shiv Visvanathan offer critical insights about modern science. Visvanathan (1988a), argues that Western development agendas in South Asia use science to justify their claims that the "underdeveloped" world is Hobbesian – that its people would perish if left to their own so-called unscientific ways. He maintains that it is the development agencies themselves which are Hobbesian in that they have internalized strategies of violence and projected them on to others. "The Hobbesian state justifies intervention as modernist resolution to the unappealing 'state of nature': nasty, brutish, short. . ." Science is vivisectionist by definition, for it treats the world as a laboratory and "triages" those in the "Third World" as its experimental guinea pigs. It replaces local cultural logic and notions of sacred and secular truth with notions of universal objective truth. But scientific truths, he suggests, are only stories told as objective and universal. In fact, they really reflect the society from which they emanate, its cultural priorities, and its vision of its place in the world. In the Indian case, colonialism began this process and the post-colonial state has continued it through instruments of Western technology and epistemology.[3]

When are truths in medicine simply a politics of representation serving the interests of the state or of political elites? Visvanathan (1988b) offers an example from the work of an early anti-science author, Carl Jungk, on the "atomic clinic" built atop Hijayama Hill by scientists working for the United States government to study radiation sickness after the bombing of Hiroshima. According to Jungk (quoted by Visvanathan 1988b:137):

> It was built ultra-modern style with the newest technologies and medical resources. But no patient that visited the "clinic" was ever to receive treatment for their suffering: If a patient were ever to ask the scientist at the clinic, "What do you advise, doctor? What can I do to get well again?," the doctor's reply was always the same, "This is not a therapeutic establishment but a scientific institute founded in collaboration with the Japanese health authorities with the exclusive object of carrying out research."

What sort of science is this? A science that cannot see the patient for the object of study he has become. Citing Jungk again, Visvanathan writes of science as a field of war: "The battlegrounds of the new frontier lie in the science laboratories and workshops" (1988b: 139). Joining him, Nandy writes, "Science violates not merely through the super-bombs powered by paranoia and super-greed; science violates also through bureaucratization of human suffering and through 'scientization' itself" (1988: 21–22).

Medicine is not exempted from the critique; it is a central target of it. South Asian scholars caution about the iatrogenesis of modern medicine and the capitalist production of its own damaging side-effects (Kothari and Mehta 1988), about the violent outcomes of the inherent reductionism of scientific practices including medicine (Shiva 1988), about the psychological violence of modern science (Nandy 1983), and about the inevitably anti-democratic consequences of a science that uses the state for its own purposes rather than vice versa (Nandy 1988). Modern scientific medicine, they claim, always contains within it the seeds of destruction of humanity and humanism in vivisectionist approaches all the while justifying its existence on the basis of its humanistic intentions (Marglin 1990; Visvanathan 1988a, 1988b).

Critiques of science emerge from a view that pays attention to the conditions of scientific production and dissemination in a global arena wherein societies do not share equally in power or privilege, benefit or blame. Science, the critics say, has always unfairly benefited the rich donor nations while disrupting the recipient poor nations and then blaming them for its failures. Sandra Harding, paying close attention to the critics, clarifies this problem (1994: 14):

> Modern science's accounting practices – the ways Northerners account for the consequences of modern sciences – appear distinctively Northern. These accounting practices mask the actual distribution of sciences' benefits and costs. Bad consequences are externalized and good ones internalized; benefits are disproportionately distributed to elites in the North and their allies in the South, and the costs disproportionately to everyone else. . . . All consequences of sciences and technologies that are not planned or intended are externalized as "not science" (cf. Alvarez 1988:108). Such an accounting need not even be intended; critics argue that such an "internalization of profits and externalization of costs is the normal consequence when nature is treated as if its individual components were isolated and unrelated. . . (cf. Bandyopadhyay and Shiva 1988: 63).

Science, these critics suggest, is a closed discourse. In a system wherein dissenters are immediately called unscientific and thereby discredited, how does one reconcile science's claims to moral, logical, or rational supersedence over other systems of knowledge? The critics' supposition is that those who adopt a Western rational view of the world via science are necessarily (though not of their own volition) post-colonially "colonized." Nandy (1983: xi) explains that this "second form" of colonization "colonizes minds in addition to bodies and it releases forces within the colonized societies to alter their cultural priorities once for all. In the process, it helps generalize the concept of the modern West from a geographical and temporal entity to a psychological category. The West is now everywhere, within the West and outside; in structures and in minds."

Ultimately, the critics tap into the view, long held in some fields of anthropology, that modern science is an ethnoscience. Extended to the non-Western world, science has played a role in undermining non-Western knowledge systems, even though it has borrowed from and built upon non-Western knowledge and non-Western knowledge offers useful and efficacious methods for intervention (Harding 1994; Ziauddin 1988; Marglin and Marglin 1990).

Many critics argue that science is a destructive instrument of modern development, and in many ways these criticisms *might* have been instrumental for the political goals of the revolutionary Nepali medical professionals. Not only do these arguments address the salient issue of Western domination but also they articulate the problem of an objectified science which claims political neutrality – a type of science opposed by many radical medical professionals in Nepal. Finally, they might have embraced these critics because Nepalis' own desires to preserve a domain of the sacred in Nepal as a hallmark of its national identity resonated with the critics' insights and desires to recuperate that for their formerly colonized nations. The convergence of interests is ironic, given the differences in their programs: the post-colonial critics might resist biomedical science in order to achieve political freedom and to valorize their traditional culture, whereas Nepali medical professionals embraced it in order to achieve political freedom and preserve their traditional culture.

Science, democracy, and nationalism

The perspective offered by Nandy would perhaps lead one to criticize the Nepalis for their uncritical and unreflective embrace of science, arguing that it makes them agents of neocolonialism, although Nandy would surely add that this is not something over which they have had much choice. Echoes of his complex position on this process of colonialism are found in his discussion of nationalism itself (1993: 16): "Not learning from the experience of the West, South Asia has merely telescoped the

Western model into its own societies. A kind of self-hatred is involved in the exercise of remodelling ourselves according to someone else's history. That is the tragedy of virtually every society in this part of Asia."[4] But, as if responding to Nandy, Nepalis did, as we have seen, voice concerns over the preservation of distinctive Nepali culture. As one physician put it, "We think that the democracy we have fought for will be different from the democracy of the West. We have seen the way that it works in the Soviet Union and China, and we have seen the democracies of the West and we will take something from both of these and make a democracy that is our own. We will take the best from each system." A desire to recover local traditions rather than importing patterns from abroad was also expressed by Parajuli (1992: 4):

> Justifications for more egalitarian and collective forms of livelihood in Nepal do not have to be imported from abroad. They are present in the remnants of our own collectivity. In fact, this is where Nepali men and women who still are less alienated from the collectivist perspective can contribute to a world shattered by the market economy of individual interest. This is where the most oppressed of the so called under-developed world like us can show the way to the over-developed, mal-developed world.

At the same time, many Nepali intellectuals in the medical field were convinced that science and democracy would not endanger the preservation of a society *unlike* the West. Science and democracy in Nepal were constructed as signifiers for both the objective and the politicized conscience of the typical Nepali citizen but they were not signifiers of sacred culture. They were the means to recuperate sacred culture.

Many medical professionals held the idea that one could be both scientific in professional outlook and a Nepali who revered and preserved the cultural practices upon which Nepali society was still largely organized, particularly religious practices. For most of them, there was no conflict between a spiritual life and one's life as a practitioner of medical science, although I only found a few who actually tried to combine them into the same set of practices. One of these practitioners who argued for the importance of spiritual healing within biomedicine was Dr. S. K. His office smelled of incense, rather than the sterile cleaning fluids of the hospitals I had been in. His desk was wood, worn into a polished surface by the years of use, and he had a glass top over the ink blotter on his desk. Beneath it, he had placed several photographs of popular Hindu religious figures: Ramakrishna Parmahansa, guru to Swami Vivekananda, Sai Baba. I noticed that on the walls where his credentials were not, he had placed an image of Milarepa, the Buddhist adept, and a framed Muslim calligraphic phrase, "Allah Bismillah" ("God is Great" as he translated it). In the course of explaining to me that the spiritual side of healing is very important, in a style not unlike many other Hindus in his profession, he offered a lengthy ecumenical reading of religious pluralism, noting that Hinduism itself encompasses the other religions, whether Buddhist, Muslim, or Christian. His personal spiritual guide was Swami Vivekananda:

This man was. . . he practiced all religions. He was a worshipper of Kaali, and went on to the worship of Krishna. . . . He went on to the worship of Ram. And when he worshipped Ram, you know how he worshipped him? He was literal and figural in his worship. He had to speak the truth, do the truth. Ram and one of Ram's greatest devotees is Hanuman [the monkey god]. He said worshipping Ram is not enough. I must worship he who is Ram's greatest worshipper, that is Hanuman. So what he did was, his "dhoti" the cloth that he ties here [around his waist and groin], he made a tail out of it and lived in the top of a tree eating fruits like a monkey. He became like a monkey worshipping Ram. He went on worshipping different forms of Hinduism and then he started on Christian religion. Somebody came and taught him the Bible, and he left the temple and all his Hindu gods were eliminated. He went out and then he went to this "sadhana." He meditated on Christ, the great Christ who was crucified for the sake of humanity. That is how he puts it. And on the third day, he sees a figure in his garden he's never seen before. A bearded person, long locks and he's got this long flowing look and he is coming. And he says who is this man? I don't recognize him. I've never seen him before. And he says, "This man came towards me and suddenly I said, my god, this is the Christ." And you know the result was when later in his life, when he was an ordinary Brahmin, great people, the scientists, all came to him later in life, and he asked them "Tell me. You know so much about Christ. You've read about him. Tell me his description." So they gave the classical description: he's got an aquiline nose, fair complexion, bearded. They said this, and he said "No, the tip of his nose was flat." That's what he said. He said, "I have seen him and the tip of his nose is flat."

And then, after that somebody came and initiated him into the Allah mantra. And he went from Christianity and out of India, to Allah. Three days later, he sees the same thing [vision of Allah]. So he went through all of the religions and he said "I am convinced now that Mother has shown me there is no difference. Mother in one form is the Christ, in one form is the Krishna, one form is that person – that leper [victim of leprosy] out there. For me there is no difference."

He started with the worship of Kaali. You look at a god from a distance, you see him sitting on a throne. You come close to him and what do you find? You can find water is blue, but pick it up and it's nothing [clear]. So Ramakrishna says Kali is the same as the imperceptible Brahmna who is called "no attributes." When the infinite, that is cosmic intelligence – you see Hinduism has got the term Brahma, cosmic intelligence. The cosmicity which is indescribable, that is the universe. I mean think of that: the creation of the universe from cosmic intelligence. When that creation takes a form, to create it takes a form and that is Shakti. Shakti is power. And we believe it always takes a female form. Never as male. Now Ramakrishna says Kaali and the imperceptible Brahma are the same. It's fire and it is the power to burn you. It is like ice and it is the power to cool you. So, he says this is Kaali and that is Kaali – there is no difference. It is like this, Ramakrishna said, "Listen, if you acccept the good you must accept the bad because they are two parts of the same thing. You must go beyond the good and the bad, beyond this and that, beyond the darkness of the mind, if you say darkness it implies light. If you say god is all god, it cannot be. There must be bad. There must be a balance of it in the Universe."

[I ask: "And you incorporate this spiritualism into your medical practices?"]

I say you must do your duty to your family and to your people and your country . . . . to your everything. Do it hard. Do it to your full capacity because it is like godliness. You've got to work but the results are not in your hands; that is the god's [responsibility]. You may work so many experiments. You may not have the Nobel prize. Somebody else will get the Nobel Prize, but if you don't, you don't get upset because the whole aim of life is godliness. There's no other aim in life. That's what I believe. There is no other purpose in life. If you realize it you call it realization, call it your own realization.

He continued for a long time with an inspired discussion of spirituality and the importance of knowing yourself. This, he felt, was also a key not only to health, but also to godliness. "Come, I'll give you a book on Sai Baba and what I have written about his life. Take it with you. You might like it." He gave me the book and walked me on a tour of his compound. He had a fragrant garden for walking. There was a small bird aviary, benches for sitting, a large shrine for the living Hindu saint, Sai Baba. He gave me an example of his religious medico-philosophy: "Always ask yourself, 'Who am I?' Say you are working and you are angry. So you say, 'I am angry.' You are very much disturbed. So you say 'Who is disturbed?' And so on. Every two steps you come back to the center [to yourself]. This way you keep yourself always. You find out who you are, constantly. When you go out, you will then know – if you are not tanned, or if you are not. The heart can be transplanted, liver can be transplanted. Then, are you the liver which is gone out or the liver which has gone in? The point is to always ask yourself who you are. You do your work but center yourself. Ramakrishna simplified religion to the question:'Who am I?'" Dr. S. K. was unique in his particularly rich descriptions of the relationship between spirituality and medicine, noting that having spiritual guides, taking spiritual retreats were all part of maintaining a healthy life. He was also unique in his willingness to include the sacred in his secular medical practice. Maintaining a distinction between science and religion was critical for most practitioners. But I quote from Dr. S. K. at length because his perspectives say much about a modern secularist Nepali attitude towards the professional place of the "sacred." He attempts to hold on to the sacred by rendering it highly individualized, repeatedly asking "Who am I?" as a mandate for health. He also asserts that the sacred must be highly ecumenical, in a manner that is well-suited to a multicultural, multiethnic society like Nepal. Most important, he assumes that sacred truths are as objective as scientific medical ones. Dr. S. K. was not unique in his commitment to the idea that if one's professionalism demanded one take on one's job as a sacred duty, one had to fulfill it, but that holding on to a sense of one's religious devotion would not interfere with good scientific practice; on the contrary, it would embolden it.

Nepali debates about democracy in the post-revolutionary period have, in fact, produced at least one form of preservationism regarding religious sentiment. In multiethnic Nepal, debates about nationalism have often been articulated about the need for retaining Nepal's rich and plural religious heritage. As a result, the debates have spawned controversy over whose culture, and whose religion, should be taken as paradigmatic for the nation. The idea of ethnic representation has emerged in contemporary debates in fields from politics to education and health. Some have argued for an "ethnopolitics" and an "ethnodevelopment" sensitive to the particular needs of each specific ethnic or religious group.[5] At a minimum, some argue, a unified Nepali culture must not be based on the brahminical Hinduism which has dominated for the past several hundred years.

Krishna Bhattachan, a Nepal and US-trained anthropologist/sociologist at Tribhuvan University and a Thakali (an ethnic minority), phrases the problem this way (1995: 129–30):

> From the Bahun–Chhetri perspective, with their internalization of concepts like caste inequality, purity and pollution of foods, drinks and castes, there has been no wrongdoing, exploitation, suppression, oppression, and domination of and against the depressed and the low caste and other ethnic groups. In contrast, looking from the Western social scientists' perspective with their concepts of equality, democracy, human rights and secularism, and from the perspective of the victims of Hindu caste hierarchy Bahuns–Chhetris are primarily responsible for their [low and non-castes'] continuing underdevelopment. . . . The national parties are dominated by particular ethnic groups – Bahuns and Chhetris – and their sectional and caste interests are rationalized into national interests, thus giving a very misleading picture of distributive justice.

It is this Western view that Bhattachan himself adopts, considering it above cultural orientations and party politics because it is based on truths judged secular, scientific, and universal, like human rights. It is this view which will preserve the ethnic diversity which, for him, gives Nepal its unique cultural identity. In fact, the debates over internal ethnic representation in Nepal contribute to debates over the politics of truth there, wherein the idea of truth is often contested by different groups. Questions about objective truth are in the new political climate often displaced by the question of *whose* objective truth one is considering.

As debates over nationalism arouse discussions about both the moral character of Nepali society, a sense of moral duty inside and outside of one's professional life, and the role of definitive ethnic and caste minority and majority labels, so too are debates aroused about the role of scientific and impartial truth in the multicultural nation. Whereas the former seem to call for a rekindling of the sorts of importance given to social partiality based on caste, ethnicity, religious affiliation, and family (the very practices critiqued in the revolution), the latter is believed capable of transforming these practices of partiality into matters of democratic truth – a form of objective truth concerning fairness and equity. Using ideas about objective truth like that found in science, and believed to be foundational to democracy, might be seen, then, as a sort of science fetishism.

Science fetishism?

Democracy in Nepal, as envisioned early on by its medical intellectuals and later by its ethnic minorities, might be seen as having anticipated the problematic posed by invoking ideas of objective truth to mediate the partiality and favoritism demanded by party, ethnic, or caste-based politics. Nepali democracy might be seen as at once an outgrowth of what might be called "science fetishism" *and* a commitment to resisting the fetishization of scientific truths by reconnecting them to their political relations of production as defined by collective interests. Just as commodities in late capitalism, as theorized by Marx and Lukacs, are reified and fetishized in relation to the social relations required to produce them, so too is science fetishized for many Nepalis in this never-colonized area of the world. Science is considered to produce objective truths detached from the social relations of their production, yet it is also believed capable of magically bestowing on all who possess it the ability to bring about an equitable distribution of resources and justice. In Nepal such equity was seen as being manageable along distinct caste, ethnic, religious and, eventually, party lines. Scientific and modern techniques for delivering truth were seen as the critical tool for this project because they would ensure fairness. Nandy (1988: 8,10) considers this somewhat delusional:

> Technology comes to represent an escape from the dirtyness of politics . . . a form of social change which ensures a place in the sun for portions of the middle classes whom the democratic process otherwise tends to marginalize, an anxiety-binding agent in the public realm, and often a media-based exercise in public relations. . . the concept of science in this model of scientific growth is that of the ultimate key to all problems facing the country, scientists subscribing to the model can lay claims to the charisma which in some other political cultures belongs exclusively

to god-kings. In the process, scientists become one of the two ultimate sources of legitimacy for the . . . state among middle classes – the others . . . are the development experts and experts on national security. . . . Science is the new reason of state.

Nepali medical professionals are by most measures members of the elite. Physicians and government medical administrators are nearly all high-caste, most are wealthy, and most are very well-connected to the resources of wealth and power inside and outside the country. I have shown that, along with most Nepalis in the post-revolutionary milieu, many still benefit from and are forced to use networks of affiliation and social influence. The preservation of these networks can be thought of as an outgrowth of both medical professionals' moral commitment to politicizing medicine (in a secular moralistic sense concerning human rights and professional duty) and their desire to retain a culturally distinctive and religious Nepal (retaining a sacred moralism tied to religious pluralism and valuing family, gods, and patrons). Within this environment, modern Nepal remains a place wherein it is believed good and proper to retain a sense of moral duty to one's status superiors, including medical professionals who are at times revered as what Nandy has called "god-kings." Thus it is possible to ask – although it requires a good deal of cynicism – whether the medical professionals have invoked a scientific objectivism which ultimately serves to conceal their elite status and privilege while entitling them to even more of these benefits. Beyond adopting science to conceal a naive idealism about objective ways to ensure multiethnic, multicaste, or multiparty representation and welfare (which means ensuring exclusionary privilege), such objectivism might actually conceal elitist favoritism and the partiality that comes with being a purveyor of source and force in the new democracy.

Some would argue that the medical professionals have, by politicizing their medicine, managed to advocate service to the people while preserving their own positions as elites in a still highly stratified and unequal society. In their participation in a "science in the service of the poor" medical professionals' elite status was elided with their status as bearers of *modernity*, wherein being modern came to mean being scientific, fair, and impartial – participating in a system that claimed to treat all persons as equal and as having equal potential for health. The political nature of this conflation in the minds of both care-givers and patients is partly what true believers of science feel makes it effective. It is an elision carried out under the guise of benefiting others. It is possible, however, that in this sense the idea that truth is objective is a way of evading questions about the elite's privileges accrued from these truths. In the same way that ideas about democracy often conceal the privileging of specific groups by being founded on a collective belief in the fairness of "the system," so too would this view suggest that privileges of the existing elite were concealed by their revolutionary calls for objective and impartial truth and justice for all. Does not science merely mask the ongoing elitism of professionals who, revered for their sacred status and their secular knowledge, seem above reproach when it comes to outcomes of science that only reproduce social inequality?

One way to assess this possibility is by asking what would have happened had circumstances been different in the revolution. If the doctors had used their authority as arbiters of truth to support the panchayat system against the public uprising, they would have been accused of using medical truth for political goals, for preserving their elitism right from the start. Their ability to tell the truth might itself have been questioned. But because they aligned themselves with the masses, the issue of their own ability to utter truth as elites was never raised. They were applauded for using politics for medical goals and for setting aside their interests as elites. Their own elitism was obscured by the foregrounding of claims to objective, and inherently beneficial, medical truth.[6] The truth, literally and figuratively, was on their side, but I would say they too were on the side of the truth that happened to be winning that day.

Taking seriously the claims of the post-colonial critics of science, then, one might want to ask to what extent medical professionals served as agents of neocolonialism, despite their stated desires for an independent and culturally distinctive Nepal. Although notions of democracy in Nepal are associated with a long history of neocolonial and unequal relations between foreign aid institutions, donor nations, and Nepali subjects, this history tends to be overlooked when science and technical solutions to development are invoked. How long would it be before people realized that nothing regarding social inequality had really changed, and that actions by the medical professionals only exacerbated the situation by treating social problems as scientific ones, thereby effacing social solutions that would be deeply tied to their own elite class and caste status and their dependency on foreign aid? How long before calls for preservationism of a distinctive Nepali way of life were interpreted as calls for a renewed Hindu elitism, masked again by scientists who claimed that the sacred is as important as the secular and that preserving the former would not infringe on the sort of truths found in the latter because it transcended culture? If it is true that Nepali medical professionals have fetishized science, why shouldn't the Nepali medical professionals be accused of acting as agents of neocolonial hegemony?

The obvious response is that Nepali medical professionals could just as easily be said to have specifically worked against a fetishization of medical truth during the revolution and after by ensuring that their truths served the interests of the people and by disclosing the politics of truth production. The practice of science among Nepali medical professionals was one that aimed to keep visible the conditions of the production of its truths by referring to social inequality as a cause of disease, by politicizing patients to be skeptical of corrupt medical practices, and by noting that if medical truth was to serve the people as opposed to privilege, everyone would have to be political about its uses. This stance both reinforced a belief in the objective truth of their medical insights, and treated these as if they were capable of fetishistically bestowing democratic freedom, health, and security on those who lived by them. But this works only if people remained aware of the possibility of such truths obscuring caste or class elitism. Democracy would only work if patients remained vigilant about not treating their doctors as god-kings but as fallible citizens just like themselves. This stance mitigated science's ability to mystify its users as to the conditions of its production. If possible, one might think of their practices as fetishizing without mystifying. The many criticisms health professionals heard as they politicized but tried to avoid accusations of political bias attest to the presence of such public vigilance.

A politics of privilege

Science and democracy in Nepal could be seen as not simply fetishized signs but also enabling practices. Nepali medical professionals constantly struggle to find a way of engaging in objectivist science while resisting partiality. Retaining commitments to political concerns which tap into a demand for social affiliations based on party, but also ethnic and caste groups (in the terms of the new democracy), has, however, made their commitment to objective standards difficult. Holding on to commitments to family, religion, ethnic group, as well as profession and party arises inevitably from the process of politicizing truth, but it also arises from more general Nepali desires to hold on to ideals about the moral dimensions of Nepali culture as a nationalist project. These moral dimensions lead to situations in which Nepalis feel a moral duty to help friends, relatives, and political allies as part of an objectivist and democratic concern wherein caste and ethnic needs as well as family values were seen as legitimate democratic idioms for expressing political demands. Many of the doctors I spoke with discussed how they felt a need to resist the sort of partiality that was targeted as corrupt during the revolution by maintaining a commitment to an objectivism that always questioned who in the social hierarchy was most likely to benefit from their truths. But ironically, this effort to remain vigilant about the politics of truth often dragged its practitioners into political eddies called corrupt because they were seen by others as new forms of partiality. One response was to invoke ideas about moral responsibility to counter these accusations, noting that moral duty to one's profession required them to speak for the poor and underprivileged, for the opposition parties, and for the minority caste and ethnic groups. Health professionals thus made a distinction between the processes resulting in this perception and those which evaded it: As Dr. N. expressed it:

Social pull and pressure exist. So do examples of yielding to it even by the most exemplary figures in the revolutionary movement. But the point is that that is not our premise. There has to be a conscious resistance to such pressures, to work towards the elimination or reduction of such pressures by establishing systems and bringing structural change which make people less motivated to seek favours at the expense of others. If we succumb to that, it should be considered our weakness.

In this practitioner's view, succumbing to social pressures of favoritism was entirely distinguishable from the social pressures that came with ensuring specific interest groups were represented, that the moral character of the nation was not eroded, and that medicine remain political. His idea was to avoid corruption as it was known in the old regime – nepotism, favoritism, bribery, *aphno manche*, "source-force" – by sticking to "the truth." But he did so by keeping in mind the political implications of his medical actions and making sure they served democratic, that is, scientific, goals. By forcing truth to be located in the domain of democracy and science (as opposed to patronage and partiality), new political practices through which truth was contested came to be seen by him as legitimate forms of democratic process. But the distinction between corrupt and good politicized medicine has, as I have shown, become quite blurred in post-revolutionary Nepal, partly because of the way that scientific truths emerge as politically constituted entities to most Nepalis. Many note that democratic politics itself has come to rely on the ongoing presence of patronage, favoritism, and other social preference repackaged into parties, ethnic and minority groups, and moral responsibilities. Anirudha Gupta (1996: 41) describes the situation as one in which in the new democracy "the politics of jobbery, intrigue, and patronage has invaded every walk of life." Under multiparty democracy, these political processes are not taken as instantiations of the success of the revolution but rather as new forms of the practices of an old corruption. Medicine is not exempted. Thus the more political medicine is made, the more it runs the risk of being seen as corrupt.

Rather than seeing patronage and favoritism as an inevitable part of any democracy, they are in post-revolutionary Nepal labeled as corruptions of a true democracy, bolstering the belief that one could ideally separate politics from modern impartial institutions like medicine. Gupta sees through this: "Such scandals under a dictatorship usually lead to its fall, [whereas] in democracies they are treated as non-events" he writes (1996: 41). But his concern is that this belief conceals the true source of ongoing troubles for Nepalis: an emerging parasitic elite who garner foreign aid resources for their own benefit. For him, the true source of democracy will come not from following the examples set by other democracies who fund these elites – India in particular – but rather by realizing that these democracies have similar problems of parasitism, those who usurp not only from their own citizens but also from those of other nations. But if Gupta sees the solution in turning to his own traditions, he might still have to contend with the possibility that the very traditions he hopes to recuperate might in fact rejuvenate the sorts of actions which have been labeled corrupt.

Perceptions that traditional Nepali culture should and could be preserved under democracy focus on its rich religious heritage, its tolerance for ethnic and caste pluralism, its family values, and its nurturing of the social and personal dimensions of social life over the technocratic or bureaucratic demands of industrialization. Intellectuals in particular mark these qualities as worthy of retaining while reaping the benefits of all that development and modernization can offer to eradicate those qualities of Nepali culture deemed problematic. But the distinctions between culture worth preserving and culture needing to be rejected is sometimes difficult to decipher. When is the promotion of religion, family, and social bonds something that will preserve traditional Nepali culture and when does it endorse corruption in the form of favoritism and patronage? When does promoting respect for Nepal's sacred religious traditions contribute to the preservation of a distinctive nation and when does it reinforce the cultural logic of moral duty to status superiors? Or worse, when does it reinforce Hindu hegemony and caste elitism? The ambiguity is well captured in the aforementioned response of one Nepali to the question of the meaning of *natabad/kripabad*. It means gratitude, he said at first, then added, "there's a good form and a bad form." The idea that something meaning "corruption" could also mean "gratitude" suggests that it is indeed sometimes unclear to many Nepalis how to reconcile traditional priorities for social reciprocity with new ideals about fairness and individualized merit-based privilege. Corrupt behaviors favor one group of people, or one person, over another who might be more deserving on the basis of "objective" measures. But morally valued behaviors among Nepalis are those which reiterate values of social cohesion in families and caste and ethnic groups; they even instill a sense of moral duty into one's modern professional activities and into one's political parties.

Thus one dilemma faced by Nepali professionals today is that Nepal is a society which has tried to eliminate social corruption in the form of favoritism of family, friends, *aphno manche* or even political party members but it still wishes to hold on to notions of the sacred which are expressed in these sorts of relationships. Moreover, Nepalis do not simply desire to use such relationships of affiliation because they see them as a way to remain moral, nationalistic, or democratic. On the contrary, Nepalis seldom have the choice to avoid using them. It could be argued that Western democracies have been able at least in the late twentieth century to legitimize themselves by providing enormous social securities to a majority of their citizens in the form of infrastructure, medical and public health care, education, and economic welfare (the so-called feminization of the state), but the Nepal government's ability to provide these things has been hampered by enormous difficulties (not least of which has been the development paradigm). This has meant that instead Nepalis are still forced to rely on their families and friends for securities and benefits when it comes to things like income, health, education, and other forms of social security. Whereas we might think of the state as being the extended family for many European and North American citizens, it is the actual extended families, and networks of friends and obligated associates, among Nepalis who are relied upon for providing what the state has, as of yet, failed to adequately provide. Coupled with the already deep-seated sensibility held by many Nepalis that expressions of reciprocity and patronage are partly tied to one's sense of moral duty to others, and with the emerging calls for a Nepali national identity that includes preservation of its rich history of upholding the sacred, we get a modern Nepali dilemma. Even if Nepalis did not consider such nationalist goals as the preservation of family and religious values, ethnic pluralism, and political party freedoms to be worth preserving, Nepalis cannot afford to operate as if the social networks emerging from these were not important.

Using the rubric of objective standards brought by both development and biomedical science (among other professions), Nepalis face a dilemma from yet another angle: by invoking scientific truths as objective and impartial but then insisting that these be put in service to political goals for the sake of health, medical professionals become occasionally mired in debates over the legitimacy of their truths. In fact, what would seem like an unproblematic endeavor in other places, in other ways, becomes in Nepal viewed as a means of corrupting truth. As multiparty politics have become the modern instrument for negotiating social privileges and rewards, so too have they become the instrument for reciprocity, patronage, and partiality. In these negotiations, truth becomes a visible marker of conquests and denials of social affiliation, not an impartial objective fact. Thus, medical professionals persistently work to remind fellow citizens of the opposite – that the nature of their truths is scientific, objective, impartial – despite the risk they run of undermining this by keeping them political.

Ashis Nandy may be right after all, then, in the sense that Nepalis may have come to think of some traditional ways of being Nepali as corrupt because they have internalized a Western vision of their culture. This interpretation is risky, however, for it undermines the position held by many Nepalis that the corollary institutions which are identified as being able to replace "corrupt" culture – namely, science and democracy – are in fact constitutive institutional mechanisms by which people in any society may achieve development; they are not "owned" by the Western nations, nor are they inherently damaging to the colonized, formerly colonized, or "neocolonized" of the world. In fact, Nepali intellectuals maintain, science and democracy are neither inherently violent nor instruments of neocolonial hegemony; they are beneficial tools that can help institutionalize freedom, independence, and the survival of Nepali culture. That Nepalis seek a way to both hold on to notions of truth which transcend social and political bias, while insisting on rendering visible the political uses to which they might be put is laudable. It is not that this is not true in other places, but that the conditions which enable it to be so in Nepal are extraordinarily demanding. Thus I would suggest that the critical stance one adopts on these themes of science and democracy have ultimately more to do with privilege than with truth.

Soon after completing this manuscript, I endeavored to write about these events with one of the Nepali physicians whom I had come to know in the course of research. After he had read my manuscript and we had discussed it, the problem of our respective privilege in regard to these issues became obvious to both of us. His commitment to exploring the links between human rights, truth, and medicine led him towards analysis of the inviolability of objective truths, while I was much more inclined towards a critical analysis of the ways in which an objectivist rendering of medical truths served some but not all political agendas. His position, as a Nepali intellectual still engaged in the struggle for democracy, was a vulnerable one. He had to reiterate the objective truthfulness of his claims because he was still involved with the struggle to make them work for democracy. I was conflicted about my position, feeling the need on the one hand to write in a manner that would support his and his fellow Nepalis' interests and on the other hand, perhaps as a consequence of my own privilege, to contextualize their movement in a broader analysis of medical science, truth, and democracy. In the long run, we realized that we would have to write two articles, one foregrounding his concerns and the other mine. Taking the truth claims of medical science to be objective and universal is not a debatable issue if one is trying to use these truths in order to stabilize one's democracy, no matter what form that democracy takes.

Although the perspective of this book will not be wholly shared by all of the Nepali professionals I worked with, my hope is that it offers an analysis of the medical professionals' role in the People's Movement which will engage them and inspire contemplation over at least one unconventional Western view of their efforts. From my perspective, Nepali medical practitioners offer insights about the possibilities of practicing a non-fetishized medical science that attends to sociological and political realities.[7] Their attempts to maintain the fine distinctions between secular and sacred in a nation wherein the very idea of the sacred was historically infused through most everyday and professional actions and particularly in relations within family, with friends, king, and even the gods, are remarkable. Accomplishing the distinction in popular discourse is imperative, for without it these professionals become vulnerable to accusations of elitism. When preserving family and religious values also legitimates the use of morally charged social affiliations for obtaining rewards (medical or otherwise), the lack of a distinction between sacred and secular results in accusations of corruption. When political parties become the primary means by which professionals are able to invoke truth for the benefit of "the people," a lack of clarity over a "political truth" and a "politicized truth" is aroused. How well and the extent to which Nepali medical professionals are able to maintain these distinctions means negotiating skillfully through the political minefields of cultural preservationism, religiously based nationalism, elite privilege, historical inertia, politicized medicine, scientific truth, and last but not least, effective medical interventions.

Perhaps, as I have suggested, in the long run, the practitioners I met have found a way to accomplish what Nandy (1988: 22) citing Chinua Achebe, suggests: "Let no one be taken in by the fact that we deal with western issues in a western language; we want to do unheard-of things with them." The unheard-of things that Nepalis do with these signs and practices of truth demonstrate to me that science and the democracies based on such notions are in fact fragile institutions, built upon fragile truths. But Nepali medical practitioners show me that however much these "universals" may be thought of as culturally and politically contingent and constructed, they are critical to the projects of social justice in many parts of the world today as non-contingent, non-constructed reality. The idea of "opting" for not retaining objectivity is not a possibility; the very idea is oxymoronic. I would only add to this that the Nepali case reveals that science does not seem to disappear any sooner than democracy once it is recognized as socially, culturally, or politically contingent, constructed, or fragile. All that disappears is the notion in Nepal that either science or democracy can exist without the other.

Notes

1 INTRODUCTION

1 My use of the term "medicine" in this text is almost entirely in reference to biomedicine as opposed to the many traditional scholarly and spirit-based medical practices found throughout Nepal. I make reference to these traditions but have not explored them here.

2 I note that the term "social science" did not yet exist, but was probably something more like "a science of the social." In a volume of translated Virchow works (1985: 3), a translation of this passage on the aims of his journal *Medical Reform* offers a slightly different translation.

3 The conference marked a radical shift in health development orientations away from high-technology, cure-based, vertical programs aimed at eradicating single diseases towards appropriate technology and preventive, basic health care programs for the masses. Its goals were simple. The stated goals were: "education concerning prevailing health problems and the methods of preventing and controlling them; the promotion of food supply and proper nutrition; an adequate supply of safe water and basic sanitation; maternal and child health care, including family planning; immunization against the major infectious diseases; prevention and control of locally endemic diseases; appropriate treatment of common diseases and injuries; and provision of essential drugs." Ultimately, they declared, the goal was "the attainment by all peoples of the world by the year 2000 of a level of health that will permit them to lead a socially and economically productive life" – "Health for All by the Year 2000."

4 The panchayat system was a single-party system of partially elected, partially appointed (by the king) government. It was organized on the principle of hierarchical tiers of representatives, representing, respectively, village, town, district, zone, and national interests. Each tier of representatives was selected from the tier beneath and elected to office, joining at the national level a group of ministers appointed by the king. It is called panchayat because at the village level it consists of a council of five persons. After the referendum of 1980, district elections to the National Assembly were allowed, and known supporters of the multiparty system were elected through them. Nevertheless, the revolution was against the lack of political freedom this system offered and its close intertwining with the monarchical institutions of power.

2 MEDICINE, SCIENCE, AND DEMOCRACY IN THE DEVELOPING WORLD

1 Locke's possessive individualism can be seen as distinctly modern. Macpherson (1962: 263–64) listed its assumptions: (i) what makes a man human is freedom from dependence on the will of others; (ii) freedom from dependence on others means freedom from any relations with others except those relations which the individual enters voluntarily with a view to his own interest; (iii) the individual is essentially the proprietor of his own person and capacities, for which he owes nothing to society; (iv) although the individual cannot alienate the whole of his property in his own person, he may alienate his capacity to labor; (v) human society consists of a series of market relations; (vi) since freedom from the wills of others is what makes a man human, each individual's freedom can rightfully be limited only by such obligations and rules as are necessary to secure the same freedom for others; (vii) political society is a human contrivance for the protection of the individual's property in his person and goods, and (therefore) for the maintenance of orderly relations of exchange between individuals regarded as proprietors of themselves.

2 I note that Shapin and Schaffer point out that at this historical moment "facts" were generated from collectives, not individuals, in the sense that experiment was always carried out under conditions of collective observation. This contrasts with my discussion of Nepali perceptions of human rights and their utility as "factual" primarily only when associated with individuals. (I note that human rights rhetoric changes its terms when speaking of the rights of indigenous groups.) Later, I bring a discussion of collectives back into the analysis when I describe the ways that medical professionals deploy scientific facts on behalf of collective interests. That is, I see competing concerns within Nepali professionals over the idea of the individual as a unit of scientific analysis when it comes to human rights and modern subjectivity and the importance of the collective when it comes to making medical facts work for the social good.

3 HISTORY AND POWER IN NEPAL

1 Some groups were loyal to more than one sovereign, according to Burghart.

2 Alternative readings of the Rana period are numerous, including those which note that these years "marked the transition from a semi-feudalistic Gorkhali empire to a centralised agrarian bureaucracy" (M. C. Regmi, cited in Whelpton 1992: 185).

3 These are the children of unions between high-caste Rana men and low-caste (often non-Rana) women, by the dictates of the Muluki Ain lower in status than their fathers. These lower-status Ranas were denied many of the patronage privileges accorded to "pure" Ranas and Chettris.

4 Ironically, although new Rana family members were banished from the post, even after Tribhuvan regained the throne, the Rana Mohan Shamsher remained prime minister.

5 He distinguishes this sort of monarchy from a feudal monarchy in which the king is beholden to noble families that have a great deal of power and grants

these families rights in return for their services. Shaha says that in Nepal the king is a patrimonial elite and, as such, rules through "peremptory commands because he is master in his own house" (1993: 2). I use his notion of patrimonialism here but stress that one of the main principles of the king's power and, by association, of those in the palace is a system of granting privileges in exchange for loyalties and services. There are no noble families to which the king is beholden (other than, some would say, the Ranas), but he used reciprocity and patronage invested with sacred importance in order to rule.

6   David N. Gellner, personal communication.

7   So, for example, soldiers could not only expect housing, subsidized electricity, pensions, etc., but their families also received informal and non-contracted preferential treatment when it came to bureaucratic processes, receipt of privileges, etc., not related to the military *per se*.

8   Children of intercaste marriages are exceptions to this rule, for they often have different caste status from their fathers or mothers. Interestingly, if the status refers to one's ethnicity, it tends to follow one's father, but if it refers to one's caste it follows one's mother. A child of a Sherpa father and Rai mother will be called a Sherpa, while a child of a low-caste mother and twice-born father (high caste) will be called low caste.

9   See Parish (1994) for a good description of this among Newars.

10 One might interpret the typical Nepali greeting of Namaste – translated roughly for tourists as "I bow to the god in you" – with this in mind. On the idea that one can discuss a unique Hindu polity, see Burghart 1984.

11 I am unable to find exact dates for their appearance in Nepali.

12 Mike Malinowski, chargé d'affaires for the US Embassy and Teddy Wood Stervinov, head of USAID at a series of talks for the official American community in Nepal, 1993.

13 US Embassy source information on Nepal, 1993.

14 Joshi (1993: 211) offers some of this information, the infant mortality figure comes from Mahesh Maskey, personal communication. (Joshi reports an 8.5 per 1,000 infant mortality rate.)

15 Clarke's is a review article of Graham Hancock's book, *Lords of Poverty: The Power, Prestige and Corruption of the International Aid Business* (Atlantic Monthly Press), in which he outlines many of these arguments and more but does not agree with everything he finds in the book.

16 See Rana, Shrestha and others in *Himal*, Mar./Apr. 1992; Justice (1987). This volume of *Himal* "What To Do with Development Aid," is devoted to critiques of development aid which range from demands for restructuring of Nepal's loans and withdrawal of aid to campaigns for reform of aid programs to improve efficacy. Other volumes of *Himal* also offer critiques (Gyawali in Jan./Feb. 1990 and see also May/June 1991).

17 Although it is not accurate to offer a generalization, democratic government and multilateral aid agencies held ambiguous attitudes in rhetoric and practice towards the Nepali monarchical system. On the one hand, there was an enormous skepticism about the regime, articulated in criticisms of corruption. On the other hand, there was a feeling that the government was basically stable and that disrupting this stability might drive Nepal into the hands of

communist insurgents, which was not desired. This was one reason that the Western countries' foreign aid positions on the revolution were largely ones of silence until nearly the end of the revolution.

18 Here again, the term *baksheesh* implies for most Westerners a sort of corruption but is translated by many Nepalis as "commission."

19 He writes, "From the fragments of the Lokayata that survive – and on the basis of which we are obliged to judge it today – it appears that all its insistence on accepting and enjoying life remains far too inadequate to inspire people to have real confidence in their heads and hands, so that they can move forward towards a greater mastery of nature and effectively intervene in the existing state of social affairs – to change the world and to work for the real emancipation of the real human beings. We are not aware of the Lokayatas ever visualising an extension of human control over nature and, in spite of their bitter protest against the priestly exploitation of the people, we do not get from them a consistent social norm as an alternative to the prevailing one, nor any programme of action for changing the prevailing social relations" (Chattopadhyaya 1976: 612).

20 Again, he writes, "The Lokayatas are the only philosophers of India to assert – though inevitably in their own way – that the socio-ethical values propagated by the philosophers are not necessarily the outcome of detached theoretical considerations. These are also connected with – and are sometimes the instruments of – maintaining the economic and other privileges of certain classes of people. These days we talk of the ideological instruments of the ruling class and of the class-interest lurking behind ideologies. Had the Lokayatas been able to speak in these terms, they would have been revolutionaries in our sense. . . . It is true that the Lokayatas appear to realise only one aspect of this connection, and that too in their own way. Certain types of ideology are propagated for the purpose of feeding the social parasites, as they say in so many words [the buddhi-paurusahinah, those who have neither intelligence nor manliness]. This is one way of connecting the mode of living with the mode of thinking. And there is no error in the connection conceived. Ideology is often a source of livelihood for the privileged minority. It is often an instrument for exploiting the people" (Chattopadhyaya 1976: 613).

21 Contrast this reading with Pfaff-Czarnecka (1996) and with the argument summarized by Gellner (1996a) that national integration in the modern sense was not an ideal until the beginning of this century and even then was combined with more traditional "dharmik" forms of legitimation.

22 Ironically, many of the most activist health workers were supporters of communism, even though they held fast to the idea that medical science could promote a multiparty democratic system. Only under democracy would their truths as medical scientists be effective – only under *democratic* conditions could their concerns for *communist* uplift be met. Scientific truth was allied with democracy, but communist activism and social perspectives on health would help to bring democracy about.

23 Shaha (1993: 176) discusses the Universal Declaration of Human Rights as a combination of the ideals of the American, French, and Russian revolutions for all mankind. Specific issues taken up by the human rights organizations are listed by Shaha as: the lack of independence of the judiciary; a "rubber-

stamp" parliament; arbitrary laws (Public Security Act) which give broad powers of repression to police; denial of peaceful assembly and association; retroactive punishment for alleged criminals; the death penalty, especially for alleged treason; imprisonment without trial; the creation of special courts which supplanted ordinary courts of law; trial by television in which the government telecast public defamation programs aimed at specific political individuals; "drumhead justice," or unfair representation in trials and unfair sentencing; denial of freedom of religion; persecution of Christians; denial of the right of political asylum; and the fettering and handcuffing of prisoners. Other human rights abuses are listed by FOPHUR as the arrest of over 25,000 persons for political reasons, the wrongful death of at least eighty persons involved in political protest (some reports were as high as 500 deaths), government refusal of information about the arrested and detained, arrests of a wife in place of a husband in hiding, torture of prisoners and failure to provide them with medical care, religious persecution of prisoners resulting in psychological abuse (particularly caste infractions), and impeding attempts to locate persons who had "disappeared" (Kaphley 1990: 27, HR Bulletin).

24 There are numerous ethnographic studies of the medical pluralism and convergence of biomedical with other medical resources in Nepal. It is not a simple topic, nor one which reveals homogeneity among communities throughout Nepal.

25 Arjun Karki, MD of Syracuse and Prativa Pandey, MD of Kathmandu in the opening paragraphs for the America-Nepal Medical Foundation, devoted to improving the health care system of Nepal.

4 REVOLUTIONARY MEDICINE: SCIENTISTS FOR DEMOCRACY

1 Commission agents are the persons through whom one is allowed to conduct business as a foreigner in Nepal. They are Nepali citizens and receive a commission (baksheesh) for their assistance. There were other popular explanations for the blockade also circulating. One had to do with the sale of arms to Nepal by China, which angered India and led to its refusal to renegotiate their trade and transit treaty. Another was that a visit made by Nepal's Hindu king to India had angered Rajiv Gandhi because the king had been allowed passage into a major Hindu temple (being a manifestation of Visnu) to which access had been denied Rajiv. Other explanations abounded.

2 Janata Dal is a "third party" coalition (anti-Congress) in India. See Shaha 1993: 183 for names of others.

3 Ravana is the king of Lanka in the Hindu epic *The Ramayana*. He is notoriously evil. He captures Sita, the wife of Ram, and is eventually defeated by Ram. One interpretation of this statement could be that this citizen has substituted the king as Ram with the king as Ravana, ironically the enemy to Visnu. Another might be that he identifies the system, not the king, with Ravana.

4 Bir Hospital is the main public hospital in downtown Kathmandu. I was told that employees at all of the public hospitals and even the Ministry of Health, were, eventually, involved in protests (especially black armband strikes among civil servants).

5 Although one physician with whom I spoke noted that the prime minister was targeting physicians as elites, another delegate suggested that he was referring not to physicians *per se* but to other elite members of the delegation, for example, members who were descendants of courtiers.

6 For example, physicians often refused to work in rural areas because they said they were often threatened by villagers who became angry at them for not having enough supplies or medicines that were needed. The lack of supplies was blamed on the government.

7 Allegedly arrested on grounds that he was involved in political organizing in the terai. Reports, or rumors, had emerged over the years which claimed that witnesses had seen him being transported in full leg and body casts by the army from one place to another. Some suspected that he had actually decided to work for the government after years of torture. Others assumed that he was dead. His father continued a campaign to recover him. He has not, to my knowledge as of the writing of this book, been found.

8 This nurse was mortally wounded when police bullets entered into her second-floor window while she was peering out at street activities.

9 The person who released these files to me asked that I refrain from copying any signed names. Thus, I have included only those who signed on behalf of groups or regions.

10 One suspects that the same interest in creating a government run by the principles of a professional and educated majority was responsible for the election of three ministers of parliament in the Lower House who were physicians.

6 MEDICINE AND POLITICS: A TRIAGE OF TRUTH IN THE PRACTICE OF MEDICINE

1 Here, too, the field of anthropology did not yet exist, although this is the translation given. I guess that the original was something more like "a science of the social."

2 The "New Man" is not defined in this text but presumably refers to the typical communist party cadre who has made himself over under the new system, eliminating his old ways and customs.

3 There are examples of politicized medicine from Latin America which I have not included here.

4 Fox-Keller (1992) notes that the idea of an *applied* science offers more credibility than is deserved to the idea of a *pure* science.

5 The branch of social constructivism in studies of science and technology, the Edinburgh School (e.g. David Bloor), at one time maintained that "science was interestingly and constitutively social all the way to its technical core: scientific knowledge itself had to be understood as a social product" (Pickering 1992: 1). This view included the idea that science is inherently political (e.g. expressing interests of various interest groups or classes). Later scholars of science and technology (e.g. Bruno Latour, Michel Callon) came to envision a greater role for the operations of an objective reality in the production of science and its truths. These researchers "placed human and non-human agents on a symmetric footing as 'actants' " (Wise 1996: 325), giving the idea of an objective "nature" equal status with social factors in determining scientific products. By the 1980s, studies of science often began to focus

not on what could constitute objective nature versus what would constitute a more contingent or culturally configured "nature" and "fact" in the world of science but on the "practice" of scientists and the cultural system constituted by these practices (Pickering 1992). This approach treated culture as practice, practices as culture, as opposed to treating culture as an ideological system that drives material action. Earlier, Thomas Kuhn offered in *The Structure of Scientific Revolutions* the insight that scientific pursuits proceed by matter of "paradigmatic" thinking in a manner that both conditions the questions posed and enables science to distinguish itself as a discipline by virtue of the fact that it can legitimately forget its past. The field of social studies of science and technology is vast and my presentation here of a very few cases is truncated and so should not be taken as anything like an exhaustive or complete overview.

6 For another example, see Martin 1991, 1994 who illustrates the cultural foundations to scientific knowledge for other cases.

7 POST-REVOLUTIONARY POLITICAL MEDICINE: CORRUPTION OR VALIDATION OF TRUTH?

1 There are citizens in the USA who consider this sort of lobbying a form of corruption, calling it a politics of "pork" or "special interests."

2 A quick glance through several volumes of Nepal's medical journals reveals this orientation. In just two volumes, 31 (nos.106–7), of the *Journal of the Nepal Medical Association*, one of Nepal's most technical journals, for example, twenty-two articles are offered and of these seven are focused on public health and make reference to social problems as a factor in ill health. This abstract from one of the articles is exemplary: "During 2049 Baisakh to Asar, 757 carpet factory labourers were admitted and another 375 treated as outpatients in Teku Hospital, making them the most important occupation group attending the hospital. 90% of them were suffering from gastro-enteritis, while others had enteric fever, infective hepatitis, pneumonia, measles, chickenpox, worm infestation, etc. This was mostly the result of overcrowding, poor sanitation, unhygienic personal habits and a lack of health consciousness. A significant number of patients had pneumonia with severe gastro-enteritis. Anthrax bacilli has not been isolated from them." (Vaidya, et al.1993; 31: 222). In their conclusion they state: "It is most unfortunate that neither the carpet manufacturers nor the authorities has seriously shown any concern for the health of the carpet factory labourers. Although child labour is prohibited by law, children as young as 5 years and working in carpet factories have been attending hospital, hence drawing attention to the need for strengthening the law. It has become imperative for the government to implement some laws immediately to provide basic health needs for the carpet factory labourers, like proper sanitation, safe drinking water, housing facilities, proper lighting and ventilation in the working place, protective garments, gloves and masks, periodic medical check-ups, medical benefits and insurance, and also for provision of health education" (Vaidya et al. 1993: 225). For every article like this one, it should be noted, there are three or four which do not address the social conditions or political solutions to the medical problems discussed.

8 SCIENCE FETISHISM, TRUTH AND PRIVILEGE

1 His perspective could also be contrasted with many of the German critical theory authors who, writing at the same time, also embraced science as an instrument that could oppose fascism but not through democratic but rather through socialist politics. Affiliated with these thinkers was Walter Benjamin who, for example, embraced modern technologies for their ability to eliminate the sort of power associated with pre-modern and also fascist regimes, what he called the power of the "aura."

2 Concerns like this were also discussed by philosophers and social scientists in Europe, notably Emile Durkheim and Marcel Mauss.

3 These authors are joined by critical voices from other nations that have been marginalized for questioning the cultural hegemony of development (Doyal 1979; Gunder Frank 1966; Foster 1987; Stone 1989; Escobar 1995). Stone in particular writes about the ways in which concerns expressed in the popular imagination in the United States come to be definitive for international health planning.

4 Ashis Nandy offers the insight for the argument that the idea of nation is itself an import from the European context (Anderson 1983; Burghart 1984; Gellner 1996a), that nationalism which is predicated upon the principle of a singular ethnic identity is itself distinctly non-South Asian. Most people in South Asia, he maintains, considered themselves to be plural in identity, not singular, until colonialism. The current nationalist debates in India, in which we see Muslim against Hindu, Sikh against Hindu, Christian against Sikh, Buddhist against Christian, etc. emerged as a legacy of colonialism.

5 There are critics of this position and it should not be taken as a majority view, if there is one. See Bihari K. Shrestha, quoted in an essay by a staff reporter for *The Nation* in "Economic Policies, Programmes Discussed" September 11, 1996: 3, who says that ethnic groups are not primarily economic or political units and therefore not a basis for development programs. He points out that much class exploitation occurs within rather than across ethnic groups. Apparently (Hu 1996) there is a constitutional ban against political units based on ethnicism, religion, and geographical region.

6 Similar problems obtain in the United States. Marxist analyses of medicine and science (Aronowitz, for example) suggest that scientists, like doctors, are elites by virtue of their monopoly on knowledge. The science they use serves as an instrument of mystification.

7 Morgan (1993: 80) might call this the vulgar Marxist practice of medicine, which "rejected the development establishment's assertions that health was above politics, and went on to place health squarely within the arena of issues to be contested in civil war or class struggle. . . . In other words, 'health' is so inextricably entangled with politics that its definition should be expanded to encompass oppression and social inequality." Although influenced by vulgar Marxism, I would say the historical condition leading to this practice in Nepal, including the social ambivalence regarding social alliances, make it somewhat different from the position defined in the sociological critique.

Bibliography

Adams, Vincanne 1996 *Tigers of the Snow and Other Virtual Sherpas*. Princeton: Princeton University Press

Adhikary, Kamal R. 1995 "The Fruits of Panchayat Development." *Himalayan Research Bulletin*, 15 (2): 12–24

Alvarez, Claude 1988 "Science, Colonialism and Violence: A Luddite View." In Ashis Nandy, ed., *Science, Hegemony and Violence*. Delhi: Oxford University Press

Anderson, Benedict 1983 *Imagined Communities*. New York: Verso

Andreski, Stanislav, ed. 1983 *Max Weber on Capitalism, Bureaucracy, and Religion: A Selection of Texts* London: George Allen and Unwin

Armstrong, David 1983 *Political Anatomy of the Body*. Cambridge: Cambridge University Press

Bachelard, Gaston 1934 (1984) *The New Scientific Spirit*. Trans. Arthur Goldhammer. Boston: Beacon Press

Baer, Hans 1982 "On the Political Economy of Health." *Medical Anthropology Newsletter*, 14(1): 1–2, 13–17

1989 "Towards a Critical Medical Anthropology of Health-Related Issues in Socialist-Oriented Societies." *Medical Anthropology*, 11: 181–194

Bandyopadhyay, J. and Vandana Shiva 1988 "Science and Control: Natural Resources and their Exploitation" in Ziauddin Sardar, ed., *The Revenge of Athena*. London: Mansell

Bhattachan, Krishna B. 1993 "Public Debate on Development: Sociological Perspectives on the Public Philosophy of the Development of Nepal." Ph.D. dissertation, Department of Sociology, University of California, Berkeley

1995 "Ethnopolitics and Ethnodevelopment: An Emerging Paradigm in Nepal" in Druba Kuma, ed., *State Leadership and Politics in Nepal*. Kathmandu: CNAS

Bista, Dor Bahadur 1991 *Fatalism and Development: Nepal's Struggle for Modernization*. Hyderabad: Orient Longman

Boyd, Byron A. 1991 *Rudolf Virchow: The Scientist as Citizen*. NY: Garland Publishers

Brown, T. Louise 1996 *The Challenge to Democracy in Nepal: A Political History*. London: Routledge

Burghart, Richard 1984 "The Formation of the Concept of Nation-State in Nepal." *Journal of Asian Studies*, 44 (1): 101–25

1993 "The Political Culture of Panchayat Democracy" in Michael Hutt, ed., *Nepal in the Nineties: Versions of the Past, Visions of the Future*. Delhi: Oxford University Press

Caplan, Lionel 1971 "Cash and Kind: Two Media of 'Bribery' in Nepal." *Man*, 6: 266–78

Chattopadhyaya, Debiprasad 1976 *What Is Living and What Is Dead in Indian Philosophy*. New Delhi: People's Publishing House

Chen, C. C., M.D. 1989 *Medicine in Rural China: A Personal Account*. Berkeley: University of California Press

Chen, Haifeng and Zhu Chao 1984 *Chinese Health Care: A Comprehensive Review of the Health Services of the People's Republic of China*. Boston: MTP Press Ltd.(a division of Kluwer)

Clarke, Thurston 1990 "Charity that Strangles the Poor." A review of *Lords of Poverty: The Power, Prestige, and Corruption of the International Aid Business*, by Graham Hancock, *Himal*, Jan./Feb. Lalitpur, Nepal: Himal Association, p. 28

DeGeyndt, Willy, Xiyan Zhno and Shunli Liu 1992 *From Barefoot Doctor to Village Doctor in Rural China*. Washington DC: World Bank.

Dixit, Kanak Mani, ed. 1992 "What To Do With Foreign Aid?" Special Volume, *Himal*, Mar./Apr. Lalitpur, Nepal: Himal Association

Donzelot, Jacques 1977 *La Police des Familles*. Paris: Editions Minuit

Douglas, Mary 1970 *Natural Symbols*, New York: Routledge

1986 *How Institutions Think*. Syracuse: Syracuse University Press

Doyal, Lesley 1979 *The Political Economy of Health*. Boston: South End Press

English, Richard 1985 "Himalayan State Formation and the Impact of British Rule in the Nineteenth Century." *Mountain Research and Development*, 5(1): 61–78

Escobar, Arturo 1988 "Power and Visibility: The Invention and Management of the Third World." *Cultural Anthropology*, 3(4): 428–43

1995 *Encountering Development: The Making and Un-making of the Third World*. Princeton: Princeton University Press

Ferguson, James 1994 *The Anti-Politics Machine: "Development," Depoliticization, and Bureaucratic Power in Lesotho*. Minneapolis: University of Minnesota Press

Fisher, William 1998 *Fluid Boundaries: Forming and Transforming Identity Among the Thakali of Central Nepal*. Columbia: Columbia University Press

Fleck, Ludwik 1935 (1979) *Genesis and Development of a Scientific Fact*. Chicago: University of Chicago Press

FOPHUR 1990 *Dawn of Democracy: People's Power in Nepal*. Forum For the Protection of Human Rights, P.O. Box 5457, Kathmandu, Nepal

Foster, George 1961 "The Dyadic Contract: A Model for the Social Structure of a Mexican Peasant Village." *American Anthropologist*, 63(6): 1173–92

1987 "World Health Organization Behavioral Science Research: Problems and Prospects." *Social Science and Medicine*, 24(9): 709–17

Foucault, Michel 1973 *The Birth of the Clinic: An Archaeology of Medical Perception*. New York:Vintage

1979 "On Governmentality." *Ideology and Consciousness*. 6: 5–22

1981 *The History of Sexuality, Volume One: An Introduction*. New York: Vintage

1988 "The Art of Telling the Truth" from the lecture "Was ist Aufklarung?," from Kritzman, ed., *Interviews and Other Writings, 1977–1984*. New York: Routledge

Fox-Keller, Evelyn 1992 *Secrets of Life, Secrets of Death: Essays on Language, Gender and Science*. New York: Routledge

Frankenberg, Ronnie 1980 "Medical Anthropology and Development: A Theoretical Perspective." *Social Science and Medicine*, 14B: 197–207

1981 "Allopathic Medicine, Profession, and Capitalist Ideology in India." *Social Science and Medicine*, 15A: 115–25

Gellner, David N. 1993 "From Sacred Centres to Communist Strongholds? On the Cities of the Kathmandu Valley, Nepal." In A. Uherek, ed., *Urban Anthropology and the Supranational and Regional Networks of the Town*. Prague Occasional Papers on Ethnology. Prague: Institute of Ethnology

Gellner, David N. 1997a "Introduction: Ethnicity and Nationalism in the World's Only Hindu State." In D. N. Gellner, J. Pfaff-Czarnecka, and J. Whelpton, eds., *Nationalism and Ethnicity in a Hindu State: The Politics of Culture in Contemporary Nepal*. Reading: Harwood

1997b "Caste, Communalism and Communism: Newars and the Nepalese State." in D. N. Gellner, J. Pfaff-Czarnecka, and J. Whelpton, eds., *Nationalism and Ethnicity in a Hindu State: The Politics of Culture in Contemporary Nepal*. Reading: Harwood

Gluckman, Max 1955 *The Judicial Process Among the Barotse of Northern Rhodesia*. Manchester: Manchester University Press

Gunder Frank, Andre 1966 "The Development of Underdevelopment." *Monthly Review*, September

Gupta, Anirudha 1996 "Pitfalls of Nepal's Democracy." *Himal*, 9(6): 40–41

Gyawali, Dipak 1991 "Troubled Politics of Himalayan Waters." *Himal*, May/June Lalitpur, Nepal: Himal Association, pp. 5–10

Haifeng, Chen and Zhu Chao, eds. 1984 *Chinese Health Care: A Comprehensive Review of the Health Services of the People's Republic of China*. Boston: MTP Press (Kluwer)

Hansen, Joseph 1967 *Che Guevara Speaks: Selected Speeches and Writings*. New York: Merit Publishers.

Harding, Sandra 1991 *Whose Science? Whose Knowledge? Thinking from Women's Lives*. Ithaca: Cornell University Press

1994 "Is Modern Science an Ethnoscience? Toward a Postcolonial Epistemology for Science Studies." Women's Studies Seminar, University of Pennsylvania, Nov. 3

Himal. Himalayan magazine, vols. 2(5), 1989 and 5(2) 1992. Lalitpur, Nepal

Höfer, Andras 1979 *The Caste Hierarchy and the State in Nepal: A Study of the Muluki Ain of 1854*. Innsbruck: Universitatsverlag Wagner

Hollinger, David 1983 "The Defense of Democracy and Robert K. Merton's Formulation of the Scientific Ethos." *Knowledge and Society: Studies in the Sociology of Culture Past and Present*, 4: 1–15

1995 "Science as a Weapon in Kulturkampfe in the United States During and After World War II." *Isis*, 86: 440–54

Hu 1996 "A Question of Delegation." A book review essay in *The Rising Nepal Friday Supplement*, Oct. 11: 3

IDS (Integrated Development Systems) 1983 *Foreign Aid and Development in Nepal*. Conference proceedings. Kathmandu: IDS

Illich, Ivan 1976 *Medical Nemesis: The Expropriation of Health*. New York: Bantam Books

1981 "The Delinking of Peace and Development." *Gandhimarg*, 3: 257–65

Joshi, Bhuwan Lal and Leo Rose 1966 *Democratic Innovations in Nepal*. Berkeley: University of California Press

Joshi, Sudan 1993 "Health Services Planning in Nepal." *Journal of the Nepal Medical Association*, 3(106): 211–14

Jungk, Robert 1954 *Tomorrow is Already Here*. London: Rupert Hart Davis

Justice, Judith 1983 "The Invisible Worker: The Role of the Peon in Nepal's Health Service." *Social Science and Medicine*, 17(14): 967–70

1987 *Policies, Plans and People*. Berkeley: University of California Press

Kaphley, Prakash 1990 "People's Movement and the Violation of Human Rights." *Human Rights Bulletin*, 2(4): 27–29

Kaufert, Patricia and John O'Neil 1990 "Cooptation and Control: The Construction of Inuit Birth." *MAQ*, 4(4): 427–42

K.C., Lok Bahadur 1993 *Recent Nepal: An Analysis of Recent Democratic Upsurge and Its Aftermath*. New Delhi: Nirala Publications

Kondos, Alex 1987 "The Question of 'Corruption' in Nepal." *Mankind*, 17(1): 15–29

Kothari, Manu L. and Lopa A. Mehta 1988 "Violence in Modern Medicine." In Ashis Nandy, ed., *Science, Hegemony and Violence: A Requim for Modernity*. Delhi: Oxford University Press

Kuhn, Thomas 1962 *The Structure of Scientific Revolutions*. Chicago: University of Chicago Press

Langford, Jean 1995 "Ayurvedic Interiors: Person, Space, and Episteme in Three Medical Practices." *Cultural Anthropology*, 10(3): 330–66

Latour, Bruno 1987 *Science in Action*. Harvard: Harvard University Press

Latour, Bruno and Steve Woolgar 1986 (1979) *Laboratory Life: The Construction of Scientific Facts*. Princeton: Princeton University Press

Leve, Lauren n.d. "Languages of Nation and Practical Dialogue: A Study of the Development of Nepali Nationalism." Unpublished manuscript, Department of Anthropology, Princeton University

Lunbeck, Elizabeth 1994 *The Psychiatric Persuasion*. Princeton: Princeton University Press

Macpherson, C. B. 1962 *The Political Theory of Possessive Individualism: Hobbes to Locke*. Oxford: Oxford University Press

Marglin, Fréderique Appfel and Stephen Marglin, eds. 1990 *Dominating Knowledge: Development Culture and Resistance*. Oxford: Oxford University Press

Marine Division (3D) Memorial Children's Hospital Information Brochure 1968, US Marine Corps

Martin, Emily 1991 "The Egg and the Sperm: How Science has Constructed a Romance Based on Stereotypical Male-Female Roles." *Signs*, 16(31): 485–501

1994 *Flexible Bodies: Tracking Immunity in American Culture from the Days of Polio to the Age of AIDS*. Boston: Beacon Press

Maskey, Mahesh 1991 "Strengthening District Health System: Policy and Management Issues in Nepal." *Journal of the Nepal Medical Association*, 29: 99–103

Maskey, Mahesh, Ms. K. L. Bhandari, and Prof. M. P. Shrestha 1994 "Role of IOM in Health System Development." *Journal of the Institute of Medicine*, 15: 294–304

Mauss, Marcel 1937 (1967) *The Gift*. New York: W. W. Norton
McHugh, Ernestine 1989 "Concepts of the Person among the Gurungs of Nepal." *American Ethnologist*, 16(1): 75–86
McKeown, Thomas 1979 *Medicine: Dream, Mirage or Nemesis?* Princeton: Princeton University Press
Mendelsohn, Everett 1974 "Revolution and Reduction: The Sociology of Methodological and Philosophical Concerns in Nineteenth Century Biology." In Y. Elkana, ed., *The Interaction Between Science and Philosophy*. Atlantic Highlands, N.J.: Humanities Press
Merton, Robert K. 1942 "A Note on Science and Democracy." *Journal of Legal and Political Sociology*, 1: 116
Misra, Chaitanya and Pitamber Sharma 1983 "Foreign Aid and Social Structure: Notes on Intra-State Relationships." IDS Foreign Aid and Development in Nepal, Proceedings of a seminar, October 4–5
Morgan, Lynn 1989 " 'Political Will' and Community Participation in Costa Rican Primary Health Care." *Medical Anthropology Quarterly*, 3(3): 232–45
1993 *Community Participation in Health: The Politics of Primary Care in Costa Rica*. Cambridge: Cambridge University Press
Morris, R. J. 1832 (1976) *Cholera*. New York: Holmes and Meier Publishers
Nandy, Ashis 1983 *The Intimate Enemy: Loss and Recovery of Self under Colonialism*. Delhi: Oxford University Press
1988 "Introduction: Science as a Reason of State." In Ashis Nandy, ed., *Science, Hegemony and Violence: A Requiem for Modernity*. Delhi: Oxford University Press
1993 "Nation, State, and Self-Hatred." *Himal*, 9(5): 16–18
Navarro, Vicente 1976 *Medicine Under Capitalism*. New York: Neale Watson
1984 "A Critique of the Ideological and Political Positions of the Willy Brandt Report and the WHO Alma Ata Declaration." *Social Science and Medicine*, 18(6): 467–74
New, Peter Kong-ming and Mary Louie New 1977 "The Barefoot Doctors of China: Healers for All Seasons." In David Landy, ed., *Culture, Disease, and Healing*. New York: Macmillan
Osmanczyk, Edmund Jan 1990 "Alma Ata Health Care Declaration." *The Encyclopedia of the United Nations*. International Relations, San Francisco
Parajuli, Pramod 1992 "Beyond Parliaments and Elections: Democracy and Political Culture in Nepal." *South Asia Forum Quarterly*, 5(1): 1–4
Parish, Steven M. 1994 *Moral Knowing in a Hindu Sacred City*. New York: Columbia University Press
Patton, Cindy 1990 *Inventing Aids*. New York: Routledge
Pfaff-Czarnecka, Joanna 1997 "Vestiges and Visions: Cultural Change in the Process of Nation-Building in Nepal." In D. N. Gellner, J. Pfaff-Czarnecka, and J. Whelpton, eds., *Nationalism and Ethnicity in a Hindu State: The Politics of Culture in Contemporary Nepal*. Reading: Harwood
Pickering, Andrew 1992 "From Science as Knowledge to Science as Practice." In Andrew Pickering, ed., *Science and Practice and Culture*. Chicago: University of Chicago Press
Pigg, Stacy 1990 *Disenchanting Shamans: Representations of Modernity and the Transformation of Healing in Nepal*. Ph.D. Dissertation, Department of Anthropology, Cornell University

1992 "Inventing Social Categories Through Place: Social Representations and Development in Nepal." *Journal of Comparative Study of Society and History*, 34(3): 491–513

1993 "Unintended Consequences: The Ideological Impact of Development in Nepal." *South Asia Bulletin*, 8(1and 2): 45–58

1995a "Acronyms and Effacement: Traditional Medical Practitioners (TMP) in International Health Development." *Social Science and Medicine*, 41: 47–68

1995b "The Social Symbolism of Healing in Nepal" *Ethnology* 34(1): 17–36

1996 "The Credible and the Credulous: The Question of 'Villagers' Beliefs' in Nepal." *Cultural Anthropology*, 11(2): 160–201

Raeper, William and Martin Hoftun 1992 *Spring Awakening: An Account of the 1990 Revolution in Nepal*. New Delhi: Viking

Rap, Rayna 1988 "Chromosomes and Communication: The Discourse of Genetic Counseling." *MAQ*, 2(2):143–57

Regmi, Mahesh C. 1978 *Thatched Huts and Stucco Palaces: Peasants and Landlords in 19th Century Nepal*. New Delhi: Vikas Publishing House

Rose, Leo 1965 "Communism Under High Atmospheric Conditions: The Party in Nepal." In Frp, Rpbt/ Scalopino, ed., *The Communist Revolution in Asia*. Englewood Cliffs, N.J.: Prentice-Hall

Seddon, David 1987 *Nepal: A State of Poverty*. Delhi: Vikas Publishing House

Shaha, Rishikesh 1992 *Ancient and Medieval Nepal*. Kathmandu: Ratna Pustak Bhandar

1993 *Politics in Nepal: 1980–1991*. Delhi: Manohar Publishers

Shapin, Steven and Simon Schaffer 1985 *Leviathan and the Air-Pump: Hobbes, Boyle, and the Experimental Life*. Princeton: Princeton University Press

Shiva, Vandana 1988 "Reductionist Science as Epistemological Violence." In Ashis Nandy, ed., *Science, Hegemony and Violence: A Requiem for Modernity*. Delhi: Oxford University Press

Stiller, Ludwig 1973 *The Rise of the House of Gorkha: A Study of the Unification of Nepal, 1768–1816*. New Delhi: Manjusri

1993 *Nepal: Growth of a Nation*. Kathmandu: Human Resources Development Research Center

Stolfi, Captain Russel H. USMCR 1968 *US Marine Corps Civic Action Efforts in Vietnam, March 1965–March 1966*. Historical Branch G-3 Division, Headquarters, US Marine Corps

Stone, Linda 1986 "Primary Health Care for Whom? Perspectives from Village Nepal." *Social Science and Medicine*, 22(3): 293–352

1989 "Cultural Crossroads of Community Participation in Development: A Case from Nepal." *Human Organization*, 48(3): 206–13

Stone, Linda and J. Gabriel Campbell 1984 "The Use and Misuse of Surveys in International Development: An Experiment from Nepal." *Human Organization*, 43(1): 27–37

Tagore, Rabindranath 1917 (1972) *Nationalism*. Calcutta: Rupa and Co.

Taylor, Rex and Annalie Rieger 1984 "Rudolf Virchow on the Typhus Epidemic in Upper Silesia: An Introduction and Translation." *Sociology of Health and Illness*, 6(2): 201–217

Temkin, Oswei 1949 "Metaphors of Human Biology." In Robert C. Stauffer, ed., *Science and Civilization*. Madison: University of Wisconsin Press

Townsend, Peter and Nick Davidson 1982 *Inequalities in Health: The Black Report.* Report by Sir Douglas Black, Professor J. N. Morris, Dr. Cyril Smith, and Professor Peter Townsend. Harmondsworth: Penguin Books

Tuting, Ludmilla and Kunda Dixit Bikas-Binas 1986 *Development/Destruction: The Change in Life and Environment of the Himalaya.* Munich: Geobuch

Virchow, Rudolf 1959 *Die Cellularpathologie.* 2nd edn. Berlin
  1985 (1879) *Collected Essays on Public Health and Epidemiology.* 2 vols., ed. Lelland J. Rather Canton, MA: Science History Publications, Watson Publishing International

Visvanathan, Shiva 1985 *Organizing for Science: The Making of an Industrial Research Laboratory.* Delhi: Oxford University Press
  1988a "On the Annals of the Laboratory State." In Ashis Nandy, ed., *Science, Hegemony and Violence: A Requiem for Modernity.* Delhi: Oxford University Press
  1988b "Atomic Physics: The Career of an Imagination." In Ashis Nandy, ed., *Science, Hegemony and Violence: A Requiem for Modernity.* Delhi: Oxford University Press

Waitzkin, Howard 1991 *The Politics of Medical Encounters.* New Haven: Yale University Press

Weber, Max 1958 *The Protestant Ethic and the Spirit of Capitalism.* New York: Charles Scribner and Sons

Weiner, Saul J. 1989 " 'Source Force' and the Nepal Medical Profession." *Social Science and Medicine,* vol 29 (5): 669–75

Whelpton, John 1983 *Jang Bahadur in Europe: The First Nepalese Mission to the West.* Kathmandu: Sahayoki Press
  1992 *Kings, Soldiers and Priests: Nepalese Politics and the Rise of Jang Bahadur Rana, 1830–1857.* Kathmandu: Ratna Pustak Bhandar
  1995 "Nepalese Political Parties: Developments Since the 1991 Elections." *European Bulletin of Himalayan Research,* 8: 17–41
  1997 "Political Identity in Nepal: State, Nation and Community." In D. N. Gellner, J. Pfaff-Czarnecka, and J. Whelpton, eds., *Nationalism and Ethnicity in a Hindu State: The Politics of Culture in Contemporary Nepal.* Reading: Harwood

Wildavsky, Aaron 1976 "Why Planning Fails in Nepal." *Administrative Science Quarterly,* 17(4): 508–28

Wise, M. Norton 1996 "The Enemy Without and the Enemy Within." An essay review, *Isis,* 87: 323–27

World Health Organization 1983 "Introductory comments by James P. Grant." Interregional Seminar on Primary Health Care, Geneva

Young, Allan 1981 "The Creation of Medical Knowledge: Some Problems in Interpretation." *Social Science and Medicine,* 15B: 379–86
  1982 "The Anthropologies of Illness and Sickness." *Annual Review of Anthropology,* 11: 257–85

Ziauddin, Sardar, ed. 1988 *The Revenge of Athena: Science, Exploitation and the Third World.* New York: Mansell Publishing Ltd, 1988.

Index